THE DOCTRINE OF FAITH

The Doctrine of Faith

A Study of the Augsburg Confession and
Contemporary Ecumenical Documents

Nestor Beck

Publishing House
St. Louis

Some quotations from the Lutheran Confessions are taken from *The Book of Concord,* translated and edited by Theodore G. Tappert, copyright © 1959 by Fortress Press. Used by permission.

Passages quoted from various volumes of *Luther's Works,* © 1957–71 by Fortress Press, are used by permission.

Copyright © 1987 by Concordia Publishing House
3558 South Jefferson Avenue, St. Louis, MO 63118-3968
Manufactured in the United States of America

All rights reserved. No part of this publication may be reproduced, stored in a retrieval system, or transmitted, in any form or by any means, electronic, mechanical, photocopying, recording, or otherwise, without the prior written permission of Concordia Publishing House.

Library of Congress Cataloging in Publication Data

Beck, Nestor, 1942–
    The doctrine of faith.

    Bibliography: p.
    1. Confessio Augustana. 2. Justification—History of doctrines—16th century. 3. Justification—History of doctrines—20th century. 4 Lutheran Church—Missouri Synod—Doctrines. 5. Lutheran Church—Doctrines. 6. Christian union conversations—Controversial literature. 7. Ecumenical movement—Controversial literature. I. Title.
BX8069.B385   1987   234'.2   86-31717
ISBN 13: 978-0-758-61840-5

---

1 2 3 4 5 6 7 8 9 10 BC 96 95 94 93 92 91 90 89 88 87

Contents

Chapter 1:	The Significance of the Augsburg Confession	7
Chapter 2:	The Purpose of the Augsburg Confession	11
Chapter 3:	The Sources of the Augsburg Confession	19
Chapter 4:	The Doctrine of Faith in Catholic Polemics	33
Chapter 5:	The Christology of the Doctrine of Faith (Art. III)	46
Chapter 6:	The Doctrine of Faith in Art. IV	52
Chapter 7:	The Doctrine of Faith in Arts. V and VI	92
Chapter 8:	Defense of the Doctrine of Faith (Art. XX)	106
Chapter 9:	The Doctrine of Faith in "Justification Today" (1963)	120
Chapter 10:	The Doctrine of Faith in the "Leuenberg Agreement" (1973)	130
Chapter 11:	The Doctrine of Faith in Lutheran-Catholic Documents (1972–83)	142
Chapter 12:	Retrospect and Perspectives	171
Notes		184

Abbreviations

AC Augsburg Confession
Ap Apology of the Augsburg Confession
BS *Die Bekenntnisschriften der evangelisch-lutherischen Kirche.* 4. Auflage. Göttingen: Vandenhoeck & Ruprecht, 1959
CR *Corpus Reformatorum,* I–XXVIII. Ed. C. G. Bretschneider and H. E. Bindsell. Halis Saxonum/Brunsvigae: C. A. Schwetschke et Filium, 1834–60. New York and London: Johnson Reprint Corporation/Frankfurt am Main: Minerva, 1963 reprint
LW *Luther's Works,* American Edition. St. Louis: Concordia, and Philadelphia: Fortress, 1955–1975
Tappert *The Book of Concord: The Confessions of the Evangelical Lutheran Church,* trans. and ed. Theodore G. Tappert. Philadelphia: Fortress, 1959
WA *Weimar Ausgabe. D. Martin Luthers Werke: Kritische Gesamtausgabe.* Weimar: H. Böhlaus Nachfolger, 1883–
WA Br *Weimar Ausgabe, Briefwechsel*
WA RN *Weimar Ausgabe, Revisionsnachtrag*

CHAPTER 1

The Significance of the Augsburg Confession

The Reformation struggle for the truth of the Gospel and freedom of conscience changed the face of Europe and produced a new social order striving for liberty and progress. This attempt to renew the Christian church from within, however, divided Western Christianity into territorial and confessional churches that have failed to achieve unity in truth and love.

To vindicate their cause, the leaders of the German Reformation in 1530 read an apologia before the Imperial Assembly in Augsburg. Their Augsburg Confession (AC) has thereafter been the basic source for the study of the Lutheran Reformation, as it explains how the "Lutherans" understood and wanted others to understand their movement. For the signers of this document the Reformation was the inevitable result of the "doctrine of faith" (*doctrina fidei*), of the conviction that faith in Christ is Christian righteousness and is the only way of salvation. As Martin Luther affirms in the Smalcald Articles, "On this article rests all that we teach and practice against the pope, the devil, and the world. Therefore we must be quite certain and have no doubts about it. Otherwise all is lost, and the pope, the devil, and all our adversaries will gain the victory (Tappert, p. 292).

From Dissent to Consensus

The Catholic controversialists of the time branded this doctrine as the Lutherans' basic and foremost error. They held that it contradicted Catholic teaching and destroyed Christian morality.[1] The Council of Trent, the epitome of the Catholic response to the Reformation, condemned this doctrine, at least in the form in which the controversialists understood it.

In the last decades, however, a remarkable consensus is said to have developed. According to the 1972 "Malta Report," titled "The Gospel and the Church," theological discussions between representatives of the Lutheran World Federation and the Vatican Secretariat for Christian Unity succeeded in outlining a consensus on justification.[2] The Joint Lutheran-Catholic Commission reaffirmed such a consensus in a declaration on the AC, "All Under One Christ" (1980), and in a statement on "Martin Luther, Witness to Jesus Christ" (1983).[3]

Lutheran and Reformed churches in Europe claim to have reached a common understanding of the Gospel, including the doctrine of justification, in the "Leuenberg Agreement" (1973).[4]

These developments raise questions: Have the Lutheran spokesmen adequately represented the Reformers' stance? Is the agreement real or does it conceal divergences? How do the consensus formulations relate to the basic confession of the Lutheran Church?

Furthermore, the Lutheran World Federation itself failed to express a common understanding of justification at the 1963 Helsinki Assembly.[5] This leads observers to ask: Why were the Lutheran churches unable themselves to express unequivocally the doctrine whereby the church stands or falls? Yet the agreements with the Catholic and the Reformed churches were reached within 10 years of the Helsinki Assembly. One wonders how Lutheran churchmen could agree with Catholics on Malta and with representatives of the Reformed churches at Leuenberg if they failed to agree among themselves at Helsinki.

These observations point up the need for an investigation of the doctrine of faith in both the AC and in contemporary ecumenical documents. One must determine what Luther and Melanchthon intended to say when they affirmed that people are justified by faith, and how their teachings were transmitted in subsequent theological agreements.

Originality and Catholicity

The AC presents an original and virtually definitive formulation of the doctrine of faith as Luther and Melanchthon understood and proclaimed it. Other confessional documents do not correct it but rather reaffirm it. It is significant, too, that the AC as charter of the Lutheran Church found legal recognition in the Peace of Augsburg (1555), which granted religious tolerance to the imperial estates adhering to its doctrinal stance.

The AC is, therefore, a perfect source for any study seeking to recover the original Lutheran affirmation of the doctrine of justification by grace through faith for Christ's sake. Moreover, while defending the Reformation, the AC claims to affirm nothing but the teachings and rites which the Christian church has upheld since its beginning. As a result this confession has provided the basis for dialog with all movements and churches that are, or intend to be, catholic.

The catholicity of the AC received wide attention in the decade preceding its 450th anniversary. It was expected that Rome would recognize it in order to open the way for fellowship between the Catholic and the Lutheran churches. Its catholicity was confirmed to a high degree by a group of experts in a "Joint Commentary."[6] The Joint Lutheran-Catholic Commission announced that, having reconsidered the Confession, it had reached a far-reaching agreement in fundamental truths of the Christian faith, including the doctrine of justification.[7]

In view of this catholicity one must examine whether the AC upholds a "catholic" view of faith and righteousness on the basis of the New Testament, the ecumenical creeds, and the early church fathers. Whatever one concludes, on this score as in others it did not *intend* to dissociate itself from the sources of Christian tradition.

One may arrive at a clear and unequivocal understanding of the AC by remembering that it was written for ordinary people and not for the learned few. It was directed at a Christian audience, but hardly one familiar with theological distinctions. Therefore, in order to get its message across, it uses relatively simple language and relies on the reader's common sense. Obviously, one must read the AC in its historical and theological context and in light of its purpose and development.

Luther and Melanchthon

Does the AC reflect the theology of Luther or of Melanchthon? Recent scholarship has established that it should be read in the light of

Luther's writings, but that Luther in turn should be interpreted on the basis of the AC.[8] The present investigation assumes that the difference between the positions of the two Reformers in the period 1528–31 was not as wide as sometimes supposed.

Melanchthon composed the AC as spokesman of the Lutheran party—on the basis of official documents. It must therefore be regarded not as an expression of his "private" theology but as the culmination of a joint effort to define and defend the Lutheran Reformation.

The joint nature of the effort is evidenced by Luther's publication of the *Instructions for the Visitors of Parish Pastors in Electoral Saxony* written by Melanchthon, and by their collaboration on the Schwabach Articles. On the basis of these latter articles Luther set up the Marburg Articles—all of this under the Duke of Saxony's oversight.

The AC therefore represents the official position of the churches in whose name the political leaders reported to the emperor. This consideration must neutralize attempts to isolate Luther's or Melanchthon's personal contributions in the common confession.

Nonetheless, the AC was composed by Melanchthon. He expressed the Lutheran stand in his own language. This makes it necessary to draw upon his works, particularly those of 1528–31, in order to understand the terminology employed in it. Luther's works will remain in sight as theological background for both its formulations and content.[9]

CHAPTER 2

The Purpose of the Augsburg Confession

The Augsburg Confession (AC) spells out, defends, and applies the doctrine of justification through faith. The significance of this doctrine becomes evident if one considers the function it had in relation to the purpose of the whole document.

To ascertain this purpose, one must examine the prefaces and epilogs drafted at different stages of composition. These reveal the Lutherans' agenda when stating their case before the Diet by means of this document. They also indicate the role the doctrine of justification through faith had played in the Reformation according to Lutheran understanding.

The Historical Setting of the Preface and Epilog Drafts

Emperor Charles V, ruler of the Holy Roman Empire of the German Nation, summoned the Diet from Bologna on Jan. 21, 1530, to convene in Augsburg in April. His declared intention was to unite the empire for the struggle against the Turks and therefore to hear everyone's opinion as to how the religious schism in Germany could be overcome. Differences should be reconciled and all Christians reunited in the fellowship of the one church, even as they lived and battled under the one and same Christ.[1]

The summons reached John the Constant, Duke of Saxony and aspirant elector, on March 11, 1530. He took the emperor at his word. He asked political and theological advisers to prepare a "report" that would account for the teachings and rites promoted in his domains in the course of the Reformation (*WA Br,* V, 264). It was necessary to explain and defend the measures which he had authorized in connection with the visitation of churches and schools in electoral Saxony. He had publicized them through Luther's edition of Melanchthon's *Instructions for Visitors,* the *Unterricht der Visitatoren* (*LW,* 40, 269–320).

The visitation had roused the opponents. Two papalist controversialists, John Fabri and John Cochlaeus, decried Luther's inconsistency and halfhearted return to traditional teachings on penitence, good works, infant baptism, and similar matters.[2]

Meetings in Wittenberg and Torgau resulted in the composition of a series of documents that formed the basis for the second part of the AC (Articles XXII–XXVIII). They have been called the "Torgau Articles" or, at Heinrich Bornkamm's suggestion, the "Wittenberg-Torgau Articles."[3]

On May 11, 1530, Melanchthon sent a draft of the AC to Luther. He called it "our apologia," but defined it as "more properly a confession." It is not known for sure whether it included doctrinal articles corresponding to the first part of the AC, or whether doctrinal arguments had been incorporated into the apologia for changes in the church's worship and order.[4] In any event, by the end of May the Saxon "report" definitely included a summary of articles of faith (first part) besides a defense of religious reforms (second part).

As he explained to Luther, Melanchthon had included "just about all the articles of faith" in order to neutralize the "most diabolic" attacks of John Eck's *Articles.*[5] An extensive preface aimed at defending the Saxon elector introduces the report on the teachings and reforms promoted.[6] The epilog was not yet available.[7]

In the first weeks of June it became clear that the Lutheran estates would have to take a united stand before Charles V and the Diet. The Duke of Saxony, attempting to promote his prospects of becoming an elector, had tried to reach a private settlement with the emperor through special envoys sent to Innsbruck.[8] The emperor, however, responded by prohibiting Lutheran preaching in Augsburg. Upon his arrival (June 15), Charles asked the Lutheran leaders to take part in the Mass and procession of Corpus Christi. At the opening of the Diet (June 20) he warned, through the "proposition" read by Count Palatine Frederick, that he was ready to act as defender of the faith and protector of the church.[9]

The Lutheran leaders understood that the emperor's stance was not as impartial as the summons to the Diet had suggested. Rather than accepting him as judge, they agreed to submit the religious issue to a free, general council.

This course of action had been urged by Philip, Landgrave of Hesse, as his instruction of March 27, 1530, and letters exchanged with Melanchthon and John Brenz indicate.[10] Luther, too, had disavowed the Diet's competence to judge the Reformation in his "Exhortation to All Clergy Assembled at Augsburg" (*LW*, 34, 3–61), which had sold 500 copies by the first week of June.

The Lutheran leaders' united stance affected the composition of the AC. The Duke of Saxony's "report" was adopted and refashioned as the single defense and confession of the Lutheran party. This demanded a new preface and an epilog as well.

The definitive preface and epilog reflect the consensus of the Lutheran leaders. They were composed by chancellor Gregory Brück and translated into Latin by Justus Jonas.[11] Work on them was not concluded until the eve of the date originally set for the presentation of the document. The delay was due to the diplomatic negotiations between the Lutheran princes and city representatives,[12] if not to Melanchthon's secret talks with Alfonso Valdes, the imperial secretary, which might have resulted in the AC not being presented to the Diet at all.[13]

Be that as it may, the new preface provides, together with the epilog, the diplomatic framework in which the AC was submitted to the Imperial Assembly.

The Preface and Epilog

The preface is less an introduction to the content of the AC than a delineation of the juridical context in which the document is being submitted to the Diet. It represents a compromise between the views of the Saxon elector and the standpoint of Philip of Hesse as to how the Lutherans should handle the situation created by the summons to the Diet of Augsburg.[14]

The Lutheran princes and cities, says the preface, have come to the Diet in obedience to the summons of the emperor in order to discuss the religious schism in Germany. At the opening of the Diet the emperor asked the estates to submit in writing their evaluation

THE DOCTRINE OF FAITH

of the religious crisis.[15] Therefore they are submitting a confession of faith in order to report what has been taught in their territories.

The emperor suggested that the opposing parties should negotiate a friendly settlement. The Lutheran estates declared that they were willing to do so, provided the other side would also present a written statement of its position. If the other party would refuse to comply with the emperor's request, the Lutherans would nevertheless do everything they could in order to promote religious peace, as their Confession clearly indicates.[16]

At the same time, the preface recalls that in previous Diets the emperor had promised not to judge the religious issue by himself, but to urge the convocation of a universal Christian council to settle the issue. The negotiations at the Diet possibly would not lead to the settlement outlined by the imperial summons. Therefore the preface renews the appeal for a Christian council. It stresses that the Lutheran estates are determined to uphold this appeal until Christian concord is reached.[17]

According to the preface, then, the document to be presented should serve as a point of departure for negotiations leading to a Christian settlement of the religious schism.[18] The document itself is called a "confession" of faith and teachings, that is, a report which enumerates the articles taught and describes the shape of the teachings dispensed on these articles. It is implied that both the selection of the articles and the character of the teachings were determined by the Holy Scriptures.[19]

The preface, however, must be read and understood in connection with the conclusion of the first part and the introduction to the second part, together with the epilog.

In the conclusion to the first part the Lutherans claim to have presented a summary (*summa*) of the doctrine preached and taught in their lands. This doctrine is firmly based on Scripture and does not contradict the Catholic Church. There is dissension only on certain traditions and abuses which the church has never sponsored. The opponents, therefore, must agree with the Lutherans on the articles of faith and stop demanding that they be punished as heretics. In the same way, the bishops ought to tolerate the Lutheran churches, regardless of any deficiencies in their rites.

This contention is based on the presupposition that the unity of the church does not consist in uniformity of human rites, but

THE PURPOSE OF THE AUGSBURG CONFESSION

rests on faithful proclamation of the Gospel and correct administration of the sacraments, as maintained in Art. VII of the Confession.

In support of their contention the Lutherans argue that canon law does not require universal uniformity in church rites and that such uniformity has never been achieved in the church. They affirm that they do keep most of the ancient rites, having merely suspended certain abuses that had insinuated themselves into the church.

The introduction to the second part opens with an appeal based on the conclusion just described. Since the Lutheran churches do not dissent from the Catholic Church in any article of faith, but have merely suspended abuses not authorized by the canons, the emperor should listen to their report both on the changes made and on the reasons for these changes (Tappert, pp. 48–49).

At this point the texts follow different lines. The Latin requests the emperor not to give credence to detractors of the Lutheran cause, since the shape of Lutheran teaching and ceremonies will please him more than he would ever have expected. According to the German text the emperor should perceive that God's command had forced the Lutherans to admit certain changes.[20]

In the conclusion of the second part the Lutheran princes and cities make clear that they had not reviewed all the abuses which troubled the church. In order to avoid prolixity they had presented only those points necessary to prove that neither in their teachings nor in their ceremonies had they promoted anything contrary to Scripture and the Catholic Church.[21]

In the epilog the Lutheran estates declare: We have submitted these articles in obedience to the emperor's request. They present our own confession and the summary of the doctrine taught by our theologians. If anyone should fault our confession, we are ready to submit a fuller account on the basis of Scripture.[22]

The sections examined suggest that the AC had the purpose of rejecting the charges made by the opponents. These were meant to incite the spiritual and political authorities to eventually violent action against the Lutheran estates and congregations. The opponents contended that the Lutherans had taught or at least tolerated heresy and therefore should be treated as heretics, that is, excommunicated by the bishops and prosecuted by the emperor. They insinuated that the Lutherans had suspended all ancient rites and therefore ought to be punished as subversive elements.

In order to refute these charges the AC delineates the teachings of the Lutheran theologians and reports the changes which had been made in the rites of the church. With this procedure the Confession pursues a double goal: to prove that the teachings of the Lutherans are based on the Scriptures and consistent with the Catholic Church, and to demonstrate that they had merely suspended certain abuses connected with the rites of the church and that their action was justified on several grounds.

It should be noted that the Lutherans' insistence on public reading of their "report" is connected with the realization of this goal. Only if read in public would the confession carry out the apologetic function of proving to both Germans and foreigners that the Lutheran princes and cities had been slandered by the opponents who had charged them with heresy.[23]

The ultimate goal of the confession, however, was to raise before the Diet a single claim: Since the Lutheran estates together with the churches they represent are still within the unity of the Christian church, the bishops must allow them to preach the Gospel and must tolerate the changes they have legitimately made.

The AC, therefore, intends not only to defend the Lutheran estates but also to submit a viable proposal concerning the restoration of religious concord in the Holy Roman Empire. It calls for benevolent toleration of the Lutheran churches by the Roman Catholic bishops on the premise that these churches are at one with the universal Christian church, for they teach nothing but the Gospel and perform only rites which are in keeping with that same Gospel.

This proposal evidently entails a specific understanding of the Gospel and of church rites which are "in keeping with the Gospel." This understanding must be ascertained by careful study of the articles.

As the AC defends the Lutheran Reformation and claims the Lutheran churches' right to be and act within the unity of the Christian church and the realm of the empire, it does not relinquish but rather sustains the changes made in church rites and customs. It strives to demonstrate that these are legitimate since they were undertaken for valid reasons. As the articles of the second part indicate, the doctrine of the righteousness of faith (*iustitia fidei*) was regarded as the main cause of and reason for drastic changes in such worship practices as the Mass, distinction of foods, monastic vows, and ordinances decreed by bishops.

The purpose of the AC, therefore, relates as follows to the doctrine of justification through faith: Inasmuch as it is a *confession,* it presents the Lutheran teaching of faith in Christ as enjoined by the Gospel (Arts. IV–VI); inasmuch as it is an *apologia,* it defends the doctrine of faith in Christ as Christian, necessary, and beneficial (Art. XX) and demonstrates that it necessitates the suspension of abuses and the promotion of Christian worship (articles of the second part).

In this precise respect the doctrine of faith in Christ is fundamental or central to the AC.

Implications

Our aim in this chapter was to establish the thrust and scope of the AC in order to comprehend the function and significance of the doctrine of faith in this document.

It should be observed, too, that the AC expresses a specific understanding of catholicity in its prefaces and epilog. It has its own conception of what is Christian or catholic in matters of doctrine and worship. It does not provide a formal definition, but spells out from article to article which teaching, rite, or practice it views as catholic.[24]

One might conclude that the AC regards as catholic that which is taught by the Gospel, confessed by the church in the creeds (and ecumenical councils), and upheld by the best authors of the Christian tradition.[25] It certainly is a complex conception, since it is not established or used formally but is determined by the *matter* which Christian teachings and rites convey, namely, Christ's significance for salvation.

The AC judges whether teachings or rites are Christian or catholic not simply by establishing whether they conform to a formal definition of catholicity, but ultimately by determining whether they put Jesus Christ to the right use God intended in the Gospel. This, in turn, indicates that the catholicity of teachings and rites cannot be established apart from the doctrine of justification by grace through faith for Christ's sake, since this doctrine alone conveys the right use to be made of Jesus Christ.

This connection between catholicity and the doctrine of faith explains why the recent discussion on the recognition of the AC by the Roman Catholic Church could not succeed. The well-intentioned authors of the proposal were not able to set up an approved criterion by which to measure and establish the catholicity of the AC. Was it to be the catholicity of the Roman Catholic Church as extant in its dogmas and decrees or as (re)interpreted by some of its contemporary ecumenically minded theologians? Or else could Protestant and Catholic theologians establish together, on the basis of a "common tradition," what is to be regarded as catholic—and then measure the AC against this standard?[26]

The AC could not but elude such attempts. Its catholicity challenges and questions the formal criteria by which benevolent ecumenists have sought to enhance its significance for the church universal. As the analysis of pertinent material in ch. 9 will show, the ecumenical discussion has failed to ascertain in which sense the AC itself means to be—and is to be regarded as—catholic. This remains a challenge for the years ahead.

CHAPTER 3

The Sources of the Augsburg Confession

The doctrine of faith in Christ is affirmed in Arts. IV–VI, defended in Art. XX, and adduced to justify reforms in several articles especially of the second part of the Augsburg Confession. In writing the Confession, Philip Melanchthon drew upon authoritative documents which had commanded the reformation of schools and churches and aligned the Lutheran estates in defensive alliances. For this reason the doctrine of justification through faith in Christ as formulated, defended, and used in the AC must be interpreted on the basis of the sources from which it was drawn.

Most studies have in fact used the sources as aids to understanding specific terms, expressions, or statements pertaining to the doctrine of faith in Christ. They have not recognized, however, that the same sources provide the clue for the structure which characterizes this doctrine in the AC.

The doctrine of justification through faith is affirmed in three articles, IV, V, and VI, and defended in Art. XX, which is made up of three parts. This simple observation serves to indicate that the "doctrine" is formed by a number of assertions that correspond to a certain number of questions.

As a careful reading will show, all of the sources raise and answer the same set of questions concerning the issue of righteousness. If one succeeds in identifying these questions, one will know which of them the AC is trying to answer in its Arts. IV–VI and XX. By knowing those questions which are answered, one will be able to understand what each assertion intends to affirm and how they relate to each other as a cluster of answers directed to a particular set of questions. Above all, one will understand why Art. IV makes two assertions concerning faith, a fact which most studies have either overlooked or failed to explain.

After characterizing the pertinent sources, we shall consider how they structure the doctrine of faith in Christ.

The Sources

The AC is made up of two clearly discerned parts: first, the "articles of faith and doctrine," originally numbered from I to XXI and, except for Art. XX, not identified by titles; second, seven articles on abuses that had been originally set apart by titles, though not numbered, as in later editions, from XXII to XXVIII.

The main sources for the second part were the Visitation Articles and the *Instructions for Visitors,* either directly or through the Torgau Articles. The other articles of the first part were drawn mainly from the Schwabach Articles, which restated Luther's confession of 1528 and provided the basis for the Marburg Articles. We will not here consider the Proposals written by theologians and pastors of Nürnberg and the Margravate of Brandenburg, for they contributed relatively little to the articles on faith and works.[1] Melanchthon's *Outline of the Epistle to the Romans* will be used later to clarify expressions in the articles on faith and works, like "through faith" and "because of Christ."[2]

Melanchthon wrote the Visitation Articles to provide internal guidelines for the visitation of churches and schools in Electoral Saxony, which Duke John had authorized on June 16, 1527.[3] They were published without his knowledge and were unduly criticized by John Agricola for their teaching on repentance. They served as draft for the more extensive German version.

The *Instructions for Visitors* was written by Melanchthon and discussed with Luther besides John Bugenhagen, George Spalatin, and other members of the Wittenberg team. It was published with Luther's preface under the auspices of the elector. Its official publication was meant to explain why and how the elector had authorized visitations in the bishops' stead.[4]

The work drew the attention of two papalist controversialists, John Fabri and John Cochlaeus. They decried it as evidencing Luther's inconsistency and halfhearted return to "Catholic" teaching on penitence, good works, infant baptism, and other issues. Cochlaeus depicted Luther as having seven heads that would never agree with each other.[5]

Such partisan criticism, however, did not prevent the Saxon elector from using the *Instructions for Visitors* and/or the Visitation Articles to document his faithfulness to the church and his loyalty to the empire, if indeed they are the (printed) report on "ceremonies" which he sent to the emperor just before the Augsburg Diet.[6]

While the Visitation documents underlie the articles of the second part, Luther's Confession of 1528 started the process which, through the Schwabach and Marburg Articles, resulted in the "articles of faith and doctrine" in the AC.[7]

Luther formulated his Confession as a theological testament. Reckoning that soon he would face the Judge of the living and the dead, he confessed his faith definitively, so that his contemporaries and the coming generations would know for sure what he taught and believed. He wanted to prevent people from misquoting him in support of erroneous teachings especially with regard to the sacraments. In its sober definiteness it is comparable to the Smalcald Articles, although differing from them in scope.

The Schwabach Articles were composed on the basis of Luther's Confession by the Wittenberg theologians and jurists at the request of the Elector of Saxony and Margrave George of Brandenburg. They were intended to provide the confessional basis not only for an alliance of Lutheran princes and cities but also for a reconciling delegation to the emperor.[8]

The elector would allow as partners only the princes and cities that concurred with the articles in rejecting the "Sacramentarians," as Luther had done in his Confession, for otherwise he saw no chance for an agreement with the emperor. At the Epiphany meeting in Nürnberg the Seventeen Articles were approved by the representatives of Electoral Saxony, Brandenburg, Hesse, and Nürnberg, as well as (indirectly) by Lüneburg, Anhalt, Mansfeld, Reutlingen, Windsheim, and Weissenburg (Nordgau).[9]

Even after the failure of the alliance and delegation plans, the elector still regarded the articles as a viable instrument for achieving a reconciliation with the emperor. Shortly before the Diet, in May 1530, he sent them together with a printed work on "ceremonies" to Innsbruck, in order to prove his orthodoxy and loyalty to the emperor. He intended to demonstrate especially that he did not support the errors of the "Sacramentarians."

The elector instructed his envoy, Hans von Dolzig, to submit the documents through the Counts of Nassau and Neuenahr, should they decide on this course to offset the misconstruing of his actions as leader of the Reformation.[10]

In fact the papal delegate, Lorenzo Campeggio, reported that the Duke of Saxony had submitted a confession of faith. As reported to him it was "the world's most holy and catholic" in the beginning, but "full of poison in the middle and the end." He sent it along with the letter.[11]

Shortly after the elector's diplomatic venture a clandestine edition of the Seventeen Articles appeared in Augsburg under the title "Luther's Confession of Faith for the Diet." The theological consultants of the papalist Elector Joachim I of Brandenburg produced a refutation. They charged the presumed author with being inconsistent, since he had modified his "theological testament."[12]

Luther set the record straight by writing from Coburg Castle: The articles had been published without his knowledge, and he was not the sole author, although he had taken part in their composition.[13]

These facts enhance the importance of the Schwabach Articles as source of the AC. Since they were held in common by the Lutheran estates and, once delivered to the Imperial Court, were known to the opponents as well, Melanchthon followed them rather closely in outlining and formulating the "articles on faith and doctrine." It has been observed that after the contacts with the emperor had failed, Melanchthon kept even more closely to the wording of the Seventeen Articles.[14]

It must be recalled, however, that some of the 21 articles were written or expanded right in Augsburg to offset Eck's pernicious articles. Three, Arts. VIII, XII, and XIV, were inserted into the sequence, while four, Arts. XVIII–XXI, were appended to the body of the Seventeen Articles.[15] Melanchthon evidently did not want to disrupt the original sequence with apologetic articles.

This explains why the doctrine of faith is discussed twice, both in Arts. IV–VI (on the basis of the Schwabach Articles) and in Art. XX (on the basis mainly of the Visitation documents).

The Marburg Articles, the last source to be considered, were composed by Luther at the Marburg Colloquy, promoted by Landgrave Philip of Hesse. They succeeded in drawing together the Swiss and the German reformers, but failed to unite them in a common stand on the Sacrament as required for a political alliance. In composing them Luther followed the Schwabach Articles, but rearranged and adapted the statements to meet the specific demands of the situation.[16]

The Visitation Articles

In the Visitation Articles Melanchthon established a list of 20 items which he wanted to investigate in the Saxon churches and schools. The first question was whether Saxon pastors taught the Decalog; the second, "how they teach faith, what faith is, how we get it" and "how they teach that men are justified."[17]

Melanchthon raised these questions in order to determine whether preaching in Electoral Saxony conformed to the pattern of Christ's own proclamation of the Gospel. He preached repentance and the forgiveness of sins. The Saxon pastors must follow His example and teach both repentance and the remission of sins.

The evangelist's summary of Christ's proclamation (Luke 24:46–47) provides both a pattern for the teaching of faith and a criterion for evaluating Christian preaching. Melanchthon, therefore, discerns three "parts" in Christian doctrine—repentance (also called the doctrine of the Law or of the fear of God), the doctrine of faith or of forgiveness (also called the doctrine of justification), and the fruits of the Spirit (also called the fruits of faith).[18]

Melanchthon makes several observations on how the second part should be taught. The pastors should, first of all, explain what faith is[19] and "how it justifies."[20] Faith is not just acquaintance with Christ's story; it is believing in the forgiveness of sins.[21] It justifies as it believes that *because of Christ* God forgives us our sins and consequently is with us, rules, guides, and is going to save us. The Holy Spirit teaches that Christ is the Satisfaction and Propitiation, and therefore we are justified by faith.[22]

Second, the pastors should point out that there can be faith only in people who are contrite, whose hearts have been terrified by the Law. Third, they must explain "how the heart receives faith": A person whom the Law has terrified receives faith if and when he hears and believes the Gospel, that God has forgiven his sins on account of Christ. Then such a person also receives the Holy Spirit, as well as hatred of sin and the intention to lead a godly life. The Holy Spirit brings along the fruits of faith or fruits of the Spirit, which constitute the third part of Christian teaching.

In the discussion of the third part Melanchthon argues that it is necessary and possible to "mortify" the flesh, augment the fear of God, and do good works. He insists, however, that our good works do not satisfy God, because Christ is the Satisfaction and Propitiation, and we are therefore justified through faith in Christ. In short, faith is the Christian's righteousness.[23]

The *Instructions for Visitors*

In the *Unterricht der Visitatoren* Melanchthon again operates with three parts of Christian life—repentance, faith, and the doing of good works (*LW,* 40, 276–77, 287).

Christ, he says, told His disciples to preach repentance and forgiveness (Luke 24:47). Pastors must, therefore, preach penitence and point out how faith is obtained, for otherwise people will not understand what faith is or what the term "faith" denotes.

Toward the end of the section on "doctrine" Melanchthon defends the sequence he proposes for Christian preaching. It is true, he says, that repentance is properly speaking a result of faith. Nevertheless it can be said that faith is preceded by the Law, fear of God, repentance. These belong to general or common faith, which Scripture demands, for instance in Heb. 11:6b, as it says: Man must, first of all, believe that God, who threatens, commands, and evokes fear, exists. Melanchthon believes that his sequence will help the common people to have a more distinctive grasp of faith *in Christ* or *justifying* faith.

The guidelines developed for the teaching of faith correspond to those of the Visitation Articles. The pastors must explain, in the first place, how people are justified: The person who is penitent and sorrowful over sin must believe that his sins are forgiven not because of his merits, but because of Christ. Then must follow the explanation of what faith is, which implies how faith is received: When a contrite and terrified conscience obtains peace, consolation, and joy from hearing that our sins are forgiven because of Christ, that is called "the faith which justifies us before God." Finally, it must be explained in whom faith exists: Faith can exist only in those who have true contrition and regret over their sins.

Several of these points reappear in the sections concerning penitence and satisfaction, which may have been influenced by Luther.[24]

In his exposition of the third part of Christian life, Melanchthon emphasizes that we must do good works, for God requires them in the Decalog, and suffer the tribulations which God imposes. Good works, however, do not make satisfaction for our sins and must not be regarded as the reason why God forgives us (*LW,* 40, 297; cf. p. 280). Melanchthon adds in the section on Christian liberty and free will that we can do good works only because the Holy Spirit rules and protects us.

The texts examined indicate that, in Melanchthon's estimation, pastors and schoolmasters were misrepresenting the doctrine of faith, and people in the parishes were not receiving its benefits. The texts explain how this doctrine should be taught in keeping with Christ's will in order to achieve its proper goal. Proper teaching provides the correct answer to a number of questions referring to the manner of justification (*modum iustificationis*), the nature and origin of faith, and the relation between faith and works, namely:

1. How are people justified?
2. Why does faith justify?
3. What is (justifying) faith?
4. How is faith obtained, or in whom does it exist?
5. Why and how does faith result in good works?

This means that the author of the Visitation documents structured the doctrine of faith, that is, he cast it in a sequence of connected statements on a number of basic issues. At issue is whether this doctrine displays the same structure in the other sources of the AC as well.

The "Great Confession"

As Luther confessed his faith article by article, he meant to affirm nothing but the common, Christian faith: "This is my faith, for so all true Christians believe and so the Holy Scriptures teach us" (*LW,* 37, 372). Therefore it was most natural for him to use the Apostolic and especially the Niceno-Constantinopolitan Creed as basis and framework for his affirmation of the Christian faith.[25]

The doctrine of justification through faith issues from the assertion of Christ's and the Spirit's self-giving on behalf of man. It is a corollary of Luther's consistent confession of Christ's "help and grace." This means that we must consider the latter in order to grasp its function and structure.

Luther states, on the basis of the creeds, who Jesus Christ is. He sums up: Christ is "my Lord and the Lord of all, Jesus Christ, the only, true Son by nature of God and of Mary, true God and true man." Then he affirms what Christ did and does "for us poor sinners": He suffered, was crucified, died, and was buried "in order that he might redeem us from sin, death, and the eternal wrath of God by his innocent blood." He rose from death, ascended to heaven, and is seated at God's right hand as "Lord over all lords, King over all kings and over all creatures" and "over death and life, over sin and righteousness" (*LW,* 37, 362).

In the same breath Luther provides the theological justification for Christ's work. On account of the common "fall, guilt and sin," all men together with Adam "would necessarily be guilty of eternal death if Jesus Christ had not come to our aid and taken upon himself this guilt and sin as an innocent lamb, paid for us by his sufferings, and if he did not still intercede and plead for us as a faithful, merciful Mediator, Savior, and the only Priest and Bishop of our souls" (ibid.).

This confession of what Luther terms "the help and grace of our Savior Jesus Christ" (*LW,* 37, 363) provides the ground for rejecting current teachings on free will and sin, since they postulate that man still is able to strive toward and prepare for righteousness and advance toward salvation.

In view of Christ's "help and grace" Luther also condemns the persuasion of attaining salvation through monastic life. It is only through Jesus Christ's name that we are saved (Acts 4:12). There can be no other saviors or ways and means of attaining salvation besides the unique righteousness which is Jesus Christ and which He has bestowed on us and placed before God, for our sake, as our sole propitiation (*LW,* 37, 363–64).

As he affirms the orders instituted by God, namely, the office of the ministry, the family, and civil government, together with the common order of Christian love, Luther stresses that none of these is a way to salvation. The way to salvation remains above all these: It is faith in Christ.

One must distinguish between being saved and becoming holy: We are saved exclusively through Christ, but become holy both through faith in Christ and through God's institutions and orders. All those who are saved through faith in Christ keep these orders and perform the appropriate works for God's praise and honor, as He requires (*LW,* 37, 364–65).

In the third part (*LW,* 37, 365–72) Luther confesses that the Holy Spirit as God's "living, eternal, divine gift and endowment," adorns the believers with faith and other spiritual gifts, raises them from death, liberates them from sin, and makes them joyful and bold in their consciences, as He testifies that God wants to be their Father, forgive their sins, and give them eternal life.

At this point Luther inserts a summary on God as the loving Giver. The Father gives Himself to us with all He has, "heaven and earth and all the creatures." This gift, however, is marred by sin. Therefore the Son, too, gave Himself to us, shared with us all His works, sufferings, wisdom, and righteousness. Thus He reconciled us to the Father in order that, once again alive and righteous, we might know and have also the Father with His gifts.

This grace, however, would not be profitable if it remained hidden and could not come to us. Therefore the Holy Spirit, too, comes and gives Himself to us. He teaches us to perceive, preserve, use, and promote Christ's benefaction. He does it both "inwardly" through faith and other spiritual gifts and "outwardly" through the Gospel, Baptism, and the Eucharist. Through them as through means and ways He comes to us and deploys Christ's passion for our salvation.

Luther goes on to discuss the sacraments, the church, confession, purgatory, the Mass, and eschatology. He closes with a ringing affirmation that these are and will remain his beliefs.

In his Confession Luther raises the question, Which is the way to salvation, or how is one saved? It is evident that in Luther's estimation the common Christian confession establishes God, the Father, the Son, and the Holy Spirit, as the only agent of salvation. Therefore the only way to salvation is Jesus Christ.

It is significant that Luther says of faith the same as he says of Christ, namely, that it is the only way to salvation. He can do so because he assumes that there is a correlation or exchange of attributes between Christ and faith. They belong together and are so intimately connected that Christ may donate Himself to faith, and faith may receive and own Christ with His gifts. This explains why and how Luther can say of faith what he says of Christ, namely, that it is the very righteousness which He is and which He gives us: It is *glauben Christi,* faith in Christ.[26]

Luther also raises the question, What is faith? It is a gift of the Holy Spirit through which He enables us to recognize, receive, keep, use, share, and advance Christ's grace or benefaction.

Luther's third underlying question is, How does one become holy? As we have seen in the discussion of the holy orders, he states that Christians become holy through faith and the "holiness," the "holy life," or the "holy works" inherent in the divine orders or institutions.

Luther intended to evidence his oneness with all true Christians in confessing the one Christian faith, as taught by the Holy Scriptures. Therefore he approaches the issue of justification theologically, that is, from the perspective of the Trinity's action as recited in the creeds. Nevertheless he does raise and answer the three main questions which the Visitation documents raised out of a pastoral-didactic concern. The Schwabach and Marburg Articles follow Luther's approach and deal with the same basic issues.

The Schwabach Articles

As the 12th of the Seventeen Articles indicates, the Wittenberg Reformers together with the Lutheran estates were conscious of their catholicity. They took for granted that they, too, were and represented the church.

They argue toward the end of the article that the church is not tied by laws and outward pomp to place and epoch, person and bearing, but is wherever one preaches the Gospel and makes legitimate use of the sacraments. Since they presume to be preaching the Gospel and using the sacraments legitimately, they boldly assert that the holy Christian church is nothing but the believers in Christ, who hold, believe, and teach the preceding articles and on this account are persecuted and martyred in the world.[27]

This means that theirs is a *bona fide* catholicity. They assume quite authentically that the faith confessed in their articles is that of the one holy Christian church.

On account of this determined catholicity the Schwabach Articles join the church universal in confessing the Trinity, the Son's incarnation, and the life, death, and resurrection of Jesus Christ in words of the Apostolic and Niceno-Constantinopolitan creeds (Arts. I–III). They stress that God's Son, Jesus Christ, truly suffered for us, as the apostle Paul affirms (Rom. 8:32; 1 Cor. 2:8).

The significance of Jesus Christ is determined in relation to the consequences of original sin (Art. IV): This is genuine sin and as such would have condemned all men, if Jesus Christ had not substituted for us. He took this and the resulting sins upon Himself, made satisfaction for them by His suffering, and thus suspended and destroyed them altogether in Himself.

This statement includes representations usually associated with the "classical" view of the Atonement. It indicates that the Wittenberg theologians were not restricted to just one strain of tradition, as some studies are prone to suggest.

The doctrine of faith is stated in Arts. V–VIII. It responds to questions that deal with consequences of the confession concerning God, Christ, and sin.

The first question is whether man can "work his way out" by his powers and good works, in order to become righteous and good again. The answer is that he cannot, since he is a sinner and subject to sin, death, and the devil. For this reason the answer to the ensuing question, whether man can prepare or dispose himself for righteousness, is negative, too.

How, then, does one become righteous and free from sin and death? What is the way to righteousness and liberation from sin and death? The fifth article answers that the only way is to believe, without having merits or works, in the Son of God, who suffered for us, as said before in Arts. III and IV.

To the question of why believing in Christ is the way to righteousness and liberation Art. V explains: This faith is our righteousness before God, for He will count and regard as righteous, good, and holy and wants to forgive all sins and endow with eternal life all those who have this faith in His Son, that on account of Him they shall be received into grace and become children in His kingdom.[28]

Three features of Art. V deserve special notice. The first is that the authors employ the verbal formulation *so wir glauben* ("as we believe in the Son") to tell how we become righteous (*modum iustificationis*). The second is that they immediately explain why or in which respect believing in Christ is "the only way to get righteous and rid of sin." The third is the sentence which states what faith believes. By placing "on account of His Son" at the beginning of the same, the authors convey that to believe in Christ is to regard Him as God's sole reason for accepting and adopting us.

The significance of these features will become evident later in this study, as we analyze the seeming tautology "through faith as we believe" and the function of the connective *denn* in the last sentence of Art. IV of the AC.[29]

It is worth noting, too, that the Schwabach Articles call faith "the only way to righteousness" because they assume its correlation to Christ: He alone is "the sole way to grace and salvation," according to Art. XV on monasticism.

The assertions of Art. V would not be intelligible if Art. VI did not explain what faith is. It is a work and gift of God which the Holy Spirit, given through Christ, effects in us. It is a vigorous, new, live entity (*wesen*), which bears much fruit and is always doing good toward God and the neighbor.[30]

As the negatives in Art. VI indicate, the authors intend to demonstrate that the faith which leads to and is righteousness is not to be confounded with the general or common faith which people elicit by themselves, even if they are heretics. They do not intend to affirm in Art. VI that faith is righteousness inasmuch as it is a new being and does good. The question of why and how faith justifies is settled in Art. V on different grounds!

If man cannot elicit faith by his own powers, how can he get it? Art. VII responds. In order that God may give and we come to faith, He instituted the preaching office or the oral Word, the Gospel. It is through the Gospel that He proclaims and gives faith, together with the Holy Spirit, where and how He wills. Art. VIII adds that, besides the oral Word, God also uses the sacraments as means whereby He offers and gives faith and His Spirit.

The Schwabach Articles thus discuss the basic issues that make up the doctrine of justification through faith, except for one. They do not explicate "how we become holy," presumably because this matter is implicit in Art. VI, on the nature of faith.

The Marburg Articles

The first three of the Marburg Articles confess the Trinity, the Son's incarnation, and Jesus Christ's work "for us" on the basis of the Niceno-Constantinopolitan Creed, which Luther explicitly mentions.[31] The fourth article succinctly restates the Schwabach article on original sin and Christ's salutary intervention. The doctrine of faith is expressed in Arts. V–X.

How are we liberated from sin and eternal death? Art. V responds that we are liberated as we believe in this Son of God, who died, rose, and rules on our behalf and that "apart from such faith we cannot free ourselves of any sin through any kind of works, station in life, or [religious] order, etc."

Moreover, according to Art. VI, "such faith is a gift of God which we cannot earn with any works or merit that precede, nor can we achieve it by our own strength, but the Holy Spirit gives and creates this faith in our hearts as it pleases him, when we hear the gospel or the word of Christ."

Why or in which respect does faith in the Son make one righteous? Art. VII replies that "faith is our righteousness before God, for the sake of which God reckons and regards us as righteous, godly, and holy apart from all works and merit, and through which He delivers us from sin, death, and hell, receives us by grace and saves us, for the sake of his Son, in whom we thus believe, and thereby (*dadurch*) we enjoy and partake of his Son's righteousness, life, and all blessings."

How does one come to faith? Arts. VIII (the Word), IX (Baptism), and XV (the Sacrament of the Altar) affirm that the Holy Spirit effects and creates faith where and in whom He wills through and with the oral Word or the Gospel of Christ. God instituted the sacraments of Baptism and the Altar for the sake of this faith.

The fifth and final question is taken up in Art. X: How do we become holy, or why and how does faith effect good works? Luther affirms: Once we have been reckoned righteous and made holy through faith,[32] this same faith effects (*ubet*) good works through the operation of the Holy Spirit, such as loving the neighbor, praying to God, and suffering persecution.

It is plain that the Marburg Articles, just as the other sources, present the doctrine of faith as response to a number of basic questions. Assuming that Melanchthon in writing the AC was faithful to his sources, it becomes highly probable that the definitive text of Arts. IV–VI and XX, too, structures the doctrine of faith as response to the set of five questions which underlie it in the sources.

CHAPTER 4

The Doctrine of Faith in Catholic Polemics

After Friedrich Loofs challenged the traditional understanding of the doctrine of justification presented in Art. IV of the Apology,[1] scholars like Carl Stange,[2] A. Warko,[3] and Johannes Kunze[4] insisted on the need of studying the opponents' antithetical position in order to grasp the Lutheran stand on justification by faith. Hugo Lämmer and Gustav Plitt,[5] among others, drew heavily on works of the Catholic controversialists, but did not trace their position chronologically, as more recent studies have done.[6]

The present chapter will delineate both the opponents' charges against the doctrine of justification through faith and their teaching on faith and works. The term "opponents" is borrowed from Melanchthon. It is used descriptively, not pejoratively.

Sources for Study

Melanchthon states in Art. XX of the AC: Our preachers and teachers are being falsely accused of prohibiting good works (Tappert, p. 41). If the opponents really made this charge, it is likely to appear in John Eck's *Articles* for the Diet of Augsburg. In this work he compiled objectionable statements from the works of Luther and Melanchthon on the basis of excerpts which he and other controversialists had prepared.[7] The study of this work is indispensable for the adequate understanding of the AC's doctrine of justification through faith.[8]

In order to determine which features of the teaching of faith Eck opposed, it will be necessary to examine his *Articles* in the light of the *Catholica Responsio,* an extensive draft of the Confutation of the AC which cited many of them.⁹ In this work it becomes clear why he objected to certain statements attributed to Luther and Melanchthon. Indeed, Eck as the compiler of the *Articles* had a key role in composing the *Responsio*.¹⁰ It can be assumed that the reasons why the controversialists denounced certain propositions remained the same during the period in which both works were produced.

The opponents' own teaching on faith and works can be gathered from the polemical writings addressed to the Reformers between 1518 and 1528. In view of their great number, we have found it advisable to concentrate on works that are concise yet representative. For this reason the present investigation concentrates on Eck's *Enchiridion* and the *Catholica Responsio*. These works, along with the Refutation of the Schwabach Articles, provided the basis for the Confutation, which the emperor issued as his official, definitive refutation of the AC.¹¹

Eck composed the *Enchiridion* to provide people with a summary of the things they should believe, so that the "heretics" would not be able to subvert their faith. He intended also to arm educated but busy Catholics with arguments to challenge and defeat the "heretics." For this purpose he compiled the anti-Lutheran evidence gathered by a host of renowned papalist polemicists, as indicated by his *ex libris*.¹²

The Refutation of the Schwabach Articles published shortly before the Diet is very instructive.¹³ It was composed by theologians with experience in anti-Lutheran polemics. Conrad Wimpina, for instance, had recently published an *anacephalaiosis* to demonstrate that Lutheran teachings derived from ancient heresies.¹⁴ John Mensing had crossed swords with Nicholas von Amsdorf precisely over faith and works.¹⁵ Moreover, since the Refutation concerns the main source of the AC, it distinguishes quite clearly between the "Catholic" and the "Lutheran" teaching on faith.

Even though it presupposes the AC, the *Catholica Responsio* is an adequate source for the purposes of this chapter. It was composed by experts in fighting Lutheranism, like Eck, Fabri, Cochlaeus, Wimpina, Mensing, and others. It is representative for the views of the main theologians opposed to the Reformation. Its numerous sources include Eck's *Articles* and his *Enchiridion,* which provided most of the evidence against the AC.¹⁶

As mentioned earlier, John Fabri and John Cochlaeus, two most virulent controversialists, attacked the Visitation Articles and the *Instructions for Visitors,* which are regarded as sources of the AC. Their works will be used as complementary sources only, since they do not reveal the theological standpoint from which they criticize the alleged inconsistencies of Luther and Melanchthon.[17]

Eck's *Articles*

The initial 65 articles consist of older material, namely, 41 propositions of Luther condemned by Pope Leo X in the bull *Exsurge Domine,* 13 theses defended against Luther and Carlstadt in Leipzig, and 11 articles dealing with Zwingli. The remaining articles were compiled specifically for a debate at the Diet of Augsburg. They denounce "old and new errors" which Eck intended to expose for the sake of "the faith, the church, and the Christian empire."[18]

Eck begins by underscoring the condemnation of Luther's position by the pope. The very first article deals with "heretical but current" teaching concerning the sacraments' imparting of justifying grace to those who do not resist. As the *Catholica Responsio* indicates, the Lutheran position was understood as denying that the sacraments impart grace or the Holy Spirit.[19]

A similar statement is denounced among the errors "against Baptism" (Art. 215). That statement affirmed that only faith in the promising Word connected with Baptism justifies and profits, while Baptism itself does not justify or profit anyone. This statement, too, was understood as denying that Baptism offers grace to the baptized.[20]

According to the second article Luther asserts that sin remains in the child after Baptism; according to the third, that concupiscence prevents the soul from entering heaven.

For the Diet Eck supplied under the heading "sin" several statements by Luther and Melanchthon against the prevalent teachings on original and actual, mortal and venial sin. They elucidate Arts. II and III to some extent: Original sin is an "actual" depraved desire (Art. 182) and remains in man (Art. 185); concupiscence is an "actual" sin (Art. 180), every motion of concupiscence is in itself a mortal sin, and only for those in Christ is it venial sin (Art. 182).[21]

Art. 31 quotes Luther's proposition, "The righteous sins in every good work"[22]; Art. 32, his assertion, "A work excellently done is a venial sin"[23]; Art. 35, his thesis, "On account of the most hidden vice of pride no one can be sure of whether he is not constantly sinning mortally."[24] In the opponents' estimation such statements prevented people from doing good works.[25]

Against these assertions Eck formulates Art. 43, the second of his Leipzig "conclusions." He grants that venial sins happen day by day, but denies that the righteous person is constantly sinning in every good work, or that one may sin mortally while righteousness remains in him after Baptism. The reason for the denial of Luther's thesis becomes evident in the second article of the *Catholica Responsio:* Luther's teaching on sin denies the efficacy and power of Baptism.[26]

Luther's denial of free will is questioned in Art. 36: "After [the fall into] sin free will is merely a matter of a name; it sins mortally when it does what is in its power." The articles compiled for the Diet include a statement denying the activity of free will in doing good works and calling it a mere figment (Art. 331).

In Art. 48 Eck asserts that Luther erred in denying free will because it is active toward evil and passive toward good deeds. He further denies a thesis not appearing in the preceding articles but quoted later in Art. 191: Faith is destroyed by any crime. Finally, Eck deems most erroneous Luther's conviction that the penitent is absolved through faith alone regardless of his contrition.

In Arts. 11 and 12 Luther is quoted as saying that the reception of sacramental absolution depends on faith in the absolution rather than on the goodness of the penitent's contrition. According to Art. 15 Luther taught that only faith in the eucharistic promise of grace makes the communicants pure and worthy.

Even though Eck does not adduce the grounds of his objections, he implies that the Lutherans discourage the doing of good works because they deny man's ability to do good and the goodness of his works, and also because they affirm that faith alone is necessary for the reception of sacramental grace and confessional absolution.

The "new and old errors" compiled especially for the Diet of Augsburg include several that deal with faith and works. Statements listed as errors "against the Old Testament," "against the New Testament," and "against the Gospel" suggest that the law of Moses does not apply to Christians (Art. 153), that the Ten Commandments cannot be fulfilled (Art. 156), that the New Testament contains no laws or precepts (Arts. 159–162 and 165). The errors "against the commandments" (Art. 176), too, imply that it is impossible to fulfill the Decalog. In the compiler's view these statements discouraged the doing of good works as they did not uphold any law that would prescribe and demand them.[27]

Articles dealing specifically with faith and works appear under the titles "faith," "against works," "against merits," and "love." It is not clear in every instance why Eck denounced certain propositions. It is useful, therefore, to concentrate on those which the *Responsio* censured explicitly.[28]

LOVE AND MERITS

Art. 210 under the heading "love" quotes Melanchthon: "Faith in action and hope in action are not distinguished in Scripture." According to the *Responsio* this article demonstrates that the "preachers" reduced the three theological virtues to just one, while the apostle Paul insists that faith, hope, and love are three distinct virtues (1 Cor. 13:13).[29]

Luther is cited in the first of three articles "against merits": "Paul dispels the dreams of the theologians who invented the merit of congruity and condignity for the purpose of attaining grace." The first half of Art. IV of the *Responsio* indicates what is wrong with this Art. 203.[30] It demonstrates that "our merits are something through the grace and mercy of God and the merit of Christ's passion," for they are rewarded by God. It affirms that Scripture discerns merits resulting from divine impulse and prevenient grace and merits resulting from grace which renders the doer worthy of eternal life. Righteous men who do good works have merits which by virtue of God's grace are worthy of eternal life.

Since the *Responsio* assumes that this teaching has the backing of "express Scriptures," it denounces Luther's statement as an impious error, for it denies our merits—both those resulting from God's impulse and prevenient grace and those resulting from the grace which renders the doer worthy of eternal life.[31]

In view of the role which grace plays in the doctrine of merits, it is not surprising that Art. 205 faults Melanchthon for saying that God's grace is not a quality in us.[32] If it is not primordially a quality

THE DOCTRINE OF FAITH

in us, it becomes difficult if not impossible to postulate merits in the strict sense of the word.

Faith and Works

The second part of the fourth article of the *Responsio* provides the clue for two articles which were placed under the heading "faith." It states that the thesis "we are justified through faith" is "the great and principal error of the preachers," for they attribute to faith alone that which is peculiar to love and God's grace. The document adduces the apostle Paul (1 Cor. 13:2) to prove that faith alone does not justify and then cites Art. 194, a conflation of passages from Melanchthon's *Loci Communes*: "It is not love that justifies, but faith, which is preferred to love."[33]

Melanchthon's proposition is impious not only because it denies that love justifies, but also because it places faith above love, contradicting 1 Cor. 13:13: "Faith, hope, love, these three; the greatest of these, however, is love." Similarly, according to Art. 191 Luther taught that "it is necessary to raise faith above all virtues, but it is taken away by any crime."[34] This teaching, says the *Responsio,* is contradicted by Col. 3:14: "Have love above all things." Later on the document stresses that when Paul says that faith is ours and justifies, he does not support the Lutheran contention for "faith alone," for his statements refer to the faith which does good works through love (Gal. 5:6).

Eck's concerns in the sections "against works" and "faith" become evident in Art. VI of the *Responsio*. It quotes the main articles of these sections in order to demonstrate that the Lutherans had preached "most scandalously" against good works, so that many simple-minded people felt that they would sin mortally if they would do a good work.[35]

According to Art. 186 Luther taught that faith and works are extremely opposed to each other, so that it is impossible to teach works without doing harm to faith.[36] Art. 198 denounces Melanchthon: "All men's works, as praiseworthy as they may seem," are merely corrupt works and sins worthy of death.[37] Luther is reproached, once more, in Art. 202: "God does not care for our works, or, if they are something before Him, they are nevertheless all equal in terms of merit." The *Responsio* makes a threefold indictment:

Luther contradicts himself in affirming merit, he restores the Jovinian heresy that all merits are equal, and he asserts the impious and blasphemous dogma that God does not care for our works.[38]

Arts. 192, 193, and 199, too, are regarded as "hostile to good works." The first states that God's promise at Baptism cannot be invalidated by any sin and that the baptized, even if they want to, cannot forfeit salvation, since no sin except unbelief can lead to damnation, and all others are instantly absorbed through faith. The *Responsio* exclaims: "Will any common person do good works if he hears that?"[39]

In Art. 193 Luther is quoted as saying: "Only faith is necessary. All the rest is most free, neither commanded nor forbidden."[40] Art. 199, in turn, is regarded as the height of folly. No Turk, Tartar, or Persian will ever believe the axiom, "Evil works do not make a man evil."[41]

The *Responsio* concludes its denunciation with a statement that seems to reflect the concerns of Eck in denouncing these propositions: "These impious doctrines have led Germany, which formerly was most Christian, to give up completely these most Christian works and devotions wherever Lutheranism has prevailed."[42] Furthermore, according to Art. XX of the *Responsio,* the assertions denounced in Art. VI demonstrate that the Lutheran preachers did indeed prohibit good works.[43]

If one views Eck's *Articles* in the light of their deployment by the *Catholica Responsio,* it becomes clear that he objected especially to "faith alone" and the presumed depreciation of love, denial of merits, and prohibition of good works. From his perspective excluding good works from justification threatened the Christian religion with extinction, for it destroyed the "Catholic" way of salvation based on the teaching of three theological virtues and two kinds of merits. If Christians would accept that faith alone is sufficient and no works are necessary, they would not do good works and consequently would not acquire merits. Without merits, however, they would not obtain salvation. If Christians would presume that faith alone justifies and for this reason would disregard love and works, their faith would remain ineffective and they would not be justified, for only the faith which does good works on account of love is able to justify. From Eck's perspective, then, "faith alone" and its sequels threatened the core of "Catholic" soteriology.

To be sure, Eck did not refrain from misquoting the Reformers and misrepresenting their position. He not only quoted passages out of context, but carefully omitted the words "in justification" from statements which "excluded" good works. His "method" definitely was not conducive to theological understanding, as Erwin Iserloh frankly acknowledges.[44]

Studying Eck's *Articles,* excerpted mainly from works published between 1518 and 1528, demonstrates that the AC was part of the debate going on since the Leipzig Disputation. It can be understood adequately only in contrast to the stand taken by the opponents of the Reformation in this long polemical exchange.

Eck's *Enchiridion*

Eck discusses faith and works in ch. V of his work. As the heading indicates, he intends to demonstrate that "faith is not sufficient without works" and that "works are something on the basis of God's accepting grace." The body of the chapter underscores these two assertions.

Eck grants that the righteous person lives by faith (Rom. 1:17) and that faith is necessary: It is "the foundation of the spiritual building because [it is] the substance of things hoped for" (Heb. 11:1). He denies, however, that the righteous lives by faith alone, or that just any kind of faith is sufficient.

Eck maintains on the basis of Augustine that faith as defined in Gal. 5:6 includes clinging to God through love. It follows that Paul regards as valid and sufficient only the faith which does good works and loves, that is, the faith which theologians have called formed or living faith. The Bible passages quoted by the Lutherans in support of "faith alone" must be understood as referring to this faith which is made alive by love and does good works of love.[45]

Once this point has been reached—that is, viewing faith as entailing works of love—the stage is set for inserting *fides per caritatem operans* in the merit scheme. This is done by affirming that the works done by this faith, driven by love, lead to the acquisition of merits which—thanks to God's accepting grace—are rewarded with eternal life.

The emphasis of *fides per caritatem operans* plainly rests on *operans,* that is, on the doing of good works. Therefore it is more accurate to speak of *work-doing faith* rather than using the common "faith active through love," which is very far from conveying Eck's meaning.⁴⁶

At the end of the chapter Eck remarks that the Lutherans, too, were beginning to distinguish true, formed faith, which they called *der liebreiche und wohltätige Glaube,* that is, faith rich in love and active in doing good, and the other kind of faith, which they called historical. This implies that the Reformers were insisting no longer that faith alone, without works, was sufficient. They were actually beginning to teach that works, too, were necessary for salvation.⁴⁷

The outline of Eck's position emerges clearly. Faced with the teaching that faith alone, without works, is sufficient, he insists that only the faith which does works through (read: on account of) love can be said to be sufficient. Faced with the Lutheran attacks on good works, he maintains that good works are meritorious of eternal life by virtue of God's accepting grace.

The Contrast

In sum, the Roman teaching on faith and works is characterized by a regular structure. Its first element is the doctrine of merits, a theory concerning the interaction between God's grace and man's free will leading to eternal salvation. The second element is the teaching of faith formed by love, which actually means "faith doing works through love." While these elements stand out clearly, their relationship requires some comment.

The teaching concerning good works and merits resulting from the interaction between grace and free will leads to the rejection of the Lutheran "faith alone" and to the affirmation of work-doing faith. Conversely this working faith is involved in the acquisition of the all-important merits.

All the Roman documents regard faith as necessary. They insist, however, that it alone is not sufficient because by itself it is unable to perform good, meritorious works. Faith alone, then, would be sufficient only if it could provide by itself the merits indispensable for salvation. But that is precisely what faith cannot do, according to the polemicists. In this respect faith depends on grace and love.

The documents do not explicate the relation between grace and love. The *Responsio* remarks that *gratia gratum faciens* is love and renders the "worker" worthy of eternal life.[48] It affirms that love performs good, meritorious deeds and operates in accordance with God's will; by doing so it provides the merits which are indispensable for salvation. Therefore it is, rigorously speaking, more useful than faith. Since it cannot be denied that faith, too, is necessary, the polemicists "put these things together" and affirm that faith *and* love justify or, more exactly, that faith formed by love, or work-doing faith, is useful and sufficient.[49] In any case, be it faith formed by love or simply love, both are useful only inasmuch as they perform good works leading to merit and ultimately to the reward of eternal life.

Since faith formed by love helps to acquire the all-decisive merits of worthiness, it functions as an integral part of the theory of merits. It has its place right in the center of the sequence *meritum de congruo* (earned through God's prevenient grace)—*meritum de condigno* (earned through His further grace).

Once the connection between the merits scheme and the representation of faith formed by love is realized, one understands the dynamics of the polemicists' argumentation. While defending "our merits" they are inevitably driven to attack "faith alone," and the polemics against this point conversely buttress the theory of merits.

Here it becomes clear, too, that justification by faith alone is the storm center of the controversy concerning faith and works. The issue is not simply whether Scripture uses *sola* or not. The cleavage goes deeper.

Luther and Melanchthon also distinguished between historical or general and loving or working faith. They stressed that historical faith is necessary, but that it is living faith that justifies (Tappert, pp. 44–45).

The peculiarity of the Reformers' view of faith stands out when one asks: What is justifying about living faith? Why is living faith useful? According to Luther and Melanchthon, faith justifies not because it conduces to merits but because it apprehends Christ, who made satisfaction for our sins and is our Righteousness before God. For the Reformers, then, faith is primordially and essentially apprehension of Christ. It is also the beginning of an incipient fulfillment of the Law. Its value, however, derives entirely from its object, Christ, not from its role within a merit scheme.

Here the full range and importance of the battle over the word *alone* becomes evident. Luther and Melanchthon were not merely debating whether faith must be preferred to love or vice-versa. They were asking: What is the ultimate basis or ground for justification? They were inquiring about the true nature and function of faith.

If Christ alone is our Righteousness and if laying hold of Christ is the peculiar and foremost function of faith, then it does justify alone, that is, without the help of further virtues like hope and love, to say nothing of works of love. Even if these virtues would help, they would help only in the same sense of apprehending and having Christ.

If, however, the basis and framework of justification is "doing good works in accordance with God's will," and if faith is by itself unable to perform good, meritorious deeds, then indeed faith justifies not alone but inasmuch as it is connected with love, for it is love that "operates in accordance with God's will" and supplies the merits rewarded with eternal life.

In short, from Luther and Melanchthon's perspective "faith formed by love" is an affirmation exclusively of "righteousness according to the Law," while "faith alone" corresponds to the righteousness established and shared by the Gospel.[50]

Luther and Melanchthon's faith evidently cannot operate within a merit scheme. For this reason the good works done by faith no longer serve the purpose of acquiring merit. (There is no merit of condignity.) The works of faith fulfill the Law, but because this righteousness of the Law remains imperfect, it is acceptable to God only because of Christ or because of faith as it apprehends Christ. As to the works one does before coming to faith, they do not serve as preparation for grace and righteousness. (There is no merit of congruity.) Thus the teaching of justification "by faith alone" entails not only a specific view of the function of faith, but also a new vision of the nature and function of good works: They are the natural fruits of faith and serve to praise God and help the neighbor.

Having said this, one must add that the Reformers and their opponents operate with diverse views of grace. Luther and Melanchthon view it as being first and foremost God's mercy, as evidenced in the sentence, "God is gracious toward us" (*Gott ist uns gnädig, Deus propitius est nobis*). Above all, however, they view it as being irreconcilable with merit. For Eck and his colleagues, on the contrary, grace and merit by no means exclude each other: God's prevenient grace establishes the merits of congruity, these obtain the grace which renders the doer worthy of eternal life, and this grace, which is love, establishes the merits of condignity which lead to obtaining eternal life.

The question for Luther and Melanchthon is whether grace is or is not an undeserved gift of God, something that God gives *gratis,* that is, because of Christ alone and therefore without regard for one's condition. If grace is a free gift imparted exclusively because of Christ, then it can be received only through faith without any merit on one's part. If, however, the reception of grace is in any way conditioned by one's acquiescence, then there is room for merit, whether or not it is made possible by Christ's death or by God's gracious aid.

At this point Luther and Melanchthon are radical: If grace is a free gift, it excludes even the merits made possible by divine aid; then, positively speaking, it can be received only through faith in God's mercy and forgiveness, totally without any merit faith may have as incipient fulfillment of the Law. Seeing things from this perspective, one could say that the controversy between the Reformers and their opponents concerns the two poles of the correlation between promise and faith. On the giving end there is God with His promise of grace, and the question is whether this grace God offers is conditioned exclusively by Christ or whether it is conditioned—at least partially—by human merits. On the receiving end there is God-given faith, and the question is whether faith alone takes hold of God's offer or whether any other virtues and merits are in some way or other conducive to the reception of grace.

In short, the contrast between the opponents' teaching and the Lutheran position expressed in the AC is plain:

1. The opponents teach that good works are meritorious of grace and eternal life. Melanchthon denies the merit of good works both before and after the reception of *gratia gratum faciens*. He insists that grace (and along with it righteousness and eternal life) cannot be merited at all, for God is merciful free of charge (*gratis*), that is, because of Christ alone, not because of one's works and merits.

2. The opponents maintain that faith justifies inasmuch as it does good works thanks to the "energy" provided by love. Melanchthon insists that, as far as the righteousness of the Gospel is concerned, faith justifies not inasmuch as it is formed by love and does good

works to fulfill the Law, but inasmuch as it takes possession of Christ, or of God's mercy and forgiveness promised and given because of Christ.

3. The opponents argue that the Lutheran teaching of faith alone implies that good works are neither necessary nor useful. Melanchthon tries to demonstrate that good works are nevertheless necessary and useful in a specific sense. In fact, he dares to say that only the Lutheran teaching of faith makes it possible to produce true, good works that are pleasing to God.

In view of such a clear contrast one may respect the good intentions but must definitely question the evidence and the interpretation of scholars who affirm that the divergences between the Confutation and the AC are merely of a verbal nature and do not concern the matter of justification itself.[51]

CHAPTER 5

The Christology of the Doctrine of Faith (Art. III)

The study of the sources of the Augsburg Confession (ch. 3) revealed the structure of the doctrine of faith and indicated that this doctrine is rooted in the confession of God and Jesus Christ in the Apostles' and Nicene Creeds. It concerns our proper recourse to Him as the only Lord of righteousness and life, the Liberator from sin and death.[1]

In keeping with its sources, notably the Schwabach and Marburg Articles, Art. III of the AC declares the Christology underlying the doctrine of faith presented in Arts. IV–VI and defended in Art. XX. It is necessary to consider this Art. III in order to comprehend the Christological presuppositions of the doctrine of justification through faith.

The Story and the Effects

As Melanchthon explains in Art XX, the true Christian faith is more than just knowing the "story" (*historia*) of Christ. It consists in believing in the "effects of the story" (*effectus historiae*) as well, namely, for what He came, acted, and suffered (*causa finalis historiae*), as summarized in the article of the forgiveness of sins.

Art. III, therefore, reports the Lutheran churches' teaching on both the "story of Christ" and its "effects," namely, how Christ's coming, passion, and action benefits us "for our salvation." It evidently presupposes the confession of God (Art. I) and implies the recognition of human sin (Art. II).

Formerly some theologians regarded Arts. I and III as an inconvenient remnant of the Middle Ages or as a political stratagem to avoid the imperial sanctions on heresy. Recent studies, however, have shown that the confession of God and Christ is not only integral but fundamental to the "main article" of Lutheran teaching, justification by faith. Nevertheless, contemporary theology still betrays a certain uneasiness, to say the least, with the assertions made in Art. III, as a critical reading of ecumenical agreements will bear out (cf. below, chs.9–11).[2]

Since the present study concerns Christian righteousness, our investigation of Art. III focuses on the "effects of the story," that is, on the purpose and benefits of Christ's coming. On the "story" itself we will make just a few basic observations.

It should be observed, in the first place, that Art. III confesses that "the Word" took on human nature in the womb of the blessed virgin Mary. This affirmation is based on John 1:1–18, especially 1:14. It presupposes the doctrine of the Trinity: *"Only* because the living God *is* eternally Father, Son, and Holy Spirit, can He *as* Son or *in* the Son *become* man, a true man, without ceasing to be God."[3]

Furthermore, the emphasis placed on "one" and "the same" Christ as subject of all the actions is meant to discard Zwingli's attempt to distinguish activities attributed to the divine and actions attributed to the human nature (alloeosis). If properly understood, it also invalidates the current distinction between "the Christ of faith" and "the historical Jesus."[4]

The point is that only the Son of God, who became man in Jesus Christ, the Son of Mary, true God and true man in one person, could perform the work described in the Creeds, namely, reconcile, redeem, and judge.[5]

Reconciliation

The purpose of Christ's coming is defined as follows in the Latin text: "in order to reconcile the Father to us and be an offering (*hostia*) not only for original guilt but also for all actual sins of men" (par. 3). The German text states this purpose somewhat differently: "in order to be an offering ... and appease God's wrath."

This formulation presupposes the teaching expressed in Art. II, that humanity is guilty and stands under God's wrath on account of sin. This teaching, again, reflects the understanding that the Law reveals man's sinfulness and God's wrath over sin, as it is stated in the sources of the AC.[6]

In short, the statement on the purpose of Christ's coming presupposes that reconciliation is necessary. It becomes meaningless if human guilt and God's wrath are toned down and the need for reconciliation is ignored.

One should not overlook that the reconciling activity is attributed to the one and same Christ, true God and true man, the very Word of God. This actually means, as Regin Prenter has shown, that through His humanity God's own Son reconciles the Father with us. The confession of Art. III, therefore, reaffirms the apostle Paul's proclamation in 2 Cor. 5:18–19, that in Christ God Himself reconciled the world unto Himself. Reconciliation, then, is an exchange between the Son and the Father in God Himself, as Luther also extols in the hymn, "Dear Christians, One and All, Rejoice."[7] In order to understand the import of the predicate, "to reconcile the Father with us," one must study Melanchthon's use of *reconcile* in the AC. He uses two verbs, *placare* and *reconciliare,* in the Latin text. With the first he refers to people's efforts to appease God's wrath (and merit grace and/or forgiveness) through the Mass and the keeping of church regulations like fasting.[8] Eventually he uses *reconciliare* to assert that good works cannot reconcile us with God. In a positive sense, however, *reconciliare (Patrem)* is applied exclusively to Christ.[9]

This indicates that the statement on Christ's coming in Art. III has polemical implications. If reconciling the Father is an exclusive attribute of Christ, it follows that we cannot reconcile or appease God through our works and acts of worship. This means that there are no God-appeasing works, but that He is appeased and favorable on account of Christ alone, as the Gospel proclaims.

The use of the present tense in Art. XX, par. 9, indicates that the expression *because of Christ,* which plays a decisive role in the doctrine of faith, refers to the *totality* of His work, including the past but extending into the present and the future. As Luther states in his "Great Confession," He stands up and steps forward day by day on our behalf as our "faithful, merciful Mediator, Savior, and only Priest and Bishop of our souls." He is "our one mercy seat" (*gnaden stuel.*)[10]

This view of Christ's continued work constitutes the basis for the frequent assertion that because of Christ we have an appeased and favorable God through faith in the same Christ.

In the Reformers' view the opponents tried to make satisfaction for sins not only through satisfactions imposed in connection with the sacrament of penance, but also through the observation of other "traditions." These included monastic vows and observances, rules about foods, fasts, holy days, and the like. According to the AC, people intended not only to make satisfaction for sins, but also to merit forgiveness of sins, justification, and/or God's grace through the observation of these traditions.[11]

Melanchthon applies *satisfacere pro peccatis* in its positive sense exclusively to Christ. In Art. XXIV he denies the theory that He made satisfaction only for original sin.[12] In Art. IV he states that "Christ ... by his death made satisfaction for our sins."[13] Even though he does not use exclusive particles, he really means that *Christ alone* made satisfaction for our sins and that none of us can make satisfaction for sin through any observance or act of worship.

It follows, according to the AC, that *Christ alone* is the consideration which prompts the Father to forgive and receive into grace those who believe that they are forgiven and accepted *on account of Christ*. This is true not only in the beginning, when they first become righteous, but also afterwards, when they already are righteous and acceptable to God.

In this way the assertion, "Christ came to be an offering for all sins," with its negative and positive connotations, points toward "because of Christ through faith" in the main sentence of Art. IV. It points also to Art. VI, since through faith in Christ we keep receiving forgiveness and righteousness after we have been justified and enabled to do really good works.[14]

Sanctification

The Latin text indicates that sanctification presupposes the sending of the Holy Spirit into the believers' hearts. Art. V explains that there He engenders faith in the Gospel or the promise of forgiveness because of Christ. Art. III says in the Latin text that He rules, comforts, and raises to life. This being comforted and quickened, as the sources of the Confession indicate, derives from hearing and believing in the promise of forgiveness; it is therefore connected with the birth and growth of faith.[15]

In the light of these observations it can be said that Christ sanctifies inasmuch as He, through the Holy Spirit, creates faith in the promise and thereby not only justifies but also comforts and quickens the terrified heart.[16]

This interpretation is confirmed by still another consideration: Christ or the Holy Spirit sanctifies, purifies, strengthens, comforts, distributes goods through the *Gospel* and the *sacraments,* which implies that He does it through faith, for these means both demand and impart faith in Christ.

This broad connotation of *sanctifying* is also documented by Luther's Large Catechism. There it applies to the Holy Spirit's activity of leading people to the Lord Christ for the reception of His gifts (Tappert, pp. 415–16).

Besides sanctifying the believers, Christ also defends and protects them with (or through) the Holy Spirit against the power of sin. This enables them to do truly good works, as Art. XX, 29–34, demonstrates.

Summary of Findings

The description of Christ's activity in Art. III explains for what purpose He has come. He came to make satisfaction for our sins and to give us not only forgiveness, righteousness, and eternal life, but also the Holy Spirit, who rules and protects us. He did not come to issue a new law in order that we may merit righteousness through certain works. In the Reformers' estimation the opponents not only regarded Him as the giver of a new law but also strove to keep His precepts in order to merit righteousness and eternal life.[17] Inasmuch as Art. III envisions Christ not as a legislator but as the Redeemer, it is implicitly attacking the opponents. A polemical thrust, therefore, is present in both sections on the purpose of Christ's coming.

Art. III recalls both the "story" and the "results" of the story. It reaffirms the teaching of the ecumenical creeds and emphasizes the benefits of Christ's work for us. In this way it provides the basis for the teaching on faith and works presented in Arts. IV–VI and elsewhere in the AC. Conversely, however, the Christology of Art. III is determined by the Lutheran doctrine of faith in a very specific sense:

Only if one knows that justification is through faith in Christ can he fully recognize the purpose of Christ's coming, according to Melanchthon.[18]

Thus the doctrine of faith and the doctrine of Christ condition each other. This should not be surprising inasmuch as faith is *faith in Christ,* and Christ is proclaimed to be *believed,* that is, to be embraced, held, and resorted to through faith in Him.

CHAPTER 6

The Doctrine of Faith in Art. IV

In Art. IV we are confronted with the declaration of that doctrine which both explains and justifies the Reformation.

The sources this article reproduces indicate that the doctrine of justification through faith results necessarily, at least in the Reformers' estimation, from the creedal confession of Christ the Lord. They warrant the conclusion that Art. IV most probably consists of *two* propositions, which respond to the questions: First, how does one become righteous? Second, what is the righteousness whereby the Christian is definitively righteous before God?

As a syntactical compound, Art. IV is made up of two sentences. The first, "Our churches also teach that ... ," comprises two clauses which depend on the transitive verb *teach*. The first of these dependent clauses expresses a negative assertion, "men cannot be justified before God by ... " The second clause is an (adversative) positive assertion, "but [that they] are freely justified for Christ's sake through faith, as they believe ... " The second full sentence comprises only a main clause. While in the Latin text it is coordinated without a particle, in the German it is connected to the preceding sentence by a conjunction, *denn*: "For God will regard and reckon this faith as righteousness ... " (Tappert, p. 30).

The Negative Clause: How Men Cannot Be Justified

In the Latin text the negative dependent clause affirms "that men cannot be justified before God by their own strength, merits, or works"; in the German, "that we cannot obtain forgiveness of sin and righteousness before God by our own merits, works, or satisfactions."

The corresponding Latin clause in Art. XX states "that our works cannot reconcile God or merit forgiveness of sins and grace"; the German, "that our works cannot reconcile us with God or obtain grace for us" (Tappert, p. 42).

All four statement emphasize the *cannot,* and this negative concerns specifically men's powers, merits, and works of satisfaction. The underlying question is not, How are people justified? It is, *Can* they be justified or obtain forgiveness and grace before God by their own powers, merits, or works (satisfactions)?

The question assumes the opinion that people *can* merit grace by these means. This opinion, however, is nothing but the opponents' teaching of *meritum de congruo,* as the Reformers saw it. The negative clause of Art. IV, therefore, questions very specifically the prevalent teaching that men could by their own powers, merits, or satisfactions obtain grace, that specific grace which is love and renders the doer of good works acceptable to God.

This fact becomes evident if one compares the fifth Schwabach article with the controversialists' Refutation of the same. The article states that man cannot free himself from sin, death, and the devil by his own powers and good works; that he cannot prepare himself for righteousness. The Refutation consists in a straightforward defense of *meritum de congruo*: Man *can* on the basis of prevenient grace prepare himself for (further) grace and righteousness through good works.

Melanchthon's formulation of the question does not take into consideration this distinction between God's initiative or prevenient grace and the (relatively minor?) role played by human free will in accomplishing *meritum congrui.* It has been suggested that he did not know the polemicists' position accurately, but it is possible that he considered their distinctions beside the point and misleading. It seems, in fact, that they were asking, *How much* can man accomplish by his powers—unaided or aided by prevenient grace? Melanchthon, however, asks whether man can *at all* merit grace and righteousness by his own powers and works.[1]

The answer given in Art. IV is: "No, men cannot at all ... "

Man's Condition

The radical "cannot" of Art. IV rests on the Lutheran conception of original sin, God's law, and Christ's work as expressed or implied in Arts. II and III. While this connection is implied in the text read at the Diet, it is stated explicitly in the first edition of the German original as well as in the Schwabach Articles.[2]

In Art. II one reads that human beings cannot merit grace by their own powers and works because all of them are conceived and born in sin; they are full of evil lust and desires and, by nature, cannot have fear of and true confidence in God. On account of this sinfulness they are subject to His eternal wrath, unless reborn through Baptism and the Holy Spirit.

This confession of Art. II in the German text implies that men have no free will except in the sense defined in Art. XVIII. As the *editio princeps* indicates, Art. II presupposes that all people should keep the Law and love God with all their heart. It assumes that His wrath against sin is so great that no creature but only His own Son could still it.

This means that the "cannot" of Art. IV rests not only on a specific view of man, but also on a certain view of God and the Law. It implies that man's natural condition is such that he cannot and will not do good on the basis of a partial remedy like prevenient grace. It implies that God's demands are so high, and His anger at human sin so severe, that He cannot and will not regard as meritorious of grace and salvation any of our feeble attempts to do good.

Christ's Honor and Glory

The "cannot" of Art. IV rests also on the concluding paragraph of Art. II, which holds that those who argue that man can be justified before God by his own powers obscure the glory of Christ's merit and gifts. In order to understand wherein this glory consists, it is necessary to examine other passages which employ *meritum Christi* and similar expressions.

According to Art. XX, "whoever trusts that he merits grace by works despises the merit and grace of Christ." According to Art. XXVI it is important that Christ's merit be recognized adequately, and therefore it is necessary to teach grace and the righteousness of faith. According to Art. XXVIII the glory of Christ's merit is hurt when people think they are justified (Latin) or merit grace (German text) by keeping the observations decreed by the bishops.[3]

The expression *gloria Christi* appears in two passages of Art.

XXVII. In par. 38 the monks are accused of having detracted from Christ's glory and denied the righteousness of faith by teaching that monastic practices "make satisfaction for sins and merit grace and justification." On the basis of Gal. 5:4 it is argued in pars. 41–43 that people who attribute justification to monastic vows "ascribe to their own works what properly belongs to the glory of Christ." This glory, as the German text suggests, consists in justifying, for it is Christ "who alone justifies."

The section of the Torgau Articles which underlies these passages accuses the monks of attributing to humans works and acts of worship the honor which belongs to Christ: He "has acquired grace, and we obtain it through faith without merit of ours." Christ's honor, therefore, consists in *acquiring grace* (AC XXVII, 38, 42–43). This is confirmed by the German text of Art. XII, par. 5. It affirms that true repentance includes believing "the Gospel and absolution (namely, that sin has been forgiven and grace has been obtained through Christ)."

The conviction that Christ alone merits grace is expressed also in Art. XXIV, par. 30: Terrified consciences learn "that through the sacrament grace and forgiveness of sin are promised us by Christ." The corresponding Latin text states that the Mass was instituted in order that the faith of the communicants may recall which gifts (*beneficia*) it obtains through Christ. On the basis of the German text it can be assumed that these "benefits" include grace and the forgiveness of sins.[4]

The teaching that Christ earned grace also underlies an assertion of Art. XX, 23, which holds that true faith believes "that we have grace, righteousness, and forgiveness of sins through Christ."

These passages demonstrate clearly that for the AC Christ's glory and honor consists in reconciling the Father and obtaining grace and justifying.

On the basis of this observation it is possible to understand the connection between the last paragraph of Art. II and the first sentence of Art. IV. Since reconciling the Father, obtaining grace, and justifying is Christ's very own work, it follows indeed, as the AC argues, that men cannot be justified before God by their own powers and works, that their works do not merit God's grace and forgiveness. Consequently, predicates like "meriting grace and forgiveness" and "justifying before God" must be attributed exclusively to Christ,

THE DOCTRINE OF FAITH

the Son of God; they do not pertain to human works. Thus the "cannot" of Art. IV is closely connected with an awesome vision of Christ's unique activity.

The first dependent clause of Art. IV must therefore be understood as asserting the negative consequences derived from this view of Christ's unique work and of man's condition as revealed by God's law.

"Before God"

The dependent clause we are analyzing denies the possibility of being justified (Latin) or obtaining righteousness (German) "before God" through one's powers, merits, or works. The expression *coram Deo, vor Gott,* implies the distinction between the righteousness of the Law or of reason, also termed human, carnal, philosophical, or civil righteousness, and the righteousness of the Gospel, also called divine, spiritual, internal, Christian, and eternal righteousness.[5]

This distinction is stated often in the Reformers' works, for instance in Melanchthon's *Outline* of the Letter to the Romans. The apostle Paul's expression *iustitia Dei,* it says, denotes the righteousness by which God reckons us righteous or by which we are righteous before God. The other righteousness we know is termed "carnal" or "human" in view of its efficient cause: It is the righteousness by which natural man or the flesh justifies itself or makes itself righteous.[6] The distinction is made also in the *Instructions for Visitors,* in the section on "Free Will" and "Christian Freedom."[7]

The AC does not explicitly define the two kinds of righteousness, even though Melanchthon knew that some of his fellow Lutherans at Augsburg had not mastered the distinction.[8] Art. XVIII, 1–3, however, clarifies the distinction as it affirms that human will has a kind of freedom to accomplish civil righteousness and to choose between the things subject to reason, but does not have the power of producing, without the Holy Spirit, the righteousness of God or spiritual righteousness. This is created in the heart as the Holy Spirit is received through the Word. In this connection the German text describes civil righteousness as "to live an outwardly honorable life" and spiritual righteousness as one's becoming acceptable to God, sincerely fearing and trusting Him, and expelling from the heart the congenital evil lusts.

In light of these passages one may conclude that the expression *before God* in Art. IV defines the extension of the predicate in the dependent clause. It conveys that human powers and works cannot justify *before God* in the sense that they cannot produce the righteousness which *God* regards as such. It does not deny the possibility of accomplishing the righteousness which human society regards as such, as the opponents construed.

The expression evidently has a "forensic" connotation. It refers to God as the Judge who operates with an unexpected criterion of righteousness: He recognizes and declares as righteousness something which no creature could ever have conceived or recognized as such, namely, faith in Christ, His Son. It follows that justification, properly speaking, can only be regarded as *forensic:* It always takes place before the throne of God's judgment and mercy.⁹

Powers, Merits, Satisfactions

As to what is excluded in Art. IV, the Latin text denies that men's own powers, merits, or works justify; the German, that merits, works, and satisfactions obtain forgiveness of sins and righteousness.

The Latin has no explicit reference to satisfactions, but it can be assumed that *opera* denotes not only works of love performed to fulfill the Law, but also the common worship practices, including the Mass and penitential satisfactions.

The German text omits the reference to men's powers. The Latin text has the plural *viribus* here and in Art. II, and both the singular *vim* and the plural *viribus* in Art. XVIII. They denote man's natural powers as summed up in the notion of free will. The other element excluded is the merit of congruity, as we have seen.

The triad of either text, then, denies all of men's possibilities. As will appear below, *propriis viribus, meritis aut operibus* stands in contrast to *per fidem*; and *durch unser Verdienst, Werck und Gnugthun* stands in contrast to *durch den Glauben* in the positive dependent clause. The contrasting terms are mutually exclusive according to the AC.

THE DOCTRINE OF FAITH

The Positive Dependent Clause: How Men Are Justified

The second dependent clause of "they teach," which states Lutheran teaching positively, comprises a dominant "but are freely justified for Christ's sake through faith" and a subordinate clause. The latter comprises a dominant "as they believe" and an object clause, "that they are received into grace and that [their] sins are forgiven because of Christ. . . ."

THE DOMINANT CLAUSE

A close analysis of the Latin text demonstrates that the object clause of "they teach" corresponds to Melanchthon's definition of the content of the Gospel, which is the "object" of faith. The subordinate clause "as they believe" is an appositive explanation of "through faith." The object clause of "they believe" restates the "object" of faith and therefore explains the key terms of the preceding object clause of "they teach."

The same relationships prevail in the German text, even though different terms are used. As the analysis progresses, the relevance of these findings for the interpretation of Art. IV will become evident.

In the Latin text the positive object clause depending on "they teach" reads as follows: "that men . . . are freely justified for Christ's sake through faith as they believe that they are received into grace and that [their] sins are forgiven because of Christ. . . ." In Art. V the Gospel is characterized as declaring that "it is not because of our merits but on account of Christ that God justifies those who believe that they are received into grace for Christ's sake." The content of the Gospel as expressed in Art. V evidently is identical with the churches' teaching reported in Art. IV.

In the German text of Art. V the Gospel is said to teach "that we through Christ's merit, not through our merit, have a gracious God, as we believe this." The dependent clause which reports the churches' teaching, however, reads in Art. IV:

"that we receive forgiveness of sins and become righteous before God by grace, for Christ's sake, through faith, as we believe that Christ suffered for us and that for his sake sins are forgiven, righteousness and eternal life is [sic] given to us." If one assumes that to "have a gracious God ... through Christ's merit" is the same as to "receive forgiveness of sins and become righteous before God ... for Christ's sake," it follows that the two statements correspond to each other in the same way as those of the Latin text.

The observation we have made finds confirmation in passages of Melanchthon's *Dispositio* of the Letter to the Romans which define the Gospel in terms that correspond very closely to the formulations of Art. IV.

Thus in the outline of ch. 11 the author distinguishes between Christ's teaching and philosophy. Human reason, he says, did not at all know the Gospel, "that we are justified freely before God, as we believe that we are received into grace by the Father on Christ's account." With Rom. 1:16 in view he writes:

"The Gospel teaches the righteousness which justifies before God.... The Gospel discloses the righteousness of faith, that before God [those] are considered righteous who believe that they are received into grace because of Christ."[10]

If the correspondence between the main assertion of Art. IV and the definition of the Gospel in Art. V is assumed, it follows that the expressions used in the two statements correspond to each other. This means, for instance, that *gratis, aus Gnaden* (Art. IV), corresponds to "not because of our merits," *non propter nostra merita, nicht durch unser Verdienst,* in Art. V.

This correspondence is confirmed by passages which explicitly interpret *gratis* as "without our merits."[11] The term *gratis*, therefore, must be regarded as the counterpart to "because of Christ." It excludes human merits and qualities as motivation for God to justify man, while *propter Christum* denotes Christ as God's only "motivation" for justifying the person who claims Him as being indeed the Father's only ground for justifying us.

The Subordinate Appositive Clause

The dependent clause of "they teach" comprises a dominant and a subordinate clause. We have examined the dominant; now we must consider the subordinate clause, "as they [men] believe that ... ," which is appended to the words "because of Christ through faith." Our question is, Which function does this clause exercise in the argumentation?

Our study of the sources of the AC indicated that the formulation *so wir glauben, daß* ... , which we have rendered, "as we believe that ... ," is not perfunctory but explicates the expression *durch den Glauben*, "through faith," and defines in which respect justification is said to be *through faith*, namely, *by believing* something very specific.[12] The present investigation of Art. IV will have to confirm these findings, or determine their correction. At any rate we cannot dare to overlook the formulation, as some studies have done.[13]

The subordinate clause we are considering comprises a dominant, "as they believe," and a dependent object clause, "that they are received into grace and [their] sins are forgiven because of Christ. . . ." In the German text one finds two object clauses, however, for the statement on Christ is formulated as an object rather than as a relative clause. Both the Latin and the German texts display a dominant clause with a transitive verb followed by the corresponding object clause(s).

The object clause of "as they believe" describes what men (are supposed to) believe, that is, the "object" of their believing. Since the "object" of faith is the Gospel, it can be said that the object clause under consideration reproduces the content of the Gospel. In this case, however, this object clause is identical with the clause depending on "they teach," since the latter reproduces the teaching of the Gospel, too.

The identity between the content of the Gospel and the "object" of faith is conveyed explicitly in the German text of Art. V, where the object of the verb "believe' is the demonstrative pronoun *solchs*, "this." The pronoun refers back to the preceding dominant clause. This clause, however, summarizes what the Gospel declares, namely, that through the merit of Christ we have a gracious God.[14]

The formulation which Melanchthon used in Art. V, therefore, confirms the supposition that in Art. IV the statements introduced by "they teach" and "they [men] believe" reproduce the content of the Gospel in similar terms.

This conclusion has a consequence decisive for the interpretation of Art. IV: If the definition of the Gospel in the main dependent clause of "they teach" is reworded in the dependent clause of "they believe," it can be assumed that the key terms of the former correspond to the main expressions of the latter. This means, among other things, that *iustificentur* corresponds to *in gratiam recipi et peccata remitti,* and that *propter Christum* matches *qui sua morte pro nostris peccatis satisfecit.* Consequently the sentence, "men ... are justified because of Christ," simply means that "they are received into grace and [their] sins are forgiven" because of Christ's satisfaction.

We shall now prove this observation by examining one by one the key terms and expressions used in these passages. Thereafter we shall try to determine conclusively the relation which prevails between *per fidem, durch den Glauben,* and its seeming reduplication, *cum credimus, so wir glauben.*

"To Become Righteous" (German Text)

In the German text, which is less technical than the Latin, "we receive forgiveness of sins and become righteous before God by grace because of Christ" (affirmative dominant clause) corresponds to "for his sake sin is forgiven, righteousness and eternal life is [sic] given to us" (subordinate clause of "as we believe"). The correspondence is perfect, except for the pair, "become righteous" and "righteousness and eternal life is given," which demands further attention.

The German *gerecht (fromm) werden,* "to become righteous," as used in the AC, is the equivalent of *iustificari.* In most of the cases it is used to describe and reject the position attributed to the opponents.[15] The same is true of the active form, *gerecht (fromm) machen,* "to make righteous or pious."[16]

Two passages besides Art. IV, however, do employ *gerecht werden* in stating the Lutheran position. Art. XX, par. 13, maintains that Augustine, too, teaches "that we obtain grace and become righteous before God through faith in Christ and not through works." Art. XXVI, par. 5, holds that Paul's struggle against the law of Moses and human tradition teaches "that before God we do not become righteous on the basis of our works, but only through faith in Christ, that for Christ's sake we obtain grace."

Both passages emphasize becoming righteous "through faith in Christ," not through or on the basis of works. This provides an indication as to where the emphasis is placed in Art. IV as well. The second passage even clarifies the meaning of "faith in Christ," as it appends a clause which defines it as believing that we obtain grace

THE DOCTRINE OF FAITH

"for Christ's sake." This formulation is very similar to that of Art. IV. Neither passage, however, explains the meaning of *gerecht werden*. The only indication concerning its meaning remains the correspondence to "righteousness and eternal life are given" in Art. IV. Therefore we shall now examine this expression.

"To Be Endowed with Righteousness" (German Text)

The term *Gerechtigkeit,* righteousness, is used several times outside of Art. IV.

According to four passages of Art. XXVII, the advocates of monasticism taught that the monks obtain or merit righteousness and God's grace. The original reads: *Gerechtigkeit und/oder Frombkeit erlangen oder verdienen.*[17] According to further passages in Arts. XXVI, XXVII, and XXVIII, the righteousness of faith was obscured, denied, or suppressed by the teachings concerning monasticism and the religious practices imposed by the bishops.[18]

According to Art. IV righteousness is *given as a present* because of Christ. Art. III, par. 5, affirms that it is Christ who through the Holy Spirit shares life and all kinds of gifts. This agrees with Luther's "Great Confession," which states explicitly that Christ has given the believers His righteousness, thus making them righteous and giving them life.[19]

As to how this righteousness is given, passages which employ *Gerechtigkeit* state the Lutheran position positively. The most important is Art. XXVIII, par. 9: Through the power of the keys or the bishops' power "are given ... eternal things and goods, namely, eternal righteousness, the Holy Spirit, and eternal life. One cannot obtain these goods except through the office of preaching and through the distribution of the holy Sacrament."[20]

This passage states quite clearly that the righteousness and eternal life referred to in Art. IV is given *through the ministry of the preached Word and the administration of the sacraments.* Since both the Word and the sacraments have in common the Gospel or promise of forgiveness and grace because of Christ, Melanchthon is able to state in a parallel passage, par. 4 of Art. XVI, that "the Gospel teaches (*lehrt, tradit*) ... an internal, eternal reality (*Wesen*) and righteousness of the heart."

Further passages explain *how* the righteousness given through the Gospel or through the preached Word and the sacraments becomes ours. According to Art. XXVII, par. 37, Paul teaches everywhere "that righteousness and goodness (*Frombkeit*) before God springs from faith and confidence, [namely] that we believe that God takes us into grace for the sake of His only Son, Christ." According to Art. VI "we receive forgiveness of sins and righteousness through faith in Christ."

The thesis that the righteousness given through the Gospel becomes ours *through faith in Christ* assumes the correlation between the promise and faith, the "argument derived from the nature of relative terms." It is stated as follows: "Every promise is received by faith. Righteousness is promised. Consequently righteousness must be received by faith."[21]

Summing up, the usage of *Gerechtigkeit* in the AC indicates that righteousness before God cannot be obtained or merited through men's works and religious practices, but is given by Christ through the Word and the sacraments and is received through faith in Christ or in the promise which declares that God receives us into grace because of Christ.

It will be recalled that the usage of *gerecht werden,* too, indicates that we become righteous not on the basis of works, but through faith in Christ, namely by believing that because of Christ we obtain forgiveness of sins.

On the basis of these findings and in view of the correspondence between the dependent clause of "it is taught" and the object clause of "as we believe," we may paraphrase the German text of Art. IV as follows: "It is taught ... that we receive forgiveness of sins and righteousness before God freely because of Christ through faith, as we believe that ... God, through the Word and the sacraments, forgives us our sins and gives us righteousness and eternal life because of His Son, Christ."

In other words, we "become righteous" by *being given and receiving* righteousness. We become righteous *freely, aus Gnaden,* because righteousness is not a reward for merit, but a *gift* given by or because of Christ. Above all, however, we become righteous *on account of Christ* because *He* imparts us His righteousness, or because *He* is God's only ground for giving us righteousness. We become righteous *through faith* because the righteousness which God promises, offers, and gives through the Word and the sacraments can be *received* only through faith in the same Word and sacraments which tell us exactly that God gives us forgiveness, righteousness, and eternal life because of Christ.

"To Be Justified" (Latin Text)

In the Latin text of Art. IV "they are justified because of Christ through faith" corresponds to "they are received into grace and [their] sins are forgiven because of Christ."[22]

The meaning of *iustificari* is not explicitly defined in the AC. The usage of the term indicates that, in Melanchthon's estimation, the opponents wanted to be justified by faith and works, by monastic vows and observances, by religious practices decreed by the bishops.[23] The use of the active form of this verb in other passages suggests that the opponents were alleged to believe that traditional acts of worship (*traditiones, cultus*), especially monastic vows, justify in God's sight.[24]

Outside of Art. IV the passive form *iustificari* is used only once to state the Lutheran position, in Art. XXIV, par. 28: "Scripture teaches that we are justified before God through faith in Christ."

The active form is used once in the Latin and once in the German text in passages stating the Lutheran position. The subjects are, respectively, God and Christ.[25]

In this way Melanchthon establishes a contrast between "God/Christ justifies" and "works/acts of worship justify," between "we are justified through faith in Christ" and "we are justified by (faith and) works, monastic observations, and religious practices."[26]

The meaning of *iustificari* can be established at least tentatively on the basis of the expressions which reproduce it in the German text, namely, "to obtain (merit) grace" (thrice), "to obtain forgiveness of sins and righteousness" (once), and "to receive forgiveness of sins and become righteous" (once).[27]

"To Be Received into Grace" (Latin Text)

In Art. IV *iustificari* is paralleled by *recipi in gratiam et peccata remitti*, "to be received into grace and to be absolved."

The expression *recipi in gratiam* plays a peculiar role in the AC. In contrast to the terms and expressions studied so far, it is used exclusively in assertions stating the Lutheran position. In all the passages but one, Art. IX, par. 2, it appears in object clauses of *credere,* "to believe," and is qualified by *propter Christum,* "because of Christ."[28] It can be said, therefore, that *recipi in gratiam propter Christum* defines most properly the object of faith in Melanchthon's way of speaking.

But what does *recipi in gratiam* mean? The AC only hints at the meaning.

According to the Latin text of Art. IX God's grace is offered through Baptism, and children ought to be baptized, for thus they are offered to God and received into His grace. According to the German text they become acceptable to God, *werden Gott Gefällig.*[29] This means that in Melanchthon's representation "to be received into grace" is to become the object of God's favor.

Art. V confirms this impression. There the Latin speaks of being received into grace because of Christ, and the German, of having a gracious God, *ein gnädigen Gott haben,* through Christ's merit.

Similarly in Art. XX, par. 15, "having a gracious God because of Christ" corresponds to "having an appeased God," *habere placatum Deum,* because of Christ. Some lines later, in par. 24, "having a gracious God through Christ" corresponds to "having a favorable Father through Christ," *per Christum habere propitium Patrem.*

As the constant use of *propter Christum* and *per Christum* indicates, the expression *recipi in gratiam* presupposes that Christ has reconciled the Father, and that the Father, on account of that reconciliation, is favorable toward those who believe in Christ, the Mediator. God's favor because of Christ finds expression first in making sinners the object of this favor and then in being permanently favorable to those who cling to Christ as ground of such undeserved benevolence.

The expression *recipi in gratiam propter Christum,* therefore, evokes the moment in which man first becomes the object of God's favor because of Christ's reconciliation. This explains why it is used precisely in connection with infant baptism. The person who has been received can "fall from grace," however, and this poses the need for being accepted again when returning to faith. For this reason *recipi in gratiam* is a technical expression of the doctrine of repentance as well.

The sources of the AC, which must also be taken into consideration, use "to be received into grace because of Christ" in passages which define the specific object and consequently the precise nature of true faith. Such is the case of the fifth Schwabach article. It affirms that God justifies those "who have this faith in the Son, that because of Him they will be received into grace and become children in His kingdom." The Visitation Articles also explain, "Faith is to hold for sure that because of Christ [our] sins are forgiven to us and that God intends to rule and defend [the person] already received into grace." While the passage of the Schwabach Articles indicates that being received into grace results in being adopted as God's child, the Visitation Articles suggest that it is closely connected, if not identical with being absolved of sin, for *iam receptus in gratiam* refers back to the person whose sins have been forgiven.[30]

The close connection between *peccata remitti* (having one's sins forgiven) and *in gratiam recipi* is signalized by the conjunction *seu* in the following passage of the *Dispositio* of the Letter to the Romans:

"The Gospel teaches that Christ, the Son of God, was given for us and that to believe that our sins are forgiven to us because of Christ or (*seu*) that we are received into the Father's grace because of Christ is righteousness before God." Another passage in the Visitation Articles defines faith as believing that "God pities us and receives us into grace," suggesting that the latter results from the former. A similar passage in the *Loci communes* encourages us not to doubt that "our sins are forgiven to us, and God already favors us and wishes us well," *iam faveat ac bene velit*.[31]

These passages indicate that, in definitions of the specific object of faith, "to be received into grace" denotes a divine action which concerns very personally the person who believes in the Gospel, an action resulting from Christ's work on behalf of men. The passages do not explain, however, what *the expression as such* means.

"Grace"

In order to establish conclusively the meaning of the expression *in gratiam recipi*, one must finally turn to the passages which define *grace*.

For instance, as Melanchthon comments on Rom. 5:15 in the *Dispositio,* the term *gratia* denotes the forgiveness of sins or, grammatically speaking, favor.[32] In the *Loci* he remarks on the same passage: "He [Paul] calls *grace* God's favor by which He has embraced Christ, and in Christ and because of Christ all the saints." He adds that he, too, understands *grace* as denoting "favor, mercy, God's free (*gratuita*) benevolence toward us." Then he summarizes, "grace is nothing else than *condonatio* or forgiveness of sin."[33]

The explanations given in these passages warrant the conclusion that "to be received into grace" is to become the object of God's mercy, to be included in the favor by which the Father embraces His Son and—with Him and because of Him—all the saints adhering to Him through faith in Him.

Summary

The object clause of "they believe" in Art. IV can, therefore, be reproduced as follows: "that they are taken into God's favor and [their] sins are forgiven because of Christ." Consequently, on the basis of the correspondence between this object clause and that of "they teach," it can be maintained that "to be justified because of Christ" is the same as "to be received into God's favor and have one's sins forgiven because of Christ."

It follows that, in Melanchthon's understanding, justification comprises two elements which are closely connected, if not identical with each other, namely, the forgiveness of sins and the reception into God's favor because of Christ through faith in Him. Being *justified* in this sense entails being at once adopted as God's child and entitled to life eternal as co-heir with the Son, as the fifth Schwabach article and the German text of Art. IV of the AC indicate.[34]

In order to visualize our findings we will incorporate them into a reformulation of both the German and the Latin texts of Art. IV. The German will then read:

> ... we receive forgiveness of sins and become righteous before God (or are given and receive God's righteousness) freely because of Christ through faith, as we believe that ... because of Christ [our] sins are forgiven and righteousness and eternal life is given to us.

Similarly, the Latin text will sound as follows:

> ... men ... are justified before God (or are taken into God's favor and have their sins forgiven) freely because of Christ through

faith, as they believe that they are received into God's favor and [their] sins are forgiven because of Christ.

If one assumes that the dependent clauses of "they teach" and "they [men] believe" indeed correspond to each other, it can be concluded that both original texts, each with its proper formulation of the predicates, envision two "moments" which are closely related, namely, that God first forgives sins and then takes into His favor or grants righteousness. The result in any case is that the former sinner or unrighteous person (*iniustus*) is now a righteous person (*iustus*) in God's sight and therefore a son of God and member of His household. The transition from being an unrighteous to being a righteous person in God's sight is called *iustificatio*.

How does this "justification" happen? Both texts answer, "because of Christ through faith." At this point there is no divergence at all, no matter how much the texts may otherwise differ. Melanchthon and his colleagues may use different predicates to describe the mysterious action which results in the qualification *righteous*, but they utilize the very same terms when it comes to saying *why* and *how* it happens, namely "because of Christ through faith."

It is to these terms that our investigation must now turn in order to solidify our findings.

"Because of Christ Through Faith"

The expression "because of Christ through faith" is the edge of the article we are considering. In view of its significance we shall successively consider first the meaning of "because of Christ," then the connection between "because of Christ" and "through faith," and finally the syntactical function of the whole expression in the argument of Art. IV.

THE MEANING OF *Propter Christum*

In the German text the expression "because of Christ" in the dependent clause of "it is taught" corresponds to the first object clause of "we believe," which reads, "that Christ suffered for us." In the Latin text it corresponds to the relative clause appended to the clause depending on "they [men] believe": "[because of Christ,] who made satisfaction for our sins by His death."

The German *editio princeps,* which also utilizes a relative clause, adds an explanation: "who reconciled God and made satisfaction for sin through His death" (*BS,* p. 57, 49–50).

The parallel text in Art. XX, par. 9, too, has a relative clause in both originals: "who alone was set up as Mediator and Propitiation, through whom the Father is reconciled."

These explanatory comments evidently point back to Art. III, which maintains that Christ alone made satisfaction for our sins and reconciles the Father with us.

A thorough exposition of *propter Christum* is found in the Visitation article on repentance. It says that there is no satisfaction except Christ's passion. This fact should enhance people's contrition and likewise "increase their faith, as they hear that the [divine] mercy was so great that Christ Himself wanted to offer His death for us. Is there any greater consolation for the afflicted heart than hearing that Christ took [our] sins on Himself and that He wants to regard His satisfaction and not regard any works of ours? For the conscience touched by the horror of judgment knows that they are not sufficient to appease God. Now faith is to hold for sure that [our] sins are forgiven to us because of Christ and that God wants to rule and defend the person who has just been received into grace."[35]

This statement indicates that *propter Christum* denotes that, on account of His or God's mercy, Christ (1) took our sins upon Himself, (2) made satisfaction for our sins or offered His death on our behalf, and (3) is resolved to have regard for His satisfaction, not for any works of ours. It indicates further that faith consists precisely in regarding Christ's reconciliation and satisfaction as God's only cause or motivation for pardoning our sins and taking us into His favor.

These passages warrant the conclusion that "because of Christ" stands for "because of Christ's satisfaction and reconciliation."

The pertinent section of Art. IV can, therefore, be paraphrased as follows: "Men [who believe in Christ] receive forgiveness of sins and are rendered righteous [German] or are justified [Latin] because of Christ's satisfaction and reconciliation." Melanchthon's point is that God is moved to forgive sins and receive into His favor exclusively by Christ's work in past and present.

This fundamental insight still is found in Carpzov, albeit in the terminology of his time.[36]

THE DOCTRINE OF FAITH

In view of the long discussion concerning Melanchthon's "doctrine of justification" (since the last century), it must be realized once for all that he knows only one kind of justification, that which takes place because of Christ's satisfaction and reconciliation and *therefore* through faith in Him.

This realization, however, raises the question, Why does this "because of Christ" require the addition "through faith"? In other words, is our underscoring of *therefore* in the preceding paragraph warranted?

THE CONNECTION *Propter Christum [Ergo] per Fidem*

In order to understand the pairing up of "because of Christ" and "through faith," one must view it in connection with the use of *faith* and *believing*.

Passages of the AC which use the term *faith* in the German text take special care always to specify its object. Some specify "faith *in God*," but most, "faith *in Christ.*"[37]

The care in specifying the object of faith indicates that *faith* and *Christ* are viewed as *correlative* terms, which means that each is regarded as demanding the other. Consequently, whenever the text speaks of Christ, it implies faith, for it assumes that this Christ must be apprehended by faith; whenever it speaks of faith, it implies Christ, for it is assumed that this faith is directed at Christ, apprehends and possesses Him.

The internal necessity which connects "because of Christ" and "through faith" is expressed by the conjunction *itaque* in the Visitation Articles on righteousness:

"The Holy Spirit teaches us that our works do not render satisfaction to God, but that Christ is satisfaction and propitiation; [that] therefore we are justified by faith."

The necessary link between the two terms is also involved in the *Instructions for Visitors,* on satisfaction: "No works of ours can make satisfaction for our sins, for Christ alone has made satisfaction" for them; consequently it is necessary in the practice of repentance "to know and believe that our sins are forgiven us because of Christ." Melanchthon adds a few lines later: "One must know, too, that God wants to forgive sins because of Christ and that one gets this forgiveness by faith (*mit Glauben*), as one believes that God wants to forgive sin because of Christ."[38]

The connection is clear. Because Christ alone made satisfaction for our sins, they are forgiven on *His* account, but since God forgives only because of Him, we get forgiveness only through *faith in Him*—assuming that Christ's satisfaction for our sins "demands" faith and is acknowledged and appropriated by faith alone.

Because forgiveness of sins and grace is given *through Christ,* it follows that it is received only *through faith,* for it is faith alone that acknowledges and confesses Christ and *His* merit as God's "motivation" for absolving and receiving us into His favor. In other words, it is only through faith that *we* become partakers of God's absolution and favor "caused" by Christ's satisfaction and reconciliation *on our behalf.*

Consequently, as Melanchthon states in Art. IV that we receive forgiveness of sins and are rendered righteous (German) or are justified (Latin) "because of Christ through faith," he presupposes that the benefit or result of Christ's work for us *becomes ours* exclusively through faith in Him. This result or benefit is that the Father, "moved" by Christ's work on our behalf, forgives our sins and receives us into His favor or, as the German text declares, endows us with righteousness and eternal life.

The argument developed below the surface is: Men are absolved and taken into favor because of Christ, and since it is on *His* account, they are absolved and taken into favor through *faith in Him*—assuming that the result of His work, God's forgiveness and favor, *becomes ours* only through faith in Him. Or, on the basis of the German text: We receive forgiveness of sins and righteousness because of Christ, and because it is on His account, we receive it only through faith—assuming that His gifts are bestowed and received only through faith in Him.

The linkage of "because of Christ" and "through faith" can also be understood on the basis of the AC passages which employ the verb *to believe.*

One of the most significant is the second paragraph of Art. XIII in the Latin text: Proper use of the sacraments requires the faith "which believes the promises that are set forth and offered" through them (Tappert, p. 35).

Art. XII states in the German text that true repentance is to have sorrow for sins and "to believe the Gospel and absolution (namely, that sin has been forgiven and grace has been obtained through Christ)" (Tappert, pp. 34–35).

According to a parallel passage in Art. XXV, par. 4, "God requires faith," so that we "believe such absolution as God's own voice heard from heaven ... such faith truly obtains and receives the forgiveness of sins."[39]

These passages make clear that faith is *correlated to the promises* inherent in the sacraments and confessional absolution, which assure that God forgives and takes us into His favor because of Christ. These promises at the same time "demand," that is, necessitate faith, for they are made in order to be believed and accepted.

The correlation between faith and promise is implicit also in the passages cited above on the correlation between faith and Christ, for He is made known and available in His role of Reconciler and Propitiation only through the promises of the sacraments, the absolution, and the preached Word. In fact, the promises offer and give precisely the things Christ procured for us, namely, God's favor and absolution. These "benefits," however, are *things promised* because of Christ; therefore they can be received only *through faith*—assuming that it is only through faith that things promised because of Christ can be received. In other words, the passages cited above operate with the "argument drawn from the nature of relative terms," as Melanchthon calls it.

The term to which faith is correlated can be either the Gospel promise or Christ, for both are inseparable. The promise offers and imparts the benefits of Christ's work, namely, forgiveness of sins and our reception into favor on His account. Conversely, the Christ to be apprehended as Reconciler and Propitiation, that is, as the "motivation" for God to absolve and accept us, is manifest and available only through the *promise* of forgiveness and grace, because Christ is inherent in the absolution, the sacraments, and the preached Word—in short, in the Gospel.

On the basis of the correlation between the promise and faith one can say also that the argument underlying "because of Christ through faith" is: We are absolved and taken into favor because of Christ and therefore through faith—realizing that the forgiveness of our sins and God's favor are offered only through the promise, and realizing further that things promised can be received only through faith, not by our own powers, works, and merits. Or, with the German text in view: We receive forgiveness of sins and righteousness because of Christ and therefore through faith, not through our own works, merits, and satisfactions—realizing that the gift of forgiveness and righteousness is imparted only through the promise and is therefore received only through faith.

It is evident, moreover, that the expression "because of Christ through faith" was placed in an emphatic position at the end of the positive dependent clause and contrasts sharply with "by their own powers, merits, or works" in the negative clause. One may conclude, therefore, that the point of Art. IV is that God justifies human beings, and they are justified by God, *because of Christ through faith,* not by their own powers, merits, or works.

The same is true of the corresponding section of Art. XX (par. 9), except that there the emphasis on "by faith" is even stronger, inasmuch as it is not coupled with "because of Christ":" . . . we obtain forgiveness and grace only by faith, as we believe that because of Christ we are received into grace."[40]

THE SYNTACTIC FUNCTION OF *Propter Christum* and *per Fidem*

The next question concerns the syntactic function of "because of Christ" and "through faith." They evidently modify the predicate "to be justified," but one may ask what kind of modification it is. It seems to be *modal,* but this has to be demonstrated. The answer is relevant because it defines more precisely what Melanchthon is trying to say in Art. IV.

It is useful to recall in this connection that one of the points Melanchthon intended to investigate in the Saxon visitation was "how they teach that men are justified."[41] In addition, several prefatory passages have the *how.* They tell us specifically that we are supposed to get forgiveness of sins and grace *through faith!*

These findings coincide with Melanchthon's remarkable statement on the intention of the Letter to the Romans: "The whole Christian doctrine concerns this topic: In what manner are we justified before God, or which thing is Christian righteousness? This definition is the head and *summa* of all Christian doctrine, that is why Paul undertook to explain and clarify this definition."[42]

We take it for granted that the AC presents the Lutheran conception of Paul's teaching (at least as Melanchthon understood it), and therefore we conclude that the answer to "How are we justified before God?" is found precisely in the *modal* qualifiers, "because of Christ through faith."

This means that the *purpose* of Art. IV is to present the Lutheran conception of *how man is justified,* that is, to assert that he is justified *because of Christ through faith in Him.*

This conclusion can be firmly established on the basis of Melanchthon's extensive draft of Art. IV of the Apology, which was replaced during the printing process. His stated intention was to describe the righteousness of faith and to present the manner of justification, *modum iustificationis.* He asks, "How then are we justified before God?" and begins to demonstrate his thesis, that "since the Son of God has been given to us so that we may become accepted by the Father *because of Him,* we are not justified by our merits but *by faith in Christ.*"[43] Melanchthon's point evidently is that we are justified by faith in Christ. In order to prove it, he demonstrates how it necessarily results from the assumption, which he takes for granted, that God accepts sinners on account of Christ alone.

The fifth Marburg article also allows a modal interpretation: "We believe that we are saved from such [original] sin and all other sins as well as from eternal death, if we believe in the same Son of God, Jesus Christ, who died for us," etc.

How are we liberated from sin and death? The answer is *so,* in this way, namely by believing in the Son who died for us.

The same is true of the fifth Schwabach article: "This is the only avenue to righteousness and liberation from sin and death, [namely] believing ... in the Son of God, who suffered for us...." Which is the way to righteousness and life? How does one get there? The answer is: *so man glaubt,* believing in the Son of God, who suffered for us.

In his "Great Confession" Luther explicitly uses the terms *Wege* and *Weise* as he states that there are no "ways or manners of being saved except that single righteousness which our Savior Jesus Christ is and has given to us and has placed before God as our only Propitiation." This assertion confirms beyond doubt that the sources of the AC deal first and foremost with the *how* of justification in the sense that they intend to demonstrate that it is *by believing in Christ* that we are justified.[44]

Finally, one can conclude from early drafts of Arts. XX and IV that the expression *through faith,* once inserted into the text, takes on the role which the dependent clause "as they/we believe" has played since the beginning, which is telling *how* we obtain forgiveness of sins and are rendered righteous. Conversely, there is no reason to suppose that the dependent clause changes its function after the insertion of "because of Christ" and "through faith." It keeps explaining, along with the preceding expressions, *how* one obtains forgiveness and is rendered righteous.

On the basis of these observations we may definitely establish that "because of Christ" and "through faith" are *modal* qualifiers of *iustificari.* They convey the specifically Lutheran answer to the question which in Melanchthon's estimation constitutes the core of Christian doctrine: "How are we justified, or which thing is Christian righteousness?" The answer is clear: We are justified because of Christ through faith, as we believe in Christ, and therefore—as will be demonstrated—this very faith is Christian righteousness.

The Appositive Nature of the Clause, "as They/We Believe . . . "

Now that the nature, function, and linkage of "because of Christ" and "through faith" have been established, it should be possible to determine the syntactic and argumentative function of the dependent clause, "as they/we believe that because of Christ . . . "

The Latin *cum* and the German *so* can mean *when* or *if.* For this reason some studies have argued that the dependent clause tells when or under which condition justification takes place. Most translations actually render the connectives as *when,* implying that the clause under consideration indicates the moment when justification takes place. Such translations give credence to the interpretations which hold that justification occurs when (and if) faith is born.[45]

These interpretations fail to take into consideration the polemical context and the development of Arts. IV and XX.

As far as the polemical context is concerned, Melanchthon and his opponents were not arguing about the time justification takes place. They were discussing whether and in which respect faith is necessary for justification. The "storm center" of the controversy was the Lutheran contention that man is justified by faith *alone.*

The opponents charged the Lutherans with attributing justification to dead, formless faith, for this is how they understood *faith alone*. They argued that justification must be attributed to faith formed by love, for only this faith quickened by love could perform the good works and acquire the merits which God's accepting grace would reward with eternal life.

This explains why in Arts. IV and XX Melanchthon cannot afford simply to state that man is justified by faith in Christ. He is bound to explain why and in which respect faith is said to justify. For this reason he specifies to which (kind of) faith he is referring, and to that end he defines precisely what this faith believes. He assumes with Luther that the nature of faith is determined by its "object," Christ as proferred in the Gospel. Thus he makes clear what kind of faith he is talking about.

As to the development of Arts. IV and XX, a study of pertinent materials evidences that the expression *through faith* does not figure in the first drafts, but was inserted later in the revision process. Originally the dependent clause "as they/we believe" modified directly the predicate of its dominant clause, stating *how* we obtain forgiveness of sins and grace. There is no reason to suppose that the insertion of *through faith* right before the dependent clause changed its character of *modal* clause. One must conclude, therefore, that in the official text the dependent clause constitutes an apposition to the modal modifier *through faith*.

Melanchthon's reasoning can be reproduced as follows. He states in the dominant clause that human beings "are justified because of Christ through faith." But in view of the opponents' teaching he anticipates the question as to how it can be through faith—in which respect? Therefore he intentionally specifies, "because of Christ through faith, that is, as they believe that on *His* account they are absolved and accepted." The dependent clause explicates in which respect men are justified through *true* faith in Christ, seeing that there is a kind of faith which cannot be said to justify, since it does not believe in that in which true faith believes.

This becomes clear if one considers similar passages in other articles of the AC. Art. XX, par. 15, mentions how terrified consciences can be comforted, not by works "but by faith alone, as they acknowledge for sure that they have an appeased God because of Christ." The apposition, *cum certo statuunt*, explicates the modal ablative *fide*. Moreover, according to Art. XXVII, par. 37, "righteousness and goodness before God issues [*sic*] from the faith and confidence that we believe that God takes us into favor because of His only Son Jesus Christ." Here again the apposition *dass wir glauben* along with its object clause defines what faith believes in order to specify what kind of faith is meant and in which respect it attains righteousness.

In several passages the object and thus the justifying nature of faith are specified in a relative rather than an appositive clause.

This is the case in the Latin text of Art. XII, par. 5: One of the parts of repentance is "the faith which is received from the Gospel or absolution and believes that sins are forgiven because of Christ and comforts the conscience and frees from terrors."

Relative clauses are used twice in Art. XXVI as well. The fourth paragraph (Latin text) states that "the faith which believes that sins are forgiven because of Christ" must be placed above all works and acts of worship.[46] The fifth paragraph explains that for the apostle Paul Christian righteousness is the faith which believes that we are received into favor because of Christ. The German text of this paragraph is a perfect parallel to the German of Art. IV, except that the apposition is formulated differently: "that before God we do not become righteous on the basis of our works, but exclusively through faith in Christ, that we obtain grace because of Christ."

These examples indicate that Melanchthon repeatedly provided *faith* with appositive or relative clauses in order to specify *in what* the faith he is referring to believes. The additional clause makes clear that he is referring not to general but to *true* faith, for it is the apprehension of the proper "object" that defines whether faith is true or not. At the same time the additional clause explicates in which sense faith justifies, namely, by recognizing and acknowledging *Christ* as the sole ground of God's absolution and favor.

Consequently, if the stated object of *faith* is the promise that one's sins are forgiven and he is accepted *because of* Christ, it is clear that the term denotes *true, justifying faith*. It means that it justifies precisely by regarding *Christ* as the sole ground of God's favorable verdict. If, however, the "object" of *faith* is nothing but the "story" of Christ as told in the gospels or the creeds without regard for its implications "for us," it is clear that the term is referring to general or historical faith, and this, according to traditional understanding, fails to justify the ungodly and the devils, who do believe "the story."[47]

What properly distinguishes true, justifying faith from general or historical faith is not primarily its "producing much fruit" as new life engendered by the Holy Spirit. The "specific difference" lies in that which faith believes, which for want of a better term we have called its "object."[48]

If we apply these findings to Art. IV, we get the following picture: The dependent clause appended to the modal modifier "through faith," which reads, "as they/we believe that because of Christ...," specifies the object in which faith believes. By doing so it makes clear that we are justified by *true faith,* which consists in believing in the promise that our sins are forgiven and that we are received into favor *because of Christ,* who made satisfaction for us. In other words, Art. IV asserts that one cannot be justified except by acknowledging *Christ,* who made satisfaction for us, as being God's only "motivation" for pardoning our sins and taking us into His favor.

What Faith Is and Why It Justifies

Melanchthon envisions the moment in which the sinner hears the Judge's verdict, "Guilty," but also the promise of forgiveness and grace because of Christ. In this moment the sinner acknowledges his own unrighteousness in contrast to the Judge's righteousness. He looks away from himself, regards only Christ, and appeals to Him alone as the Mediator and Propitiation set up on our behalf. *This looking away from oneself to Christ, this engaging Him for one's salvation,* is true, justifying faith.

At this point it becomes clear that in justification humanity is forced to its knees to glorify Christ, as foreseen in Phil. 2:10–11. The One we crucified as the unrighteous, Him we must acknowledge as the Righteous One, the only One who can help us from unrighteousness to righteousness. The One we despised as forsaken by God, Him we must regard as the only One who enjoys God's favor and is able to extend us the same benevolence.

In short, Christ is entirely vindicated, as sinners turn away from themselves to Him alone. The moment they resort to Him for salvation, they recognize and enjoy Him in the function which the Father assigned Him, and thus they glorify Him.

Faith, then, by making use of Christ, above all gives Him His glory, the glory which the Father gave Him and which men have denied Him all the while.

Melanchthon's struggle for justification by faith alone is indeed a struggle for the glory and honor of Christ.[49] Critics who have accused him of putting faith exclusively at the service of the terrified conscience have failed to read him on his own terms.[50]

In the AC Melanchthon says over and over that the glory and honor of Christ can be acknowledged and promoted only if the doctrine of faith is preached. True, he says also that only through this doctrine can the conscience attain peace. One does not need much theological acumen, however, to realize that this second aspect derives from the first as a necessary consequence. Only if Christ is acknowledged as God's only "cause" for dealing mercifully with us can consciences experience peace, for only then will people realize that God's favor depends *on Him* alone, not on their own works, which always turn out to be imperfect and fail to meet the divine standards.

In fact, what is wrong with being terrified at God's judgment is not its being painful, as most critics seem to assume, but that it is *theologically* blasphemous against God. The terrified conscience, as long as it remains terrified, does not acknowledge that God is reconciled and favorable because of Christ. It remains in a posture of mistrust and rebellion typical of sin. *This* is the fundamental reason why Melanchthon is concerned with overcoming terrors of conscience by faith *in Christ*. He wants to promote adequate knowledge and worship of God on the basis of justification through faith.[51]

True faith, then, is truly a *theological* virtue. It is "out of this world," for it is given and created by God. It goes "out of this world" to Christ, who stands before God on our behalf as our true Advocate and Shepherd. Other virtues have their value in themselves and inside the world. Only faith has its "value" so to say "outside" of itself, namely, in the "object" which it beholds and appropriates.

If one recalls Eck's view of faith as an ineffective virtue immanent in man, and his conception of love as a virtue which ultimately derives its value from fulfilling the Law, not from embracing and "using" Christ, he will realize how far a distance separates him from Melanchthon.[52]

For the moment, however, suffice it to say that the dependent clause, "as they/we believe that because of Christ ... ," restates the correlation between Christ (as proffered in the promise) and faith, that correlation implicit in the linkage of "because of Christ" and "through faith." By doing so, the dependent clause makes clear that according to Lutheran teaching man is justified not by any kind of faith, but by *true* faith *in Christ*—and that faith justifies not as a virtue, quality, or condition, not even as an adequate relation to God, but as it recognizes Christ, the Mediator, as God's only ground for absolving and accepting the sinner.[53]

In view of these findings we cannot concur with contemporary interpretations of Art. IV which play down the correlation between faith and Christ in the promise of the Gospel and postulate that faith justifies inasmuch as it regenerates, that is, establishes a new relation of trust and love to God corresponding to primeval righteousness. In this connection faith is viewed very much like the controversialists' *gratia gratum faciens*.[54]

In our estimation such conceptions of Art. IV fail to reproduce the main feature of Melanchthon's understanding of faith and therefore cannot but misrepresent the role of faith in justification.

It seems that theologians who do not view faith as *fides actualis,* that is, as believing or apprehending the promise of the Gospel, tend to attribute justification to faith not in the relationship category (*in praedicamento relationis*) but in the category of quality (*in praedicamento qualititatis*). The interpretations we have questioned do conceive of faith as a relation to God, but still regard this relation in qualitative terms inasmuch as the new quality called *Gottesverhältnis* is regarded as the basis and condition for being reckoned righteous by God.[55]

This, however, must be discussed in connection with the analysis of the second sentence of Art. IV.

The Second Sentence: Faith as Righteousness

The Meaning of the Sentence

The subject of the sentence under consideration is God, the same God who is the active agent of the passive verbs in the preceding clause. He not only justifies those who believe in Christ, but also imputes this faith as righteousness before Him. What does it mean that God imputes faith as righteousness or, as the German text says, regards and reckons faith as righteousness?

Returning to the sources of the AC, a glance at the Marburg Articles indicates that the assertion of this sentence corresponds to the latter's seventh article, which states that "such faith is our righteousness," in the sense that on account of it "God reckons and regards us as righteous, godly, and holy" (*LW,* 38, 86).

The corresponding section of the fifth Schwabach article reads: "This kind of faith is our righteousness before God, for God intends to reckon and regard as righteous, good, and holy ... all [those] who have such faith in His Son, that because of His Son they shall be received into favor and be children in His kingdom."[56]

The articles quoted have two parts each, and the second part corresponds literally to the formulation of Art. IV, except that here the text reproduces the very wording of Rom. 4:5, presumably to avoid charges of misinterpretation. If it can be assumed that the final sentence of Art. IV corresponds to the seventh of the Marburg and the fifth of the Schwabach Articles, it follows that this sentence affirms, in its peculiar way, the same proposition which the sources uphold, namely, that "*this* faith [described in the preceding sentence] is our righteousness before God." In other words, if God imputes or regards and reckons *this* faith as righteousness before Him, it is clear that *this faith* is our [that is, the believers'] righteousness before God.

The assertion that "*this* faith" is our righteousness before God has a double negative connotation. It suggests first that our righteousness before God does not consist in any works of ours. It conveys further that our righteousness before God is not just any kind of faith, but the specific kind of faith described in the same article. It is not general or common faith, which believes only the "story" and therefore does not resort to Christ as Mediator. It is *special faith,* which believes not only the story of Christ but also and especially the "effects" of the story as they affect *us.* It is the faith which believes that God absolves and accepts us not because of any value of ours, but exclusively because of *Christ,* who died and intercedes *for us.*

The double connotation of "this faith" appears explicitly in Art.

XXVI, par. 5, in a formulation that sounds very much like Art. IV: Paul demonstrates that "Christian righteousness is something other than works of this kind, namely the faith which believes that we are taken into grace because of Christ." The righteousness of the Christian before God, then, is not the works of the Law and human traditions, but faith in Christ; and not just any faith, but a very special kind of faith which believes the specific "object" defined before and consequently entails a new relationship with God.

The theological import of the second sentence of Art. IV can also be detected on the basis of Melanchthon's *Outline* of the Letter to the Romans. It holds that Paul wrote this Letter in order to teach us what righteousness before God is. It consists in believing that we are received into the Father's favor because of Christ, without our merits. The expression *the righteousness of God,* according to the author, is used by the apostle to denote the righteousness by which *God reckons* or by which *we are* righteous before Him.

In the comments on Rom. 3:21 Melanchthon recalls the *summa* of Paul's proposition: "Righteousness before God is to believe that righteousness and forgiveness of sins is [sic] given to us because of Christ without our merits." This is the definition of Christian righteousness or, as Paul says, of God's righteousness, that is, the righteousness "by which *we are* righteous before God or by which *He reckons* us righteous."[57]

These passages indicate that the expressions "our righteousness before God," "Christian righteousness," "the righteousness of God," all denote the same reality, namely, the "thing" by which we are righteous before God or are reckoned righteous by Him. They envision a "permanent" condition: The believer is now righteous, he is counted and regarded as righteous by the same God who first absolved and accepted him in a one-time action which will be repeated only if he becomes unrighteous and must be justified again.

As it states that God reckons and regards faith as righteousness, Art. IV also has in view the condition in which those who believe in Christ *are* righteous before God. It should not be overlooked, however, that "this faith" is placed in an emphatic position at the beginning of the sentence. The emphasis indicates that the point of Art. IV actually is that we are righteous by *faith itself,* that is, by the very same faith which believes that we are absolved and accepted or that forgiveness and righteousness is given to us *because of Christ.*

This means that the faith described in the preceding clause is *itself* our righteousness before God, the thing by which we are or by which He reckons us righteous. This, however, does not mean that faith is *in itself* that righteousness by which we are counted righteous, as we shall see.

What is Melanchthon's basis for affirming that faith is righteousness? The definition of *iustitia fidei* in the analysis of Rom. 10:3–8 provides an answer: The righteousness by which we are justified before God is "to believe in Christ: whoever apprehends this One, he has the end of the Law, that is, he is righteous before God, he has made satisfaction to God."[58] Faith in Christ is our righteousness before God because it takes hold of *Christ,* the end of the Law, and thereby appropriates His attributes, notably His righteousness. In short, faith is righteousness because of its correlation and exchange of attributes with Christ.

Melanchthon's comments on Col. 2:10, *per Christum estis consummati,* express the same understanding:

"Christian righteousness is that kind of righteousness by which one renders satisfaction to God and which justifies before God. But those human works do not render satisfaction to God; Christ, however, made satisfaction; therefore only those are righteous who have been made perfect by Christ, that is, who believe in Christ, that through Him satisfaction has been rendered to the Father, and whom Christ has sanctified by the Holy Spirit." Melanchthon adds that Christian righteousness renders satisfaction to God by believing that the Father has absolved because of Christ; it is created by the Holy Spirit, who engenders faith and brings along other gifts.[59] Faith, then, is righteousness inasmuch as it believes in Christ as the One who has made satisfaction to God on our behalf.

The correlation between faith and the Satisfier is already presented in the *Loci* of 1521. There Melanchthon says that Rom. 4:5 and Gen. 15:16 make clear that faith is called righteousness *apposite*. In the same context he states the correlation quite clearly: "We teach that man is justified by faith alone, that is, that Christ's righteousness is our righteousness through faith...."[60]

It should not be presumed that in the second sentence of Art. IV Melanchthon is expressing a theological peculiarity. He is actually reproducing, in his own words, the teaching on grace and faith which Luther formulated already in the "Preface to the Letter to the

THE DOCTRINE OF FAITH

Romans." Although the New Testament and later the German Bible went through successive editions, Luther never changed it. One may assume that he and his colleagues were satisfied with the formulation of the issues.

As he defines *grace* Luther writes:

> The difference between grace and gift is that grace properly means God's favor or good will which of Himself He holds for us, by which He is led to pour in us Christ and the Holy Spirit with His gifts.... Now, since the gifts and the Spirit augment in us daily, and we are not yet perfect ... still grace effects this much, that we are altogether reckoned as fully righteous. For His grace does not divide or dismember itself as the gifts do, but takes us up altogether into His favor on account of Christ, our Advocate and Mediator, and on account of the fact that the gifts have been started in us.[61]

The statement clearly indicates that, in Luther's view, God's grace will not stop halfway. Once God has expressed His favor, He will follow through and count the whole person as totally and completely righteous in view of Christ and of the incipient renovation. Consequently, Christ can grant him eternal life without further conditions being attached. Luther can make such a bold statement because he assumes the correlation between faith and Christ.

This view of grace, with its intrinsic correlation faith–Christ, prompts Luther's understanding of faith as righteousness:

> Now this faith [which is God's work in us that transforms and begets us anew on God's part] is righteousness and is called the righteousness of God or [the righteousness] which counts in God's sight, on account of the fact that God gives it and reckons it as righteousness because of Christ our Mediator and brings it about that one gives to everyone what he owes him. For (*denn*) through faith man becomes sinless and gets a craving for God's commandments; he thereby gives God His honor and pays everyone his due.[62]

As Luther sees it, faith is righteousness for three reasons: that God gives it, that He reckons it as righteousness on account of Christ the Mediator (whom the Gospel proclaims and the same faith acknowledges as such), and that it effectively pays everyone his due. As the connective *denn* indicates, the forgiveness of sins through faith in Christ, with the ensuing renovation, is assumed in this definition of faith as righteousness very much as in Art. IV, except that renovation is not mentioned here but in the complementary Art. XX.

In brief, the Reformers regarded faith as righteousness not because it is an excellent virtue or regenerates, but because it takes hold of Christ, the Satisfier. Faith is righteousness in God's sight not *in itself,* as a "self-contained" virtue, but because it grasps and holds Christ, our only Righteousness. Consequently, as the second sentence of Art. IV affirms that faith is righteousness, it presupposes the same kind of correlation between faith and Christ which underlies the linkage between "because of Christ" and "through faith" in the first sentence.

If one overlooks this correlation, he will most certainly misunderstand and misrepresent Melanchthon's position. He will assume that faith is righteousness for other, secondary reasons rather than for the reason we have described.

Nevertheless, as the comments on Col. 2:10 and the "Preface to the Letter to the Romans" indicate, the Reformers teach also that faith is an excellent virtue and the beginning of renovation. Therefore they regard it not only as the righteousness proclaimed and imparted by the Gospel, but also as righteousness according to the Law. The incipient or partial fulfillment of the Law which faith effects, however, remains incomplete and is spoiled by sin. Consequently, it cannot by itself be our righteousness before God; only Christ's perfect righteousness, which faith apprehends and possesses, can be the righteousness which God acknowledges and crowns with eternal life.

The Relationship Between the Two Sentences

Now that the meaning and theological import of the second sentence has been determined, it is necessary to establish its relationship to the preceding one.

In the Latin text there is no connective between the two sentences. The German employs the connective *denn,* "for," which suggests that the first sentence is explained and complemented by the second: "We receive forgiveness of sins and become righteous before God ... *through faith,* as we believe that [our] sins are forgiven and righteousness ... is given to us *because of Christ,* for it is *this faith* that God wants to regard and count as righteousness before Him."

The thesis that we receive forgiveness of sins and become righteous before God *through faith* in Christ is enhanced by the additional consideration that *this very faith* is our righteousness before God, the "thing" by which we are righteous before Him. Melanchthon takes for granted that the "thing" by which the believer is (permanently) righteous and the "thing" by which he was justified are identical. If anyone is—or rather presumes to be—righteous by his works, he must assume that he is justified by works. If, however, as the sentence under consideration asserts, the Christian is righteous by faith, he must have been justified by that same faith. Conversely, if the person has been justified by faith, he is also righteous (or is reckoned righteous) by that same faith, which in both cases is focused on Christ.[63]

Our investigation, then, demonstrates conclusively that Art. IV makes *two* assertions concerning faith, namely, that we are justified by faith and that faith is the righteousness by which we are (reckoned) righteous. These two statements correspond to the questions which Melanchthon regarded as the head and *summa* of Christian doctrine: How are we justified? or Which thing is Christian righteousness?[64]

These findings also demonstrate that Melanchthon remained faithful to his sources while making use of relative freedom in formulating the Lutheran position.

Contrast with the Opponents' Teaching

As Melanchthon affirms that man cannot be justified through his own powers, merits, or works, he is denying the opponents' *meritum de congruo*. He maintains that by acquiescing in God's prevenient grace and motion, or by preparing himself through good works done in the power of prevenient grace, man cannot merit the grace which renders him acceptable or righteous. Man does not of himself acquiesce in God's inspiration. God's grace and righteousness is not a reward for merits; it is given to us free of charge because of Christ.

As Melanchthon affirms that men are justified because of Christ through faith, that is, that they are absolved and received into God's favor *by believing in Christ,* he is denying the opponents' teaching of *fides charitate formata* or *fides per charitatem operans.* Faith justifies not because it is formed by love, not because it does good works by the energy love provides, but because and inasmuch as it believes in the promise, that is, apprehends and holds Christ as God's only and exclusive motivation for absolving and accepting the terrified and believing sinner. In short, the AC holds that people are justified before God not by faith formed by love, but by faith "formed by Christ." This is how Luther expressed it in a remarkable postscript to Melanchthon's letter to John Brenz which clarifies the Lutheran position and dispels misunderstanding as to why faith is said to justify.[65]

As Melanchthon says that this faith (believing in the promise or taking hold of Christ) is regarded and reckoned by God as the believer's righteousness, he proposes an alternative to the opponents' *gratia gratum faciens.* He denies that man becomes and is acceptable to God by love inasmuch as it is a God-given gift and fulfills the Law. He holds that man becomes and is righteous or pleasing to God by faith itself, regardless of love, inasmuch as faith believes in the promise and thus apprehends and holds our only Righteousness, Christ Himself. This means that the righteousness by which we are righteous before God or by which God reckons us righteous is not love or the fulfillment of the Law in any sense whatsoever; it is the very faith by which one becomes righteous in first place, namely, the faith which believes that we are absolved, accepted, and (consequently) reckoned righteous *because of Christ, the Mediator.*[66]

It will become evident below that Melanchthon also opposes the teaching of *meritum condigni,* as he states in Arts.VI and XX that forgiveness of sins and grace is received through faith alone and is not merited by the good works of the righteous. In these articles he operates just as in Art. IV with the correlation between the promise (or Christ) and faith: Because God's further favor and forgiveness has been earned by Christ alone and is imparted exclusively through the promise, it is received exclusively by faith, just as God's initial favor and forgiveness has been received by faith, on account of the same reasons.

This description of the polemical thrust of Art. IV indicates that

Melanchthon is waging battle first and foremost for the Lutheran teaching of faith or—more exactly—for the teaching of the *righteousness* of faith (*doctrina de iustitia fidei*): We are justified and reckoned righteous by *faith alone,* that is, by believing that *exclusively because of Christ* God forgives us our sins, takes us into His favor, and reckons us righteous.[67]

This teaching rests on three main presuppositions:

1. God's grace is a gift promised and given freely *because of Christ;* it is not a reward for the merit of our works;

2. The benefit of Christ's work, namely, God's grace, that is, His forgiveness or favor and the gift of the Holy Spirit, is imparted only through the preached Word, the absolution, and the sacraments of Baptism and the Eucharist, in short, through the Gospel;

3. Things promised and given because of Christ can be received only by faith in Christ, not by love or works which fulfill the Law (argument derived from the nature of relative terms).[68]

Because the opponents failed to understand the import and function of Melanchthon's *because of Christ* and the correlation between Christ (or the promise) and faith, they were altogether unable to understand the Lutheran teaching of the righteousness of faith.[69]

Our view of the purport of Art. IV in contradistinction to the controversialists' stand is confirmed by Melanchthon's 1531 "Theses on Justification by Faith." As editor Johannes Haussleiter argues, they summarize the argumentation developed in the AC and the Apology. Thesis No. 36 reads: "As we declare that faith alone justifies, it is this that must be understood: not only that in the beginning (*initio*) it accepts the forgiveness of sins or converts, but also that thereafter (*deinceps*) faith alone is counted as righteousness by God, even though fulfillment of the Law necessarily results. In fact this fulfillment of the Law is not accepted before God except because of faith."[70]

This thesis bears out that Melanchthon discerned two moments or situations which he characterizes by the adverbs *initio* and *deinceps*. His main point, however, is that the very same faith which justifies *initio* by recognizing *Christ,* the Mediator, as the only ground for God absolving the sinner, is *deinceps* credited as righteousness, regardless of the concomitant fulfillment of the Law, because and inasmuch as it is correlated to Christ, the Mediator, as a later edition states explicitly. In short, justification is altogether by faith *alone,* rather than by faith *and love.*

Relevance of the Findings

The findings we have made suggest that the distinction between *iustum effici* (to be made righteous) and *iustum reputari* (to be accounted righteous), which for generations has fascinated—and paralyzed—scholars, is definitely of secondary importance.

This distinction is mentioned later in the Apology, but it underlies formulations of the AC as well. The German original speaks of *gerecht werden,* "to become righteous," and the Latin *iustificari* in Art. IV evidently means "to be made righteous." These expressions of and by themselves, however, say nothing about *how* the sinner ends up being a righteous person, *iustus*; they do not tell whether he is rendered righteous by being "made" righteous or by being "called" righteous, that is, whether justification is "effective" or "forensic." This must be perceived clearly, for most studies have associated *iustum effici* with "effective" and *iustum reputari* with "forensic" justification, as if the former could not be "forensic," and the latter could not be "effective" as well.

If one reads Melanchthon's formulations carefully, it will be noticed that he states with almost pedantic precision that we are both rendered *and* reckoned righteous *by faith* in Christ. In his understanding, however, faith is always correlated with Christ or the promise of grace because of Christ. Correlative terms cannot be torn apart, for they necessitate each other. The current distinction between so-called "effective" and so-called "forensic" justification, respectively *Gerechtmachung* (making righteous) and *Gerechtsprechung* (declaring righteous), however, tends to tear apart the correlation.

As they speak of "effective justification" in connection with *iustum effici,* most studies have in mind the change or transformation which takes place in man as he is endowed with faith and raised to new life; normally they do not envision this God-given faith as magnetized by its "object," the Christ "outside" of us, and as regarding exactly this *Christ* as the sole ground for being absolved and accepted.

When referring to "forensic justification" in terms of *iustum reputari*, such studies have in mind only the relation to Christ "outside" of us; they presume that the person is not changed at all when he is justified *because of Christ,* since they do not perceive that Christ together with His gifts—including the Holy Spirit Himself—is appropriated and so to say swallowed by the faith which apprehends and embraces Him.

Therefore, inasmuch as the current expressions "effective" and "forensic" justification tend to concentrate on only one term of the correlation, they are not adequate to express Melanchthon's position. The best one can do is leave them aside and formulate the "doctrine of faith" on Melanchthon's own terms. It *is* a fact that he managed to formulate the Lutheran position in the AC without insisting on the distinction between *iustum effici* and *iustum reputari.* He does insist on other points, however, and Reformation studies would be well advised to concentrate on *them!*

Summing up, according to Art. IV the sinner, terrified by the awareness of sin and of God's wrath against it, is "rendered" righteous before God *by faith in Christ* or *by believing in the Gospel,* namely, that it is *because of Christ* that his sins are forgiven and he is received into God's favor. *This* faith is imputed as righteousness (Latin text) or regarded and reckoned as righteousness (German text) *before God,* which means that faith in Christ is *itself* the righteousness by which God reckons the believer righteous or by which he is righteous before Him. In both cases the correlation faith–Christ (promise) is presupposed. In both cases the action takes place *before God.*

It must be understood, however, that man stands "before God" in a very specific sense wherever the ministers of Christ exercise the power of the keys in His name (Art. XXVIII). Sinners are justified *before God* when they are baptized and first received into God's favor (Art. IX). They are justified *before God* when, after having fallen and become unrighteous, they are once again absolved from sin and restored to God's favor (Arts. XII and XXV). Consequently Baptism and confessional absolution are the first and foremost "places" of justification before God.

Sinners as well as believers are justified before God also as they hear and believe the preached Word (Arts. IV and V) or the promises connected with the Sacrament of the Altar (Art.XIII).

In any case, to be justified *before God* means to be justified by being confronted with the Gospel or the promise of forgiveness and grace because of Christ, which both requires and imparts true faith, as Art. V clearly indicates.

Why, then, one could ask, does Melanchthon use two expressions rather than one? He uses them, in our estimation, to discern and denote diverse but intimately connected moments or situations. *Iustum effici* refers to the beginning, when the terrified sinner is first rendered righteous by being absolved and accepted *by faith in Christ*. It denotes not a process but a "punctiform" event. One is either unrighteous (*impius, iniustus*) or righteous (*iustus, pius*). One cannot be halfway righteous. *Iustum reputari,* in turn, refers to an event which issues from the former: Now that the person has been absolved and accepted into God's favor, he is also counted righteous *by the same faith in the same Christ,* which at the prompting of the Gospel embraces and regards Him as his own, his only Righteousness.

It follows that while *iustum effici* applies to the unrighteous sinner, *iustum reputari* is used only with reference to the person who already believes in Christ and enjoys God's favor.

It must be observed, however, that the AC uses the term "justification" indiscriminately for the first and the second moment; expressions such as "forgiveness" and "grace" can refer to God's *initial* forgiveness and favor as well as to His *further* absolution and continued favor. In order to determine which is the case in particular instances, one must inquire who is being spoken of, whether it is the sinner (who is to become righteous) or the believer (who has become righteous already and now is to be reckoned righteous).

CHAPTER 7

The Doctrine of Faith in Arts. V and VI

Our investigation on Art. IV grew long and complex because theological tradition has so encrusted it with interpretations as to preclude a plain reading of the relatively clear text.

While Art. IV reveals the core, it by no means expresses the whole doctrine of justification through faith. As our studies on the structure of this doctrine have indicated, it comprises several issues beyond those discussed in the previous chapter. We must now consider the issues raised in Arts. V and VI.

The Scope of Art. V

Art. V deals with the question of how one obtains (justifying) faith. As our study of the sources (ch. 3 above) has shown, this question is a regular feature of the Lutheran doctrine of faith and works.

The importance of this question can be gathered from Melanchthon's comments on the context of Rom. 10:17, a passage which he adduced in the fourth article of a preliminary draft of the AC and which Luther referred to in the eighth of the Marburg Articles.

Melanchthon views Rom. 10:14–15 as a crescendo (*gradatio*) intended to express "the manner of justification and the cause of faith, or how faith is obtained": Nobody invokes God unless he believes; nobody believes unless he has heard the Word; nobody can hear the Word unless it is preached; nobody can preach the Word unless God sends people to preach it.

This crescendo, he says, is confirmed by the prophet, who foretells the sending of people who would announce a new Word which proclaims grace and peace, not the Law, which proclaims wrath.

This new Word preaches forgiveness of sins and offers righteousness, free of charge, to those who believe.

The apostle, then, teaches that faith is born in this manner: by hearing God's Word preached by a man. The efficient cause of faith is, therefore, the Word by which God drives and moves the hearts of human beings to believe.

Melanchthon adds that the Holy Spirit is not received without the Word and that the apostle included the sending, too, in order to commend the ministry of God's Word.

In his comments on the usefulness of this passage Melanchthon states that the apostle's crescendo concerning the manner of justification or the cause of faith must be preserved against those who despise the ministry of the Word and imagine that the Holy Spirit is received without the Word.[1]

Melanchthon's interpretation of Rom. 10:13–17 indicates that the question concerning the *modum iustificationis* is closely related to the issue of the "cause of faith" or "how faith is received" (*quomodo fides concipiatur*). Whenever he speaks of the former, he must speak of the latter, too.

In the AC itself Melanchthon followed the same procedure. In Art. IV he explained how we are justified. In Art. V he shows what is the cause of faith or how we obtain the faith by which we are justified, as the initial words indicate: "In order that we may obtain this faith."[2]

The Function of the Ministry

The analysis of Rom. 10:13–17 indicates, too, why Melanchthon includes in Art. V a reference to the ministry of teaching the Gospel and administering the sacraments. He simply wants to follow the apostle's line of reasoning. According to the same, God sends preachers of the Word in order that people, by hearing this Word, may *believe* in the Lord and invoke His name. This means, in the terms of Art. V, that God instituted the ministry of the Gospel and the sacraments *in order to impart the faith* by which one is justified before Him. In other words, Melanchthon mentions the ministry only because it is involved in the *creation and preservation of faith*.

For a discussion of the ministry itself one must turn to Art. XXVIII, which also underscores the function of the ministry in creating and nurturing faith in Christ. This view of the ministry was opposed to the bishops' pretentions to other kinds of power. It was also—and it continues to be—a blow against those who do not believe, with Luther and Melanchthon, that under normal circumstances God speaks to us through the ministry of the Word and sacraments.[3] The ministry is not a human expedient; it is God's institution. It derives its lowliness, but also its awesome dignity, from being God's tool in the creation of faith.

How, then, is the ministry involved in the creation, the giving, of faith in Christ?

Art. V states: Through the means of the Word preached and the sacraments administered by His ministers God gives the Spirit, who creates faith in those who hear the Gospel. This assertion conveys three things: (a) Only through the Word and the sacraments is the Holy Spirit given; (b) It is the Holy Spirit who creates faith; and (c) Faith is created, under normal circumstances, only in those who hear the Gospel.

The formulation—God (or Christ) gives the Holy Spirit through the Word and the sacraments "as through means"—goes back to the "Great Confession." There Luther states that He "comes to us" through the Gospel, Baptism, and the Sacrament of the Altar "as through three means or methods" and exercises Christ's passion in us, making it profitable for salvation.[4]

The seventh Schwabach article states that through the Gospel "as means" God gives "faith along with the Holy Spirit how and where He wills."[5]

The conviction that the Holy Spirit is given only through the Word and the sacraments finds expression in Art. XXVIII. It argues that the power of the keys is exercised only by teaching or preaching the Gospel and administering the sacraments. It imparts not earthly but eternal things, namely, eternal righteousness, the Holy Spirit, and eternal life. These things cannot be received except through the ministry of the Word and the sacraments (pars. 8–9).

Another parallel to the formulation of Art. V is found in Art. XVIII, where Melanchthon states that divine or spiritual righteousness is produced in the heart as the Holy Spirit is received through the Word. Such statements were apt to dispel the misunderstanding promoted by Eck's articles, which claimed that according to Luther the sacraments do not impart grace and the Holy Spirit.

As the exposition of Rom. 10:14–17 and the last section of Art. V indicate, the thesis that the Holy Spirit is received only through the Word and the sacraments is directed mainly at the Anabaptists and "enthusiasts," but also at the "others (*alii*) who think that the Holy Spirit comes to men without the external Word, through their own preparations and works" (Tappert, p. 31). These "others" are, for instance, the advocates of *meritum congrui*. They teach, according to Melanchthon, that the grace of the Holy Spirit is merited by works, not received through the Word.[6]

This attack on the Roman opponents is formulated more subtly in the AC than in the Schwabach and Marburg Articles, which were destined so to say for internal consumption.[7] An open attack in the AC would have entailed the need for explanations, forcing Melanchthon to disrupt the conciseness of the first part.

Faith as Creation of the Holy Spirit

The affirmation that it is the Holy Spirit who creates faith can be traced back to the "Great Confession." It says that the Holy Spirit as a living, eternal gift and present adorns all believers with faith and other spiritual gifts.

On the same line the sixth Schwabach article stresses that faith is God's work and gift which the Holy Spirit, given by Christ, produces (*wirket*) in us.

The sixth of the Marburg Articles emphasizes that faith is a gift of God and that the Holy Spirit gives and creates (*schafft*) it in our hearts whenever He wills.[8]

The formulation in Art. V, "the Holy Spirit produces (*efficit, wirket*) faith," evidently derives from the Schwabach and the Marburg Articles. It appears in other sources as well, as in the *Outline* of Rom. 5:5: "He [Paul] adds the efficient cause of faith, for the Holy Spirit shed into the saints produces (*efficit*) faith, so that they may know that they are loved by God."[9]

As the Schwabach and the Marburg Articles indicate, the assertion that the Holy Spirit is the cause of faith has polemical undertones. It implies that by their own powers men may produce general or common faith, but are altogether unable to elicit the true faith by which we are justified before God.

This point is stated explicitly in Art. XVIII: The human will does not have the power to produce divine or spiritual righteousness, for natural man does not perceive spiritual things (1 Cor. 2:14).

In Whom Faith Can Be

Art. V furthermore points out when, where, and in whom the Holy Spirit creates faith. For the purposes of this study it is important to observe the new accents introduced here.[10]

The seventh Schwabach Article states that God, through the Gospel, gives faith and the Holy Spirit "how and where (*wie und wo*) He wills."

The eighth Marburg article says that the Holy Spirit produces and creates faith through and with the oral Word "where and in whom (*wo und in welchen*) He wills." The sixth, however, specifies that the Holy Spirit gives and produces faith "where (*wo*) He wills ... as (*wenn*) we hear the Gospel or Christ's Word."

In the AC Melanchthon omitted the "how" of the Schwabach article and connected its "where God wills" with "when He wills" from the two Marburg articles. While the sixth Marburg article specified that faith is created *as* we hear the Gospel, the AC specifies that it is created *"in those* who hear the Gospel." In this way Art. V places the creation of faith in the hands of God's sovereignty, but at the same time stresses the limits which He Himself has set to His activity.

But who are those who hear the Gospel?

The *Instructions for Visitors* stress in the section on the Ten Commandments that it is necessary to preach not only penitence but also faith. Whoever is aware of his sin and regrets it must believe that his sins are forgiven to him not because of our merit but because of Christ. Whenever the penitent and terrified conscience receives peace, comfort, and joy from hearing that our sins have been forgiven to us *because of Christ, this* is called the faith which makes us righteous before God.[11] This passage indicates that those who need to hear the Gospel are the people who have been led by the Law to acknowledge and regret their sins.

In the Visitation Articles, too, it is the heart terrified by the Law that hears the Gospel, that Christ has made satisfaction for sin and that because of Him one's sins are forgiven.[12]

The Holy Spirit, then, creates faith in the *penitent sinners* who hear the Gospel.[13]

The Gospel as the "Cause" of Faith

Several texts state that God moves terrified hearts to believe precisely through the Gospel they hear.

In the *Instructions for Visitors* the Reformers insist that God produces contrition and faith in the hearts through the preaching of the Word:

"Just as one exhorts people to faith, and God produces (*wircket*) faith through such preaching, so one must also exhort and drive to contrition, and let God decide in whom He works contrition, for He operates through the preaching of the Word."[14]

In the exposition of Paul's assertion that "the Gospel is God's power" (Rom. 1:16), Melanchthon states explicitly: "Through the Gospel God is active (*efficax*); He moves the hearts to believe and imputes this faith as righteousness."[15]

In Art. XII of the AC Melanchthon declares that faith, the second part of repentance, is received from the Gospel or absolution. It believes that sins are forgiven because of Christ, it comforts the conscience, it frees from terrors.[16]

This absolution, according to Art. XXV, must be believed as God's own voice sounding from heaven, and this faith truly obtains and receives the forgiveness of sins.

A similar statement is found in Art. XIII. The sacraments are above all signs and witnesses of God's will toward us. They were set up to call forth (*excitare, erwecken*) faith in those who use them. Therefore one must use them in such a way as to elicit the kind of faith which believes the promises that are presented and shown through them (AC, XXV, 4). In short, faith is created *in those who hear the Gospel* because it is *through the Gospel* inherent in the preached Word, in the absolution, and in the sacraments that God moves the penitent consciences to faith in Christ.[17]

The Word spoken and the sacraments applied by the ministry, then, are God's instruments or means to create faith in a double sense: Through them God gives the Holy Spirit, who creates faith, and through them God moves hearts to believe, or demands, calls forth, and strengthens faith in Christ.

THE DOCTRINE OF FAITH

This perception of the issue is evident also in Luther's "Great Confession," which says that God moves one to faith "outwardly" through the Gospel and the sacraments and "inwardly" through the witness of the Holy Spirit.[18]

Art. V states that we obtain true faith through the Word and the sacraments, or more specifically through the Gospel, for it is through the Gospel that God moves hearts to believe. The article asserts, too, that it is the Holy Spirit who is the efficient cause of faith. The Holy Spirit, however, is connected with Word and sacraments in a double sense: first because He is given through Word and sacraments, and then because He produces faith precisely in those who hear the Gospel. These self-imposed limitations of the Spirit are ignored both by the "fanatics" and by the "others" who try to get the Holy Spirit and faith without recurring to the Word preached by men. *This is the main point of Art. V.*

Which Gospel Produces Faith

Besides saying that faith is created in those who hear the Gospel, Melanchthon says explicitly what they hear or what moves them to believe. By stating what the Gospel says, Melanchthon dispels or prevents misunderstandings.

The Gospel which terrified sinners hear is not a codification of new precepts brought by Christ. It is not merely the account of Christ's life, death, and resurrection. It is rather the Word of God which offers and imparts the fruits or benefits of Christ's work to the sinner who sees no way out in the face of God's judgment. It is the Word of God which because of Christ absolves and accepts the penitent sinner who believes that he is indeed taken into God's favor *because of Christ.*

Be defining the Gospel, Melanchthon prevents the term from being understood in the way the opponents understood it, namely, as *nova lex* and *historia.*

It must be observed, however, that in this definition of the Gospel the Latin predicate is provided with a very specific object. It is stated that God justifies not "men," not "us," but those who believe that they are taken into God's favor because of Christ.

A similar emphasis is found in one of Melanchthon's comments on Rom. 1:16: "The Gospel discloses the righteousness of faith, that those who believe that they are taken into grace because of Christ are considered righteous before God."[19]

Melanchthon's point in such remarks becomes clear in his analysis of Rom. 3:21: Besides stating that God's righteousness has been revealed without the Law (main proposition), Paul explains to whom the righteousness revealed in the Gospel belongs ("circumstance"). He says that it belongs to all, but above all to those who believe.[20]

In keeping with this exegesis of Romans, Melanchthon's definition of the Gospel in Art. V stresses that God justifies *those who believe* that they are accepted because of Christ. Although God's forgiveness and favor because of Christ is [sic] offered to all, it materializes in those who believe that they are favored because of Christ. Because God ultimately justifies precisely those who believe this, one understands why and how the Gospel moves terrified hearts to believe. By telling them that God justifies precisely those who believe that they are favored because of Christ, the Gospel *moves them to become such people* by believing precisely that.

Furthermore, by defining the Gospel in the above terms, Melanchthon defines what faith believes, namely, the same Gospel which moves to faith. This is especially evident in the German text, where the demonstrative pronoun *solchs* (this), which tells what faith believes, refers back to the preceding definition of the Gospel. The "object" of faith, therefore, is the very Gospel which produces faith.[21]

It is in order to do justice to this fact that the term *object* has been placed in quotation marks, for one is dealing not with a common, passive object, but with a special, living power which produces the "virtue" which apprehends it.

By defining what the believers believe, Melanchthon makes clear once more that their faith differs radically from that of demons and godless people, who do not believe that they have God's favor because of Christ.

In other words, by defining the "object" of faith, Melanchthon implicitly clarifies the *nature* of faith. Later, in Art. XX, he states explicitly what the term *faith* denotes in Lutheran teaching, especially in the AC.

Summary

In Art. V Melanchthon tells us how we obtain the faith by which we are justified before God and which is the righteousness by which we are righteous before God (Art. IV). We obtain it *through the Word,* that is, through the preached Gospel and the oral absolution, and *through the sacraments,* that is, through Baptism and the Lord's Supper.

Melanchthon also identifies the cause of faith. It is the Holy Spirit who creates faith in those who hear the Gospel. He is the *efficient cause* of faith. Since, however, hearts or consciences are moved to faith through the Gospel, which the preached Word, the absolution, and the sacraments have in common, Art. V submits that the Gospel is the *instrumental cause* of faith. Thus faith is *caused by the Holy Spirit through the Gospel.*

With this explanation Art. V makes clear that the faith of Art. IV differs qualitatively from the general or historical faith which demons and godless people are said to have. The latter is not caused by the Holy Spirit through the Gospel and therefore does not believe in the Gospel. The result is that they do not benefit from God's Christ-motivated justification, which the Gospel promises precisely to those who believe in its promise, offer, and gift.

The Scope of Art. VI

Art. VI and the opening section of the third part of Art. XX discuss four points: the necessity of doing good works, which works are to be done, the reason for doing good works, and the purpose of doing them.[22] We will consider them in this order.

The Necessity of Good Works

The necessity of good works is expressed by two clauses in the Latin text of Art. VI: "This faith is bound (*debet*) to bring forth good fruits" and "it is necessary (*oportet*) to do the good works commanded by God." Art. XX has one clause only: "it is necessary (*necesse est*) to do good works."

The German text states in Art. VI that "faith should (*soll*) produce good fruits and good works" and that one must (*muss*) do good works; in Art. XX, "that good works should and must be done" (*sollen und mussen geschehen*).[23]

In the sources one finds that both the sixth of the Schwabach Articles and the tenth of the Marburg Articles use the indicative as they affirm that faith bears much fruit and does good works.

In short, the faith discussed in Arts. IV and V is a new nature and must therefore produce new fruits, as Art. VI says.

Which Works Must Be Done

Art. VI states in second place which works must be done, namely, those which God has commanded. This point is missing in Art. XX, which, however, includes a sampling of true good works (pars. 36–37).

The Schwabach and Marburg Articles, too, list true good works, but do not include this point.[24] It presumably derives from the *Instructions for Visitors*. This work states in the section on the Ten Commandments that good works are called good not only because they are done for the sake of the neighbor, but also because God has commanded them. The same source affirms in the section on prayer that the good works commanded by God (*die Gott geboten hat*) must be done.[25]

Which good works are commanded by God? They are the works demanded by the Ten Commandments, "for all good works are therein comprehended."[26]

By stressing that one must do the good works commanded by God in the Decalog, Art. VI implicitly criticizes the emphasis on works which in the Lutherans' opinion are unnecessary because God has not commanded them.[27] This becomes evident not only in the foreword of Art. XX, which will be discussed below, but also and especially in Arts. XXVI and XXVII.

According to Art. XXVI the former emphasis on the keeping of regulations concerning holy days, fasts, foods, and clothes led the paterfamilias, the mother, the magistrate, etc., to believe that they were living a less spiritual and less perfect life in their respective callings.

According to Art. XXVII the notion that the monks live a holy and perfect life (*status perfectionis*) led husbands, wives, magistrates, etc., to "flee the world," forgetting that one must serve God in the commandments which He has given, not in precepts which have been devised by men. "A good and perfect way of life (*genus vitae, Stand des Lebens*) is any which God has commanded."[28]

These passages indicate that the works commanded by God are stipulated in the Ten Commandments inasmuch as these are connected with one's condition or way of life as paterfamilias, mother, magistrate, pastor, and the like. In short, by saying that one must do "the works commanded by God," Art. VI is implicitly proposing the Lutheran view of true perfection and worship of God. This consists, according to Art. XXVII, in "fearing God earnestly and yet having a great faith and trust, because of Christ, that we have an appeased God, asking of God and surely expecting help in all things that must be borne according to [our] vocation, meanwhile externally doing good works and fulfilling [our] vocation with diligence" (pars. 49–50).

These observations suffice to demonstrate that Art. VI does not propose a narrow view of the fulfillment of God's commandments, but opens the way to productive involvement with society and nature.

The Reason for Doing Good Works

This, according to Arts. VI and XX, is purely and simply that God wants them to be done: "because of God's will."

The precedent for this formulation is Luther's statement concerning good works connected with the holy orders of ministry, marriage, government, Christian love: "God wants to have such works from us ... and all those who are blessed in faith in Christ do such works and keep such orders."[29]

There was little disagreement between the opponents and the Lutherans over the fact that God does require the doing of good works.

The Purpose of Doing Good Works

The purpose of doing good works is formulated positively in the German text of Art. XX, par. 27: "for God's praise." The purpose for which they are *not* to be done is formulated with the following terms in the German text of Arts. VI and XX, par. 27: "not in order to put one's trust in these works to merit grace before God through them." The Latin uses "justification" in Art. VI and "grace" in Art. XX: "not in order to have the confidence of meriting justification (grace) before God through these works."

This representation is based on passages like Rom. 3:27–28. Since God's righteousness has been revealed without the Law, Melanchthon regards it as a blasphemy against Christ to elect works with the hope and pretension that one is justified through them. Men are justified by faith without the works of the Law. This realization eliminates confidence in one's works and satisfactions. If works justified, the result would be confidence in oneself and boasting.[30]

The AC, however, gives a different reason for not trusting in one's works in order to merit grace or justification through them. It states in the German text of Art. VI: "We receive forgiveness of sin and righteousness through faith in Christ" (Tappert). The Latin has: "Forgiveness of sins and justification is [sic] apprehended by faith."[31]

These formulations are nothing but the conclusion of the argument drawn from the nature of relative terms. The "grace" or forgiveness of sins and righteousness (or justification) which people intend to merit are not a reward for merit, but things promised and given because of Christ. Since things promised can be received only by faith in Christ, it follows that grace or forgiveness and justification can be received only by faith in Christ.

The question for Art. VI is whether true good works can be trusted with the intention of meriting God's grace through them. The grace to be merited is not the initial one by which man is first accepted, but "further" grace by which the accepted person enjoys God's *continual* favor.

Melanchthon describes this in his analysis of Rom. 8:1–2. He remarks that grace comprises both the forgiveness of sins or God's favor and the giving of the Holy Spirit. He stresses that Paul connects these two things. By saying that there is no condemnation, the apostle suggests that there is sin in the saints but that it is forgiven because of faith in Christ. He also indicates that sin is overcome by the Holy Spirit given to the believer.[32]

Melanchthon's analysis makes clear that the grace one needs after he has been justified and has started to perform good works is God's forgiveness or favor which "covers" the sin still present, the grace and favor which regards one as acceptable and righteous in spite of this remaining sin. As Arts. VI and XX affirm, this "second" grace is received only through faith, and for this reason faith is said to be our righteousness not only in Art. IV but also in Art. VI. Faith is the "thing" by which God reckons righteous and by which one is righteous before God, and this not only in the *beginning*, when he has no good works, but also *afterwards*, when he already has them.

The reformulation of Art. VI in the first German edition, therefore, reads: "we receive forgiveness of sin and are reckoned righteous through faith because of Christ."[33]

Now one can see that Arts. VI and XX, as they affirm that the forgiveness of sins and grace (or righteousness or justification) are apprehended only through faith in Christ, link up to the final sentence of Art. IV, which says that God reckons faith as righteousness before Him. It is by faith that we are first absolved, accepted, and reckoned righteous. It is still by the same faith that we *continue* to be absolved, accepted, and regarded as righteous before God. Why? Because both in the beginning and afterwards faith believes in the Gospel, namely, that God forgives, accepts, and reckons us righteous *because of Christ*. Both in the beginning and afterwards faith clings to Christ, knowing and believing that God is favorable to us, forgives us our sins, and reckons us righteous on account of *Him!*

Contrast

The opponents of the Reformation affirmed that, after having received the grace which is love and makes acceptable, man may perform good works. These are rewarded, by virtue of God's accepting grace, with further grace and ultimately with eternal life. The doing of good works is thus inseparably connected with the alleged merit of condignity.

By stating that one does not earn forgiveness and grace by good works, Melanchthon openly denies the opponents' merit of condignity, just as in Art. IV he denied the merit of congruity and the theory of faith formed by love.

The confrontation is total, for the parties operate with diverging notions of Christ's work, of the Gospel, and of faith. Consequently they operate with different views of the function and purpose of good works.

Whereas the opponents boldly engage good works in the process of salvation, no matter how much they speak of the grace earned by Christ, Melanchthon engages only Christ in His Word and therefore exclusively faith in the matter of justification.[34] As a result he postulates that good works can be done for entirely unselfish purposes, namely, to praise God and to help others in keeping with one's "state" or calling in the context of Luther's common order of Christian love.[35] Yet even these good works, as indicated in the first German edition, remain imperfect and very far from fulfilling the Law. For this reason they are acceptable to God exclusively because of Christ or God's promised mercy, which is applied to us by faith in Christ.

This, however, takes us to the analysis of Art. XX, in the next chapter.

CHAPTER 8

Defense of the Doctrine of Faith (Art. XX)

As redactor of the Augsburg Confession Melanchthon reported the doctrine of faith as taught in Lutheran churches and schools. He stated that faith in Christ justifies (Art. IV), that it results from hearing the Gospel and consists in apprehending Christ as the ground for God's favor (Art. V), and that far from preventing them it produces good works in keeping with God's will (Art. VI). And yet he appended another article "On Faith and Good Works" to the "Articles of Faith."

One may not assume that in Art. XX he simply repeats the assertions of Arts. IV–VI; rather, he gives them a new slant. As a matter of fact, he composed Art. XX in order to refute the allegations concerning the pernicious effects of the doctrine of justification through faith and to demonstrate how necessary and beneficial it is for enhancing Christ's glory, renewing people's consciences, and promoting true service to God. In short, Art. XX must be regarded as a definite apology or defense of the doctrine of faith.

Since Melanchthon is dealing with the effects or results of Lutheran teaching, he extensively deploys the "argument from experience" besides Scriptural and patristic evidence.[1] This does not mean that he intends to psychologize faith, as has been charged.[2] It does mean, however, that he commends the doctrine of justification through faith on the basis of its beneficial results. This contention of ours will become clear as we examine the scope of Art. XX on the basis of its foreword after defining its outline on the basis of the sources.

Outline of the Article

The defense and commendation of the doctrine of justification by grace through faith for Christ's sake is framed by an introduction and a conclusion[3] and is organized in three parts.[4] In the course of his apology Melanchthon restates the main propositions of Arts. IV–VI in order to dispel misconstructions of the Lutheran position.

The first part explains how we are justified. It affirms that we obtain forgiveness of sins and grace exclusively through faith in Christ as we believe that because of Him God forgives us our sins and receives us into His favor.[5]

The second section clarifies what faith is, or what the term "faith" denotes according to Scripture. It shows that Lutherans attribute justification not to common faith, but to the faith which believes that through Christ we have forgiveness, righteousness, and grace, the faith which therefore produces confidence toward God (pars. 23, 25–26).

In the third section Melanchthon reports that the Lutheran teaching of faith both demands good works (pars. 27, 35) and shows how they can be done (pars. 29–40). Good works, however, do not merit grace, for we lay hold of forgiveness and grace through faith alone (pars. 27–28).

The Scope of the Article

As the foreword indicates, Art. XX deals with the allegation that the Lutherans prohibit good works.

The review of Eck's articles has indicated that the opponents did not formulate the allegation in these terms. They did, however, denounce the Lutheran attacks on the countless religious practices and the virtues of civil righteousness. They sought to create the impression that several Lutheran teachings, especially that of "faith alone," discouraged good works as being either useless or even harmful to salvation. They suggested, in short, that the Lutherans neither taught nor required good works.

This is the reason why the foreword asserts first of all that the Lutherans have taught good works, namely, those which God requires in the Ten Commandments and which are performed according to one's vocation.[6]

At this point a divergence of terminology becomes apparent. When the opponents say, "The Lutherans do not teach good works," the expression "good works" refers to the works commanded by God *and* to the religious practices imposed by bishops and religious orders. When Melanchthon replies, "We do teach good works," he is referring mainly if not exclusively to the works required in the Decalog and connected with one's vocation. The scope of the expression "good works," then, depends on whether it is used with reference to the opponents' or the Lutheran position.

With their charges against Lutheran teaching the opponents implied that their own teaching of good works prior to the Reformation was above criticism. Melanchthon does not grant this. He therefore stresses that their teaching on this subject was grossly inadequate. They failed to teach the works required by God in one's calling and taught only the "childish and needless works" connected with popular piety and monasticism. Melanchthon observes that in view of the Lutheran criticism the opponents no longer praised such works as highly as before, for they were now teaching that people are justified by faith and works, not by works alone as they had taught before.

As the opponents contended that the Lutheran doctrine of justification through faith turns people away from doing good works, they implied that it should never have been preached at all. In view of this fact Art. XX not only restates this doctrine, but also tries to demonstrate that it *has to be preached openly to all people* in order that they will stop trying to merit forgiveness and grace through self-elected acts of worship. It has to be preached also in order to enable them to know, love, and worship God and to perform in their respective callings the good works which God requires and regards as such.

The Lutherans have instructed the churches concerning faith because former preachers and teachers stressed only the doctrine of works and did not even mention faith: "It is necessary for all to acknowledge that there was in the sermons the deepest of silences concerning the righteousness of faith" (par. 8).

This short review of the foreword of Art. XX indicates that the article goes beyond stating and defending the Lutheran teaching of faith on a theoretical level. It also discusses the *effects* of this teaching on people's piety. In doing so it affirms the paradox that one must teach "faith alone" in order to call forth true worship of God and true good works.

Now it is necessary to establish how this is done in the three major sections of the article.

How We Are Justified

The first section begins by denying the merit of good works and affirming that one obtains divine forgiveness and favor only by faith as he believes that he is received into favor *because of Christ*.

The relative clause which describes Christ's work on our behalf has been discussed in the analysis of Art. IV. Now it is necessary to consider only how the Christological argument is handled.

Melanchthon presupposes that God must be reconciled before one may receive His favor. For this reason he regards the attempt to merit His grace through good works as an effort to reconcile Him on the basis of human powers. But to reconcile God and to merit His favor is the exclusive function of Christ. It follows that whoever has the confidence of meriting God's favor by works despises Christ's merit and grace and tries to get to God by his own powers, without Christ, who is the only way to God.

In this application of the Christological argument Melanchthon does not take into consideration that opponents such as Eck assigned to Christ the role of having earned the grace which makes possible good works leading to the merits of congruity and condignity.[7] He could have said, as in the Apology (IV, 80–81), that Christ is allowed to function as Mediator and Propitiator only if one believes that because of Him the Father receives us into His favor.

At any rate, it is significant that Melanchthon's first and principal argument in favor of the doctrine of justification through faith is not a simple passage of Scripture but an assertion concerning Christ's function. This assertion derives from the Ecumenical Creeds and the Catholic tradition, which rest on Scriptural evidence (Rom. 3:25; 8:34; 1 Tim. 2:5; 1 John 2:1).

Having stated the Lutheran teaching of faith, Melanchthon affirms that it is identical with Paul's. The opponents, however, had stated that the Lutheran "heresy" was a misrepresentation of Paul's position.[8] In order to prove that the Lutherans were not proposing a new interpretation of Paul, he appeals to the authority of SS. Augustine and Ambrose.

The reference to St. Augustine is rather general. The Ambrose quotation supports the Christological argument against the merit of works at least as far as the merit of congruity is concerned: If justification were due to the preceding merits, so that it would not be a gift of God but a reward to the doer of works, then the redemption by Christ's blood would be of little value and the preeminence of God's mercy over human works would be eliminated.

Having invoked the authority of Paul, Melanchthon employs an argument drawn from experience. Whereas people who have experienced neither pains of conscience nor the relief of faith despise the Lutheran teaching, pious and sensible consciences have experienced that it affords plenty of consolation. When the conscience is confronted with its sinfulness and God's wrath against sin, it cannot be quieted by any works, but only by faith in Christ.

This observation from experience is confirmed by the apostle Paul in Rom. 5:1: "Being justified through faith, we have peace with God."

Melanchthon's implicit line of reasoning is that only people who have experienced both the terrors of judgment and the consolation afforded by faith can understand and evaluate the Lutheran teaching of faith.

The argument from experience in general is expanded by a reference to past experience which underscores remarks made in the foreword of the article. Because consciences were instructed only with the doctrine of works and not comforted with the Gospel, they turned to monasticism and other works (actually religious practices) in order to merit grace and make satisfaction for sins.

The exclusive emphasis on good works is here regarded as the cause for restlessness of conscience. This restlessness results in the invention of religious practices aimed at winning God's favor. Here Melanchthon already implies what he says explicitly in the ensuing section (pars. 24–25), namely, that only true faith brings about true knowledge and worship of God.

The concluding part of the section takes up the contention implicit in the passage introducing the report on the doctrine of justification through faith: It is absolutely necessary to preach faith in Christ in order that terrified consciences will not remain deprived of consolation but will know that one apprehends grace and forgiveness of sins by faith in Christ (par. 22).

It is important to observe that Melanchthon is concerned with consolation of consciences not because he seeks to satisfy their selfish needs but because he wants to promote adequate worship of God and put a stop to the questionable religious practices resulting from restlessness of conscience.

One must say that at least in the AC Melanchthon is concerned primarily with the honor and glory of Christ, which is realized through faith in Him. The concern for the consolation of consciences is definitely secondary, a result of the former. This must be maintained against attempts to charge Melanchthon with theological subjectivism while ignoring the Christocentrism of his faith.[9]

What Faith Is

The preceding section defined faith implicitly, but an explicit definition was necessary for several reasons. As the Visitation Documents indicate,[10] some people in the Lutheran camp imagined that they had faith, but in fact had neither learned nor experienced what faith really is. Therefore the preachers had to explain how faith is born and what it is, so that people would not think they had faith when they did not have it. Above all, however, the opponents had misconstrued the Lutheran teaching of faith as referring exclusively to the kind of faith which prevails even among demons and the unrighteous, that is, the faith which does not issue in a new relationship to God and does not turn away from sin.

These were the main reasons which made an explicit definition of faith indispensable.

In order to explain what the Lutherans mean when they teach *faith* and in order to distinguish between true and presumed faith, Melanchthon defines it in terms of its object and of its necessary effects (see ch. 5 above).

The "object" of common or general faith, which even the godless believe in, is merely the story of Christ, namely, as the German text specifies, that He died and rose from the dead. The object of true faith is not only the story, but the outcome of the story as well. This outcome or result is expressed in the article of the Creed, "I believe in the forgiveness of sins." True faith, then, believes "that we have grace, righteousness, and forgiveness of sins *through Christ,*" as the Latin says, or "that we receive grace and forgiveness of sin *through Christ,*" as the German states.[11]

Because the two kinds of faith differ in what they believe, they differ also in their effects. Godless people and devils do not believe the article of the forgiveness of sins, namely, that God absolves them because of Christ. Therefore "they hate God as an enemy, do not call upon him, and expect no good from him" (par. 25, Tappert). Because they do not know God as a reconciled and favorable Father, they maintain the relationship to Him which characterizes original sin, according to Art. II of the AC. Those who believe that God absolves and receives them because of Christ, however, have learned that through Him they have a favorable Father. For this reason they know God truly, that is, the way He really is, call upon Him, and consequently are not godless like the pagans.

Melanchthon's point is, then, that true faith differs from common or general faith not only in regard to its object but also in regard to the specific knowledge of God which leads to confidence in Him and His help. It is presupposed that through the promise of forgiveness and grace because of Christ God discloses Himself as an appeased and favorable God and thus evokes a new and true knowledge of Himself. Faith does not dream up a new vision of God to which nothing corresponds "outside" of it. No, God Himself calls forth faith in Christ and thereby true knowledge of Himself through the good news and promise that He is reconciled and favorable because of Christ. Therefore the reconciled and appeased God, the favorable Father, is both the "thing" which is (passively) known and the "thing" which (actively) causes knowledge of Himself in us.

This realization opens the vista for Melanchthon's view of God and of revelation or theological knowledge. For the moment suffice it to say the following: By disclosing Himself as the propitiated Father through Christ, God convicts natural man of being in error, of living a lie in regarding and treating God as an enemy and a threat to his existence.

If this observation is correct, Melanchthon's theology is very far from placing God at the service of man and his needs. It demonstrates, on the contrary, that God's truth and glory triumph, through Christ, over man's untruth and unrighteousness or bad conscience.

Only when God conquers man does the latter attain his full well-being.

This paragraph containing Melanchthon's definition of faith (par. 26) may create the impression that the difference between general and true faith corresponds to the difference between knowledge (*notitia*) and confidence (*fiducia*). In fact, however, the terms are carefully qualified.

The German text contrasts "knowing the reports, as even the devils know them" and "having confidence in God, that He is favorable to us." The Latin insists that according to St. Augustine *faith* does not denote "knowledge of the kind which is in the godless," but "the confidence which comforts and raises up terrified consciences" inasmuch as—this is implied—it believes the promise of forgiveness because of Christ.

The distinction between *notitia* and *fiducia*, therefore, implies the distinction between the respective objects, that is, between the respective "things" which are known or trusted. The emphasis rests not on the faculties of man but on the objects which correspond to them. This fact has frequently been overlooked.[12]

These observations can be demonstrated on the basis of Melanchthon's outline of the content of Rom. 4:1-2.[13] He criticizes those who accuse Paul of having misunderstood and misused Genesis in connecting Abraham's faith with Christ. They go wrong in thinking that God's promise to Abraham has to do only with numerous descendants; their error lies in assuming that faith is nothing but the knowledge of the "story." Abraham's faith, however, was of the kind which believes that God is appeased and propitious, trusts God's help, dares to expect and demand help from God. Such a faith always comprises knowledge of Christ (*Christi notitiam*), that the Father takes us into favor not because of our merits but because of Christ. Therefore all the references to the patriarchs' faith concerning earthly goods imply confidence in God's grace and mercy (*fiducia gratiae ac misericordiae Dei*).[14] They could expect bodily goods from God only because they knew for sure that His wrath is not appeased by our merits and works; they knew that they were taken into favor because of the promised Christ.

Applying these findings to the Epistle to the Romans, Melanchthon stresses that whenever Paul uses the term "faith" one must understand not only the knowledge of the "story" of Christ's passion but also the knowledge of the reason why He suffered. This, too, pertains to the story. The demons and godless men also know that Christ suffered, but do not believe that the Father is reconciled because of Him and that God loves and defends them.

One can observe in this exposition that true faith can also be described in terms of knowledge (*notitia* or *cognitio*) as long as knowing refers to the right object, namely, to Christ or the cause why He suffered or the promise that God is favorable because of Him.

This exposition further demonstrates that *confidence*, too, is carefully provided with a genitive stating the object of the trusting, *fiducia gratiae ac misericordiae Dei*. Whether Melanchthon employs *fiducia* or *cognitio* to describe faith, he always postulates Christ Himself or the promise of grace on His account as object of the trusting or knowing. He presupposes that the whole person is affected by this faith, so that a new vision and worship of God results.

For this reason one may no longer reduce the difference between the two kinds of faith to "knowledge" and "trust" without emphasizing the all-important "objects" of this knowing and trusting.

Faith Effects Good Works

The third part of Art. XX begins (par. 27) by reasserting the necessity and purpose of doing good works. Then, however, it turns into a commendation of the Lutheran teaching of faith in its relation to good works.

The statement that one receives forgiveness and grace by faith leads into the assertion that one receives the Holy Spirit through the same faith. This transition presupposes that grace comprises both God's favor and His gift of the Holy Spirit. Whoever is absolved and taken into God's favor is endowed at once with the Holy Spirit.[15] According to the German text the reception of the Holy Spirit enables the heart to do good works. The Latin text specifies that by receiving the Spirit hearts are renewed and provided with new emotions. Thus they are enabled to give birth to good works. Both texts suppose that the rule and protection of the Holy Spirit is absolutely indispensable for the doing of good works.

Melanchthon's teaching on the Spirit's rule appears, for instance, in his comments on Rom. 8:2. "The law of the Spirit of life" denotes the rule (*gubernatio*) by the Holy Spirit, who does not allow sin and death to rule us. He sustains, comforts, and restores to life in the terrors of sin, so that sin cannot lead us to despair, and death cannot devour us.[16]

In the comments on Rom. 6:1–15 Melanchthon explains that the believers can do good works because they have a God who is appeased, who defends and helps them; furthermore, sins can neither terrify them, for they have been absolved, nor draw them to evil works, for they are steered by the Holy Spirit and protected by Christ.[17]

In the Visitation Articles and the *Instructions for Visitors* the teaching concerning the rule of the Holy Spirit figures prominently in the sections on free will and Christian liberty. These sections are also the source of the argument concerning the impossibility of doing true good works without faith and the Holy Spirit.

Melanchthon states that the human will is free to accomplish in a certain sense the righteousness of the flesh or civil righteousness. The same is required and rewarded by God, but it is not sufficient for justification. The devil, however, prevents people from accomplishing even this righteousness, driving into adultery, murder, and other crimes those who trust exclusively in their own power and do not ask for God's help. By contrast, Christian liberty consists in having forgiveness of sins through Christ and in obtaining the Holy Spirit, by whom we are liberated from the devil's rule. The Spirit rules and protects us against the devil's power.[18]

As he tries to demonstrate in Art. XX that faith and the Holy Spirit are necessary to do good works, Melanchthon argues that man's powers, without the Holy Spirit, are under the devil's control. He drives people to all kinds of sins, godless opinions, and crimes. Melanchthon argues on the basis of experience that the philosophers defiled themselves with open crimes even though they tried to live a decent life.

In the Visitation Documents Melanchthon further stresses that by his own powers man cannot cleanse his heart and produce divine gifts or spiritual works such as true contrition, true fear of God, true confidence in God, sincere love, chastity, a forgiving spirit, true patience, true prayer, liberality. This true Christian righteousness is received from God.

In keeping with this thesis concerning free will and Christian liberty Melanchthon argues in Art. XX that human powers, without the Holy Spirit, are unable to perform the works of the First and Second Commandments, such as calling upon God, expecting good things from Him, being patient in suffering. As the German stresses, these works cannot be done without Christ's help.

Melanchthon's argumentation applies the method of exclusion. Since true good works cannot be done without the Holy Spirit, it follows that they can be done under His rule and guidance. The Spirit, however, is received through faith, for it is by faith that God's grace (which comprises His favor and the gift of the Holy Spirit) is apprehended. For that reason the Lutheran teaching of faith does in fact make good works possible. Rather than being accused of prohibiting good works, the doctrine of justification through faith should be praised for requiring true good works and indicating how they can be accomplished.

The third part of Art. XX, then, does not merely state that the Lutherans require good works in order to contradict the charge that they prohibit them. It submits still another reason why the Lutheran doctrine of faith has to be preached, namely, *to enable people to do true good works* under the rule and guidance of the Holy Spirit. The Lutheran doctrine of faith, therefore, is justified not only because it honors Christ as the only Mediator and Propitiation, not only because it comforts terrified consciences, but also because it enables people to perform truly good works, works which natural man cannot accomplish by his own powers.

This may sound theoretical to the 20th-century reader. For the Lutherans and their spokesman at Augsburg, however, it was a matter of life and death. For Melanchthon the doctrine of justification through faith was the key teaching of Christianity. If it were outlawed and suppressed, the Reformation would perish, for *this* doctrine had led to the renovation of life and worship in the Lutheran territories. Therefore he tries with all means at hand to convince the emperor and the Diet that the preaching of true faith in Christ had to go on, even though it was laying waste the worship and morals of Eck's "most Christian" Germany, as the opponents alleged. The struggle of Art. XX, then, is a struggle for the survival of the Reformation.

Unfortunately Art. XX, probably composed in the last days before the public reading of the AC, shows signs of hasty composition, especially in the last part. It sounds rudimentary if compared with the reformulation inserted some months later in the first edition of the German text. We shall now briefly consider its final part in order to round out the picture.

Faith Renders Good Works Acceptable

As he prepared the first edition of the German AC, known as *editio princeps,* Melanchthon recast all of Art. XX. He produced a text which must be regarded as one of the most remarkable summaries of the doctrine of faith produced by the Reformation. Unfortunately, it has not received the attention it deserves, because the critical editions of the AC have given preference to the "original," albeit reconstructed, text. The text reproduced in the *editio princeps,* however, made history throughout the 16th century, as did the Latin edition (*Variata*) of 1540, which also displays an expanded form of Art. XX. In order to avoid repetitions we will consider here only the final part of the reformulated Art. XX.

The title of the final part clearly suggests its division into three sections: "That one ought to and must do good works, and how one can do them, and how they are acceptable to God."[19] We turn directly to the second and third sections.

In the second section Melanchthon grants that by their natural powers men are able to perform honest works to some extent. He insists, however, that the heart cannot love God unless it believes that He is favorable. Therefore the Lutherans first of all teach faith, whereby the Holy Spirit is given; they also teach that Christ helps and protects us against the devil. As the heart knows that God wants to favor and hear us on Christ's account, it can love God and call upon Him. And since it knows that Christ wants to strengthen and help, it awaits His help, does not despair, and strives against the devil. For this reason Jesus Christ says: "Without Me you can do nothing" (John 15:5). Consequently, if one does not teach faith adequately, he will not teach works profitably.

The Lutherans, Melanchthon proceeds, also instruct people on how good works are acceptable. Good works please God because He has accepted the person and reckons him righteous because of Christ. Therefore we may not presume that after regeneration we are righteous by virtue of our purity or because we fulfill the Law.

No, even then one must invoke the Mediator and maintain that God favors us because of Christ and that our works require mercy and are not so worthy as to be accepted as righteousness and be rewarded with eternal life. We must hold that good works please God because He favors the person on account of Christ. But it is only through faith that one understands that God favors the person. Consequently, good works please God only in the believer, as Paul teaches in Rom. 14:23: "Whatever does not happen in faith is sin." For good works to please God the heart must first be at peace with Him and reckon that He has regard for us (*sich unser annehme*), favors us, and considers us righteous, not because of our merit but out of mercy because of Christ.

Melanchthon's presentation is clear. God's favor rests on Christ. Christ, however, is the Mediator on our behalf. God's favor, therefore, extends to the believers who cling to Him through faith and envelops also the good works which result from their regeneration by the Holy Spirit. The main point is that Christ is and remains the Mediator even in relation to the good works issuing from the new life of faith. This means that faith must apprehend and hold the Mediator even for the approval of the believer's works.

If things are seen in this perspective, it is true indeed that one must promote faith in Christ not only to elicit good works but also to make sure that God will regard them as good.

It is clear and evident that Melanchthon envisions the believer as acting boldly on the assumption that his person together with his actions can count on God's approval because of Christ. One hears in the background Paul's word which Melanchthon esteemed so much: "If God be for us, who will be against us?"

In these formulations of the *editio princeps* one finds the conclusive evidence of the Reformers' struggle for a true Christian ethos. The doctrine of justification through faith is not restricted to standing before God and being absolved of past sins. It promotes Christian *action* spirited by confidence in God's mercy and approval on Christ's account. Ultimately only the believer sustained by God's favor can *dare*.

It is a tragedy that this clear perception was obscured in succeeding generations, and that Lutherans to this day are known for their quietism rather than being famous for their daring in God's name.

DEFENSE OF THE DOCTRINE OF FAITH (ART. XX)

At this point, however, we must leave the text of the AC and turn to contemporary ecumenical documents in order to determine how this powerful and inspiring doctrine of justification through faith has been handled in contemporary theological agreements.

CHAPTER 9

The Doctrine of Faith in "Justification Today" (1963)

Since we have established the doctrine of justification through faith as Christian righteousness, it is now important to consider how it is used in five contemporary ecumenical documents. Our main question is whether these agreements adequately represent the Reformers' understanding of the matter as expressed in the Augsburg Confession.

The document we will study in this chapter, "Justification Today," stems from discussions among Lutheran churches at the Lutheran World Federation's fourth assembly, Helsinki, 1963. It represents an attempt to recast the doctrine of justification in contemporary language. It was meant to enable the Lutheran churches to give a *Lutheran* contribution to the ecumenical movement.

Since the AC is the fundamental confession of the Lutheran churches, it is fair to assume that in the discussions their spokesmen tried to represent its stand on faith. The question to be answered is how adequately the Lutheran teaching of justification by faith is presented in the agreements resulting from the ecumenical discussions.

Historical Origins

"Justification Today" is the definitive version of "Document Number 75—Revised Form" that was "received" by the fourth assembly of the Lutheran World Federation and referred to the Commission on Theology for "discussion, final formulation, and publication."[1] In

THE DOCTRINE OF FAITH IN "JUSTIFICATION TODAY" (1963)

order to understand its content, it is useful to recall the circumstances of its composition.

The third assembly, Minneapolis, 1957, directed the Commission on Theology to study "the Lutheran Confessions in their importance for the life of the church in the present." It was later agreed that to carry out this directive the commission would investigate "what the teaching of the Lutheran Confessions on justification means for the present proclamation of the church and the spiritual life of its members."[2]

Between 1958 and 1961 the Commission on Theology discussed the doctrine of justification on the basis of papers presented by theological experts. Since it had to report its findings to the assembly, the commission decided to summarize (and simplify) them in a "study document" addressed to pastors and congregations. Vilmos Vajta, Warren Quanbeck, and Peter Brunner prepared drafts on the basis of the AC and other sources.[3]

The commission submitted this "Study Document on Justification" to the member churches to obtain their views on it for the assembly. It also submitted a further report of its deliberations on justification and other issues.[4]

The Helsinki assembly convened from July 30 to Aug. 11, 1963. Its theme, "Christ Today," as the executive secretary explained, called for reflection on "the proclamation and reality of the sinner's justification for Christ's sake." The issue was whether justification by faith and the fellowship with God that results from it were (still) determining factors of the churches' proclamation and life.[5]

The main lecturers had been advised in a special meeting to question and correct the misrepresentation of the "message of justification" as a doctrine, as an individual experience, or as a spiritual event without relation to the world. The Executive Committee hoped that the discussion of the issue would help the churches recover full comprehension of the "message of justification" in order to share it with modern man and other churches in the ecumenical movement.[6]

The debate on six issues concerning justification took place mainly in 26 study groups. The groups were faced with an abundance of materials, namely, the Commission on Theology's official report and the study document together with the churches' appraisals, a statement draft written by the federation staff, and four lectures on justification presented in the plenary sessions. Group work, however, had to be concluded in seven hours' time. As the staff explained later, the groups were not expected to produce a report on the state of research, or a dogmatic definition of the matter.[7]

The group reports and the draft submitted by the staff were consolidated by the Coordinating Committee. Its president, Bishop Hanns Lilje, presented the "Report on the Discussion on the Justification Theme—Document Number 75, First Draft" in the plenary session. He described it as a doctrinal statement on the sinner's justification by grace alone. It was to be understood as "an interpretation of God's single redeeming act" in Jesus Christ, which is "the real content of the doctrinal statement on the sinner's justification."[8]

Regardless of the expectations of the staff, the assembly assumed that a solemn resolution or consensus declaration was intended. It criticized the document and returned it to the committee.[9]

The committee held an open session to receive suggestions. It revised the text and presented it as "Christ Today—Document Number 75, Revised Form." According to Bishop Lilje, the new document conveyed the results of the group sessions, reflected the assembly's faithfulness to the forefathers' confession, and discussed the subject in view of the present spiritual situation.[10]

After much debate the assembly decided to accept this document and refer it to the Commission on Theology for "discussion, final revision, and publication." President Franklin Clark Fry closed the discussion emphasizing that the assembly had issued "a theological declaration in today's language—without vacillating on its recognition of the Lutheran Confessions and Holy Scriptures." Not a single voice had questioned the expression of the Christian faith in the terminology of the doctrine of justification as found in the AC. "This is remarkable enough!" he exclaimed.[11]

A year later the Commission on Theology made a revision of the document without substantially changing its content and character. It provided a foreword with thought-provoking questions raised especially by theologians in the German Democratic Republic.[12]

"Failure" Factors

Several explanations have been given for the assembly's apparent failure in approving an authoritative statement on justification.

According to the staff of the Lutheran World Federation the effort failed on technical grounds. The assembly misunderstood its task. It tried to act as both a church council and a theological conference. It also envisioned a consensus declaration.[13]

As a former staff member wrote recently, the outcome would have been different if delegates had voiced only their churches' stand on the preparatory document, and if the assembly had followed a conciliar method in approving the report on group discussions.[14]

It is possible that the assembly outdid itself as it tried, at the same time, to articulate the contemporary significance of the doctrinal tradition and to bear actual witness of it to the modern world.[15]

In a Catholic observers' estimation, the assembly was unable to express the "justification message" in clear, modern language because the *matter itself* remained controversial and unclear.[16] The inability to clarify *how* the message must be proclaimed reveals uncertainty on justification itself, for precisely in the case of justification it is impossible to separate the *how* from *what* is proclaimed.[17]

According to Wolfgang Trillhaas, the assembly's caution denoted awareness of the seriousness of the issue: Since a new word on the matter could not be found, it was wise to keep to traditional formulations until a new word might appear. Perhaps, as the United States Lutheran–Catholic Dialogue Group ponders in retrospect, "the main importance of the assembly is that it alerted Lutherans to a need for further consideration on the cardinal theme of justification."[18]

"Justification Today," therefore, is a discussion paper that reflects the attempt to recover and communicate the Biblical "message of justification" as received and understood in the Lutheran theological tradition. It is not a definitive statement, but does carry "moral authority, which rests with the inner strength of conviction of decisions which are submitted to the member churches for their reception," as the last assembly of the federation has established with regard to such resolutions.[19]

Outline

The document addresses itself to five questions:

1. How is contact between the justification message and modern man established?
2. What is justification? How does it take place?
3. How could justification through Baptism become a call to faith?
4. How does justification relate to the Christian community and the world?
5. How shall the church preach the message of justification, so that a life of faith and service may be the result? For the purposes of this study it will be necessary to examine especially the first and second parts, which correspond to the first two questions.[20]

Approach

The document assumes in the first part that the message of the Reformation intended to answer the question, "How do I find a gracious God?"

This assumption is questionable, to say the least. Luther's search for an answer to that question, it is true, influenced his theological development and turned him into a reformer. This, however, does not mean that it determined his whole theology. As he formulated his teachings in the "Great Confession" (1528), the Catechisms (1529), and the "Smalcald Articles" (1536), he recited God's action on man's behalf in the words of the Apostles' and Nicene Creeds and drew implications with regard to man's condition and redemption. He emphasized not human need but God's action that relieves such need even before it is realized.

The document itself forcefully argues that God, the Creator, is present and active through His goodness and judgment before human beings, His creatures, become aware of and recognize Him. It is God Himself who answers our questions and meets our needs. He comes to man as He sends His Son in order that the world may have life.

Thus the document itself modifies its initial approach and sets the stage for the discussion of justification in the second part.

Jesus Christ's Role

"Jesus Christ is God's act (*Tat Gottes*) in which God has provided redemption for all men" (No. 5).

One may question whether it is proper to speak of a person as being God's act. The meaning intended is clear: God has provided redemption for all men through Jesus. The document emphasizes: "It is God Himself who justifies man, the impious, in the Son of God who became man, the crucified and risen Jesus" (No. 5).

Later in Part 2 the document affirms that God, through Jesus' communion with sinners, descended into the depths of godlessness to justify sinners, not the righteous (No. 7). In another passage of the same part the document stresses that the Reformers, as they asserted justification by faith, were concerned not with a specific terminology but with Christ's deed and honor: He alone redeems us from our sins (No. 8).

This, however, is all the document has to say about Christ's role in justification.

It is plain that the document avoids saying that Jesus Christ "made satisfaction for our sins" and "reconciled the Father with us," as the AC does in Arts. IV and III. It follows the trend set by the study document, which unfolds its ideas from a perspective of salvation history and therefore develops "the doctrine of reconciliation and justification not as a doctrine of satisfaction, but on the basis of the Biblical concept of God's righteousness." This is retraced throughout Scripture as "the patterns of God's action."[21] Still the study document did say that Jesus "stood in our place before God, receiving in His own body and life the judgment of God upon our sin and guilt" and that He "accepted the curse of the Law in order to deliver us from its curse."[22] The final statement, however, did not incorporate these insights.

Later, as it treats of the church, the document speaks of Christ's rule, but does not describe it. Similarly, it does not explain, as Luther does in the "Great Confession," that on account of His resurrection and exaltation Jesus is Lord over life and death, sin and righteousness, able and willing to share life and righteousness, and stands before God as the high priest and bishop of our souls. While it is plain *that* Jesus Christ redeems and justified, it remains unclear *how* he does it.

The document tried to avoid the traditional confession that justification takes place "because of Christ" (*propter Christum*), but did not produce a convincing alternative.

The document is also reticent about the Holy Spirit and His role in offering and sharing Christ's benefits or gifts through the promise of the Gospel.

One reads in paragraph five that the message of justification "is based on the words and deeds of the earthly man Jesus of Nazareth" and stems "from the apostles' encounter with the risen Lord." They carried the message into the world and handed it down to us in the Holy Spirit's power. Christ's presence in the Holy Spirit is mentioned elsewhere (No. 9) as the only source of the church's life. That is all the document has to say about the Holy Spirit.

The Gospel

The role of the Gospel in justification is described in paragraph six: Through the message of justification "God's justifying Christ deed comes to each of us." Another passage states that the justifying deed of Christ comes to the individual through Baptism: God comes near, and only the new man born out of water and the Spirit is allowed to live (No. 10).

The document implies, but does not state, that the awareness of both one's perdition and God's love is connected with the realization of His judgment over sin. It extols God's justification of *the sinner* but does not care to say that the latter is subject to God's law and judgment, unless he is justified.

The document does emphasize elsewhere, however, that the Christian receives God's justifying verdict only in permanent repentance (No. 27), which implies that the sinner, too, must be repentant as he trusts in God's promise and receives forgiveness.

Faith

"Justification Today" does not mention faith explicitly in the section on justification. It implies and suggests it when it says that the message of justification leads us to "realize God's love ... as we entrust ourselves to His promise and thus receive the forgiveness of our

THE DOCTRINE OF FAITH IN "JUSTIFICATION TODAY" (1963)

sins" (No. 6). This realization of God's love, this entrusting oneself to the promise, one may presume, is faith.

The document, then, does imply that the message of justification calls forth faith, and that faith believes in the promise inherent in the message.[23] It does not state, however, that faith is necessary, nor does it specify the role it plays in justification.

In short, the text fails to clarify *how* the sinner is justified, that is, the *modum iustificationis,* as Melanchthon used to say. It remains unexplained how and why God regards sinners as righteous. The notion that faith in Christ is the Christian's righteousness before God is totally absent.

Since the document does not describe the origin, nature, and role of justifying faith, it is remarkable how much it tries to make of faith in other contexts. It says of the church that it is built up in faith in the Lord Jesus Christ (No. 9). It asks the church to take Baptism seriously, so that it may help faith (No. 10). It inquires as to the reason why the faith of the church is so poor in visible expressions, if compared to the great epochs of its history (No. 16). It stresses that faith in the crucified and risen Lord gives man courage to live in a world that is set through with demonic powers and temptations (No. 25). These statements, however, remain rather abstract. Faith as such is not discussed, and it remains unclear just how it would meet these expectations.

Toward the end of the second part the document explains that the *issue* of justification is the center of Scripture, even though different expressions are used for God's saving act (No. 8). It reaffirms that the church stands or falls with the Biblical message of justification by faith alone properly understood as witness to Christ as the only One who redeems us from sin.

The Christian Community

In Parts III through V the document establishes the proper relation between the message of justification, the church, and the world.

Because the text is so reticent on faith, it does not explain how the church is born and what it is. The document stresses that the church finds its proper function in handling the means whereby God justifies sinners (No. 13). Through the Word and the sacraments new life grows (No. 11). As it exercises its function, the church must

THE DOCTRINE OF FAITH

view itself as the communion of absolved sinners (No. 13), make sure that all people are reached with God's message (No. 15), and thus realize the new humanity under Christ's rule (No. 11).

In the final part the document describes the effects of justification on the Christian's life in the world. He is expected to follow Jesus and imitate His example by giving himself for the world in the power of the resurrection communicated at Baptism. The certainty that God rules the world enables him to face demonic powers, cooperate even with unbelievers, and express the new humanity imparted through Christ's incarnation and resurrection.

"Justification Today" insists that the church, which as Christ's body depends entirely on His mercy, must request and receive its life through His presence in the Holy Spirit (No. 9). The document, however, does not mention that the Christian, too, is continually and totally dependent on Christ's mercy: He remains imperfect, and his service will always be faulty and polluted by sin. As Melanchthon argues in the first edition of the AC in German, the Christian remains acceptable and pleases God with his deeds only on account of faith in Christ (*BS,* p. 83). This aspect of the Lutheran teaching on Christian righteousness, however, is disregarded in "Justification Today."

Evaluation

These observations show with sufficient clarity that the Lutheran doctrine of Christian righteousness, as expressed in the AC and understood in this study, did not find comprehensive expression in "Justification Today."

It is inadequate, if not misleading, to affirm that justification consists in Christ's fellowship with sinners as the result of God's condescension to the depths of godlessness. While this is part of justification, it is by no means all of it.

As the Lutheran churches of the German Democratic Republic stated in a declaration signed by five representative theologians, the document omitted essential aspects of Biblical and Reformation teaching, so that it becomes impossible to grasp the whole depth of the message of justification.[24]

In summary, several significant features of the AC are lacking:

1. There is no clear word about the role of God's law in leading the sinner to awareness of sin and the realization of God's judgment;

THE DOCTRINE OF FAITH IN "JUSTIFICATION TODAY" (1963)

2. It is not stressed that Christ died and rose "for us men and our salvation," as the Nicene Creed puts it;

3. It is not explained that the Gospel, as God's promise of Christ's gifts through the Holy Spirit, both demands and calls forth true faith in Christ for the reception of things promised and offered;

4. It is not mentioned that faith is the Christian's righteousness on account of which God permanently regards him as righteous and his good works as acceptable, since he holds fast to Christ as ground for God's mercy;

5. There is no thought as to how Christian worship and service please God and are acceptable to Him, even though imperfect and soiled by sin.

One may grant that "Justification Today" does not openly question the concepts the AC uses to express the doctrine of justification, as president Fry asserted in closing the Helsinki debate on the issue. But it is readily apparent that the document does not reflect a "systematic consensus formation" on justification.[25] It does, however, presume to convey the Biblical message of justification as the Reformers proclaimed it; therefore one must call into question its omissions and inadequacies: It definitely does not measure up to the standards of the AC.

With "Justification Today" the Lutheran World Federation had an unfortunate start in entering ecumenical dialog. If its member churches did not succeed in recovering the Lutheran heritage, how could they share it with other Christians?

CHAPTER 10

The Doctrine of Faith in the "Leuenberg Agreement" (1973)

Historical Background

The document to be studied in this chapter is the "Agreement Between Reformation Churches in Europe" (*Leuenberger Konkordie*),[1] approved in 1973 by Lutheran, Reformed, Union, Waldensian, and Czech Brethren churches.

The Faith and Order Commission of the World Council of Churches promoted a series of Lutheran–Reformed talks between 1955 and 1971. From 1964 to 1967 the Lutheran and Reformed world federations sponsored discussions in Bad Schauenburg, Switzerland. The issue was whether the division between Lutheran and Reformed churches could still be justified.

A series of theses on God's Word, the Law, and the Confessions as well as a report on the talks were positively received by 21 of the 83 churches affiliated with the Lutheran World Federation and the WCC.[2]

The Faith and Order Commission and the world federations promoted a third series of talks at Leuenberg, near Basel, in 1969 and 1970, with delegates representing most of the churches.

The 1970 report on "Church Division and Church Fellowship" encouraged the churches to elaborate and come to an agreement on measures leading to church fellowship including intercommunion and intercelebration. The churches authorized drafting an agreement and sent delegates to discuss one such proposal in 1971.

THE DOCTRINE OF FAITH IN THE "LEUENBERG AGREEMENT" (1973)

On March 16, 1973, 45 delegates representing some 60 churches approved the final text of the Agreement.

The churches were invited to manifest their formal approval by Sept. 30, 1974. By the summer of 1982, 74 European and 2 non-European churches had given assent to the "Leuenberg Agreement."[3]

In a declaration issued in July 1980 the LWF reaffirmed the member churches' agreement with their Reformed brethren in a "basic understanding of the Gospel" as expressed also in the "Leuenberg Agreement."[4]

Ecumenical Significance

It is significant, particularly for the Church of Rome, that in the "Leuenberg Agreement" two groups of Protestant churches, the Lutheran and the Reformed, tried to define the specific understanding of the Gospel issuing from the Reformation at the same time as they were also in dialog with the Roman Catholic Church.[5]

In fact, a Lutheran spokesman stressed the need for coordination between the Leuenberg talks and the dialog with the Vatican,[6] and a Roman Catholic theologian hoped that the Leuenberg document would incorporate the Lutheran–Catholic agreement on justification.[7] According to an informed source, however, it remains questionable whether the results of the Lutheran–Reformed dialog will agree with those of the Lutheran–Catholic dialog.[8] Coordination and consistency do not necessarily characterize international ecumenical organizations.

Outline

The document under consideration is made up of a prolog and four clearly identified parts.

In the prolog the churches declare that they have reached a common understanding of the Gospel and therefore are able to proclaim and bring about church fellowship. In keeping with Reformation principles, they assume that agreement in the right teaching of the Gospel and the administration of the sacraments is both an indispensable and a sufficient basis for church fellowship (Nos. 1 and 2).

This approach to the question of church fellowship was evidently inspired by the AC, especially by Arts. I–VIII. In fact, one of the issues discussed in the 1971 agreement draft had been over whether the AC could provide the framework for an agreement between Reformation churches.[9]

In keeping with this approach, the first part describes "the road to fellowship." Changes that have occurred since the Reformation make possible today a fellowship that the Reformers were not able to enjoy, even though they were unanimous in confessing the Gospel of God's free grace in Christ and the creeds of Christendom.

The second part describes "the common understanding of the Gospel." The third gives expression to the "agreement on the doctrinal condemnations of the Reformation era." The fourth deals with "the proclamation and realization of church fellowship" on the basis of principles established in the preceding parts.

The structure of the document reflects the stand taken by the 1970 Leuenberg Report: There is reason enough for church fellowship when Jesus' exclusive role in mediating salvation is recognized as the core of the Gospel and the only measure of doctrine and life.[10] The doctrine of justification by faith and regeneration must then be developed on this basis. In connection with it an agreement on the efficacy of the Word and the sacraments must also be envisioned.[11]

The document defines consensus on the Gospel and the sacraments and then draws the implications for church fellowship. We must now examine this common understanding of the Gospel (Part II, Nos. 6–16), for it entails an agreement on the doctrine of justification (Nos. 7–12).

The Gospel

The document describes the Gospel as "the message of Jesus Christ, the salvation of the world in fulfillment of God's promises to Israel" (No. 7). It defines the relation between the Gospel and justification by saying that in this doctrine the Reformers expressed the proper understanding of the Gospel (No. 8).

This distinction between the Gospel (itself) and the Reformers' doctrine of justification as an "understanding" of it is open to question. It assumes that the Reformers consciously developed a doctrine as we understand the term today, that this was a doctrine of *justification,* and that the same consisted in a (subjective) interpretation of the (objective) Gospel.

The present study of the AC suggests that Luther and Melanchthon were concerned with the proclamation and *use* of the Gospel. This concern led them to affirm a *doctrine of faith* that would ensure correct use of the Gospel, that is, the reception through faith of Christ's gifts offered and shared by the Gospel. This doctrine of faith was in their estimation Jesus' and Paul's very own. To speak of the doctrine of justification as the Reformers' "understanding" or "interpretation" of the Gospel appears anachronistic. It presumes that Luther and Melanchthon thought in categories of the 20th century.

Moreover, it should not surprise us that the document considers the possibility that the Reformers might have expressed an (adequate and comprehensive) understanding of the Gospel in the (single) doctrine of justification. This reduction of the Gospel to the doctrine of justification is characteristic of the theological method that made possible the "Leuenberg Agreement."[12]

It is clear, however, that the "Leuenberg Agreement" understands the Gospel as centered in Christ, and God's saving action (*Heilshandeln*) as linked to the conveying of salvation (*Heilszuwendung*) in justification. Thus the Agreement definitely anchors justification in Christology and in so doing dissociates itself from purely anthropological interpretations that envision the assurance of one's acceptance without any reference to Christ.[13]

Jesus Christ

The "Leuenberg Agreement" in No. 9 details the Gospel witness to Jesus Christ as the incarnate, crucified, risen, and coming One. It affirms, first, that through Jesus Christ God bound Himself to man; second, that Jesus Christ took upon Himself God's judgment and thus demonstrated God's love to sinners; and third, that as Judge and Savior He leads the world to its consummation.

This description is complemented by statements in other articles. In No. 12 the Agreement states what it regards as a conviction shared by all the Confessions of the Reformation, namely, that Jesus Christ's "exclusive role in mediating salvation" constitutes the heart of Scripture. In No. 16 the churches affirm that through Christ's death as proclaimed in the Lord's Supper God has reconciled the world with Himself.

The document does not describe in detail what it calls Jesus Christ's exclusive role as Mediator of salvation. One must draw together the aspects mentioned in several articles in order to get the picture.

The document evidently avoids saying that Jesus Christ sacrificed Himself *for us* and reconciled *God* with us, as the AC does. For this reason it does not depict the exalted Christ as Mediator and Propitiator standing before God on our behalf.[14]

One wonders whether such conceptions as Christ's "reconciling the Father" and His "interceding for us" are to be numbered among the "historically conditioned thought forms" of the Reformation that must be left behind in order to "actualize" the "message of justification" (No. 5).

The Holy Spirit

The document does not include a specific section on the Holy Spirit and God's (Christ's) action through Him. There are references to His action in statements on God's Word, the sacraments, and the Gospel.

One reads in No. 10 that God "through His Word in the Holy Spirit" calls all men to repent and believe; in No. 13, that Jesus Christ is present in the Holy Spirit in preaching, Baptism, and the Lord's Supper. In No. 14 one learns that in Baptism Jesus Christ calls people in the power of His Holy Spirit into His community and to a new life of faith. According to No. 21 the Holy Spirit and thus God Himself renders Jesus present to us as the crucified and risen One in the Word of promise and the sacraments. According to No. 24 the Gospel assures the sinner of unconditional acceptance by God.

Throughout this text the Holy Spirit is depicted as God's or Christ's medium. The document does not explain how the Holy Spirit relates to God's Word and the sacraments, but both of these are definitely regarded as effective means of Christ's presence and action among men.

The Law

In the text the nature and significance of God's law is not discussed in detail. The document assumes that man is a sinner, that he has fallen prey to sin and death (No. 14) and must repent. It explains that if man believes in the Gospel, he is liberated from the charges of the Law (No. 10) and lives in daily repentance (Nos. 10, 14). Other than that, the text stresses that God's demanding and giving will encompasses the whole world (No. 11).

In this respect the document views the Law as norm and rule, rather than as accuser. It seems to stand in contradiction to the Apology of the AC, which holds that the Law always accuses as long as man lives.[15]

The Correlation Promise-Faith

The text stresses that the Gospel consists in a promise. Thus in No. 10 one reads: "God calls men through His Word in the Holy Spirit to repentance and faith and He promises His righteousness in Jesus Christ to the sinner who believes. Whoever trusts in the Gospel is justified before God because of Christ and is thus free from the charges of the Law."

According to this passage, the Gospel offers God's righteousness in Jesus Christ. It is worth noting that this offer of righteousness is good only for those who believe in the Gospel. It would have been more in keeping with the spirit of the AC had the document said that the Gospel offers righteousness in Christ to *all* men and by this very offer moves them to believe in the promise and receive the offered righteousness.[16] The formulation seems faulty. It may not correspond to the authors' intention.

No. 24, as mentioned, states that "the sinner's unconditional acceptance by God is promised in the Gospel. Whoever trusts in it can be sure of his salvation and praise God's election." This passage regards the Gospel as the promise of God's unconditional acceptance—valid for all sinners. It corresponds to the first subtitle of Part II and No. 12, where the "message of justification" is called the message of God's grace.

No. 13 charges the church with the task of preaching the Gospel and explains that Christ is present in the Holy Spirit in preaching,

Baptism, and the Lord's Supper. The text adds that "thus"—presumably by the spreading of the Gospel—justification in Christ is imparted to man and that thereby the Lord gathers His congregation. Justification in Christ is, therefore, that which the Gospel promises and shares.

According to No. 15 the Lord's Supper "grants us forgiveness for our sins and sets us free for a new life of faith."

These passages indicate that in the "Leuenberg Agreement" the Gospel is considered as the promise of God's righteousness, of His free grace, and of our unconditional acceptance in Christ. They also indicate that the Agreement regards faith as necessary for one to receive those gifts.

In some articles the text implies but does not explicitly state that the promise calls forth the very faith demanded for its reception. In No. 10, for instance, after saying that God calls people to faith and offers righteousness to believers, it adds that those who believe in the Gospel are justified. The same sequence of promise and faith is evident in No. 24. There the believer's faith is said to trust in the promise of unconditional acceptance referred to previously.

These observations suggest that the "Leuenberg Agreement" assumes a correlation between the Gospel promise and the faith resulting from and focused on this promise. In this regard it seems to follow the AC (AC, V).

The Role of Faith

The text of the Agreement, however, does not specify exactly what the "objects" are in which faith believes as it "trusts" (in) the Gospel. Consequently, it does not tell what precisely faith is supposed to believe with regard to Christ and His role in justification. All one hears is that righteousness "in Christ" is offered in the Gospel (No. 10), which assumes that faith acknowledges that in some way it is "in Christ" that God's righteousness is offered and received—presumably because He is the One who demonstrated God's love to sinners by taking God's judgment upon Himself (No. 9).

The AC, however, takes pains to declare exactly what faith believes, and this coincides exactly with that which the Gospel promises and offers—on account and on behalf of Christ.

Because the Agreement does not tell exactly what faith believes,

THE DOCTRINE OF FAITH IN THE "LEUENBERG AGREEMENT" (1973)

it does not explain at all why faith has any role in justification, or (what comes to the same) why it is only the believer who is privileged with the offer and gift of righteousness, acceptance, or justification "in Christ."

In short, the Agreement assumes and affirms, but neither explains nor demonstrates, the justifying role of faith. In this respect it is incomplete compared with the AC, which carefully states what it is that faith believes and why it can be said to justify (AC, IV).

The Formulation "Because of Christ"

Because the Agreement does not detail the content of the promise and does not define what faith believes (in) as it trusts the promise, the text does not—and in fact cannot—explain why the believer is justified exactly "because of Christ."

If the document had presented Jesus Christ as the incarnate Son of God who suffered and triumphed on behalf of us all, if it had defined the Gospel as the promise and offer of righteousness on account of Christ, if it had portrayed faith as believing that God offers and imparts righteousness on Christ's account, then the text would be justified in saying that God justifies the sinner who trusts (in) the Gospel, because of Christ.

Since the Agreement fails to join the AC in laying these foundations, it remains questionable why it should say that God justifies the believing sinner because of Christ.

If it had been consistent with its own view of Christ, faith, and promise, the document could at the most have said that God justifies or accepts the believing sinner "in Christ" out of sheer grace and unmotivated love. That is entirely what the view of Christ set forth in No. 9 demands and all it allows.

As it is, the formula "because of Christ" in No. 10 does not make sense, inasmuch as the context does not present Christ as the One on whose account God assures, and faith is sure of having, righteousness.

Justification

The "Leuenberg Agreement" does not explain in what justification consists. The passages that deal with the matter (Nos. 10, 14, 15, and

24) suggest that *justification* means that God (Christ) imparts righteousness, accepts or receives into the fellowship of salvation, grants forgiveness of sins, calls and sets one free for a new life issuing from faith. As it employs these rather traditional expressions, the Agreement avoids using the verbal expressions "to be made righteous" and "to be reckoned righteous," which have caused so much discussion.

Since it does not establish a clear correlation between faith and Christ, the Agreement does not state that faith is reckoned as righteousness, as the AC does on the basis of the Epistle to the Romans (AC, IV, 3).

The Agreement text speaks of a new life that issues forth from faith (see for instance Nos. 14 and 15). The passages that tell how the justified person lives, however, do not describe his new activity as resulting from faith or, for that matter, from Christ's presence in faith or from the Holy Spirit's prompting. It remains unclear why and how the Christian's life is "out of faith."

The document stresses that justification introduces the believer into Christian fellowship and that the new life of praising God and serving others takes place within the community. Thus it tries to overcome an individualistic understanding of justification.

It also stresses the eschatological orientation of Christian action, as it speaks of the Christian "assurance that God will bring His kingdom in all its fullness" (No. 10).

It is remarkable, however, that the text does not explicitly mention love of God and man as the result of faith and the motivation of Christian service. The emphasis is not on love as fulfillment of the Law, but on action in this world.

It is remarkable, too, that the Agreement, while referring quite often to repentance and daily renewal, does not reckon with the fact that the believer's deeds are under God's scrutiny and fail to meet His standards, therefore standing in need of Christ's intervention as Mediator and Propitiator.

The text implies that God accepts the believer's good works without further qualification. Because this is so, the Agreement does not present and regard faith as that righteousness by which we are (and are reckoned) righteous together with our works on account of Christ, the Mediator.

THE DOCTRINE OF FAITH IN THE "LEUENBERG AGREEMENT" (1973)

In short, the document does not include any affirmation corresponding to the last sentence of the fourth article of the AC.

Limited Scope

The "Leuenberg Agreement" is limited in its scope. It describes the churches' common understanding of the Gospel only insofar as it is regarded as necessary for establishing church fellowship (No. 6). A full treatment of justification by faith is beyond its scope.

The text presents the basic views of the AC and even employs once again the expression "because of Christ" in its statement on justification. One does not have in its Christology, however, a clear affirmation that Christ came, acted, died, rose, and rules for us human beings. This *pro nobis* is necessary to support, explain, and justify the use of "because of Christ" with regard to justification.

While the document implies a correlation between the promise and faith, it could have been more explicit on the correlation between faith and Christ. As it is, the Agreement does not allow one to suppose that faith actually is the believer's righteousness to the extent that it apprehends and regards Christ as righteousness. Consequently the key Reformation insight that the believer needs to be and actually is reckoned righteous on account of faith, that is, on account of Christ as apprehended and engaged by faith, was left out of consideration. In short, even though the Agreement is traditional in its formulations, as commentators have observed,[17] it is selective in incorporating or omitting traits that make up the AC doctrine of Christian righteousness as identified in this study.

The Agreement expressly affirms that the churches have the right (!) to "actualize" the Christian message (No. 5). One must hope, however, that the exercise of the "freedom of faith" in a "continued responsible testimony to the Word" will not result in silent suppression of teachings which Luther and Melanchthon regarded as decisive for the recognition of Christ's role and the promotion of true Christian worship and service to God.

A Compromise

The last article in the section under consideration (No. 12) stresses that the understanding of the Gospel as set forth in the "Leuenberg

Agreement" is based on the ancient Creeds of the church and reaffirms the common conviction of the Reformation Confessions that Jesus Christ's "mediation of salvation" is the heart of Scripture and that the "message of justification" is the measure of all preaching in the church.

This statement is not redundant, as it might seem. It signifies that the understanding of the Gospel presented in this section (Nos. 6–12) represents a compromise between the Lutheran and the Reformed churches. While granting that the "justification message" is the touchstone of Christian preaching, as Lutherans hold, it affirms that the center of Scripture is Christ's mediatorship, as Reformed churches have tended to stress.[18]

Furthermore, as they stress that their understanding of the Gospel is based on the Creeds, the Lutheran and Reformed churches recommend their Agreement to the Roman Catholic and Eastern Orthodox churches, which have placed high value on the Ecumenical Creeds.

"Reinterpretation" Efforts

The documents examined in this and the previous chapter have the common intention of using the AC to interpret and master a new historical situation characterized by specific developments in theological research and ecumenical relations.

While preserving many Reformation accents, both documents strive to relate their (contemporary) view of Christ with the (traditional) doctrine of justification. Their "reinterpretation," however, does not quite succeed. It does not tell unequivocally what Christ does and what faith consequently must do in justification.

One can only interpret what is first clearly perceived. The "reinterpretation" could not succeed because the authors started out with an inadequate perception of the teaching of the AC. They understood it as a doctrine of justification while it is a doctrine of *faith,* faith in *Christ* in the sense of regarding Him and resorting to Him as the Mediator and Propitiator.

If one no longer wishes to see Him and recur to Him in this way, it becomes difficult, if not impossible to make sense out of a "doctrine of faith" which assumes this specific view of Christ's role and function.

THE DOCTRINE OF FAITH IN THE "LEUENBERG AGREEMENT" (1973)

In short, the documents stand with contemporary theology in their view of Christ and wish to be based as well on the AC in their understanding of justification. This is the root of their difficulties. A theology that replaces the Christ of the AC with something else, necessarily changes the role and function of faith. It will believe something else and therefore will have a different function—or no function at all in justification.

This may explain why "Justification Today" and the "Leuenberg Agreement" have so little to say on faith in connection with justification and so much to say on it in connection with service to God and neighbor. To little avail, for if one empties faith of its content, which is Christ the Lord, with His powerful Spirit, how will it ever meet the expectations placed on it?

CHAPTER 11

The Doctrine of Faith in Lutheran-Catholic Documents (1972–83)

To determine how the AC's doctrine of faith is understood and represented in ecumenical documents stemming from the international dialog between Lutherans and Roman Catholics, the present chapter will examine three ecumenical documents that have been issued between 1972 and 1983.

"The Gospel and the Church" ("Malta Report," 1972)

The Vatican Secretariat for Christian Unity and the Executive Committee of the Lutheran World Federation formed the International Lutheran-Roman Catholic Study Commission on the basis of proposals worked out by the Joint Working Group. This task force had been created to further contacts initiated at the Second Vatican Council.

The commission discussed the theme "The Gospel and the Church" in five sessions between 1967 and 1971. It approved the text of the report in San Anton, Malta, on Feb. 25, 1971 (hence the name "Malta Report"). The document was officially released on Feb. 9, 1972, with a preface signed by the general secretary of the Lutheran World Federation.[1]

Scope

As the "Malta Report" discusses the current understanding of the Gospel and its relation to the church, it does not refer to the AC, except when dealing with related issues, like the ministry and church order. It avoids reopening 16th-century controversies and tries to formulate an agreement on the basis of contemporary exegetical studies.

It is necessary to discuss the document here mainly because it is assumed and referred to in the Joint Commission's 1980 declaration on the AC.

The report is composed of an introduction and four parts, on the relation between the Gospel and (1) tradition, (2) the world, (3) the office of the ministry, and (4) the unity of the church. The present analysis concentrates on the introduction and the first part, which present the scope of the discussions and the agreement achieved on justification.

The introduction explains the origins of the document and tells how the commission understood and met its task. It did not "deal with the theological controversies of the sixteenth century as such" but examined once again "the confessional differences in the light of the findings of contemporary studies on Biblical theology and church history as well as of the perspectives opened up by the Second Vatican Council" (No. 7).

The introduction reports further that the commission members reached a consensus on the theological understanding of the Gospel and other controversial points of doctrine. They agreed on the Christological and soteriological center of the Gospel and on its importance for the church as basis and norm.

As the introduction spells out the limitations and problems of the dialog, it calls attention to a difficulty which Lutherans encounter. While Roman Catholics can quote the Second Vatican Council and other recent statements of the magisterium, Lutherans can only refer back to the 16th-century Confessions. They find it difficult to define their present confession and understanding of the Christian faith in an authoritative way.

This observation is remarkable if one recalls that the LWF made "justification today" the theme of the Helsinki Assembly so as to enable its members to share this matter in the ecumenical dialog. The Helsinki document evidently was not regarded as authoritative and quoteworthy.

The introduction therefore remarks that the "Malta Report" represents the convictions and insights of the Study Commission, has no binding character, and is offered for discussion in order to improve relations between the Lutheran and Roman Catholic churches.

Gospel and Tradition

The first section of the report deals with "The Gospel and Tradition." It assumes that the question of the right understanding of the Gospel drove Lutherans and Catholics apart and that an agreement on this issue could bring them together again. Hope for an agreement rests on a new appraisal of confessional differences deriving from changes in historical circumstances and theological methodology (Nos. 14–15).

In order to determine how Lutherans and Catholics understand the Gospel today, the commission asked first of all how, in their estimation, the primitive church's preaching (*kerygma*) is related to Jesus' proclamation.

The commission members were agreed that "the Gospel rests fundamentally on the Easter witness." Consequently the report states that "in the Gospel God's salvation is handed down in Jesus Christ and made present in the Holy Spirit."[2] As proclamation of the saving action the Gospel is itself a salvation event (No. 16).

The commission takes for granted the distinction between the church's preaching and Jesus' proclamation. It views the Gospel as a message which the apostolic church formulated on the basis of the witnesses' testimony of the resurrection of Jesus. The Reformers, however, regarded the Gospel as the risen Christ's very own message, which *He* placed in the witnesses' mouth to be proclaimed in the power of the Holy Spirit. Here as elsewhere the report does not relate its assumptions and conclusions to the churches' confessional stand.[3]

Since the Gospel must be conveyed to ever-new historical situations, the commission inquires how one could discern between legitimate and illegitimate developments. It sets up a primary criterion, namely, that "the Holy Spirit establishes the Christ event as an act of salvation" (No. 18).[4] It discusses and evaluates secondary criteria for the continuity between tradition and its original source.

Since there is concern for a single truth that remains constant throughout the diversity of traditions, the commission asks: What is the foundation and center of the Gospel that the church's manifold testimony tries to convey and unfold in ever-different historical situations? According to the report it consists "in God's eschatological action of salvation in the cross and resurrection of Jesus, which all proclamation strives to explicate" (No. 25).

The search for the center of the Gospel in turn makes the commission ask how the dialog partners understand justification. The commission comes to the conclusion that "in the interpretation of justification a far-reaching consensus is becoming evident today" (No. 26).[5]

Even though "a wide agreement in the understanding of the doctrine of justification appears possible," the commission questions whether Lutherans and Catholics assign the same role to this doctrine and have the same regard for its consequences for the life and teaching of the church (No. 28). It concludes that both sides are convinced that the Gospel engenders Christian liberty and that the church must be an institution of freedom (No. 30).

This review of the argumentation developed in the first part of the "Malta Report" indicates quite clearly that the discussion of the problem of justification is subservient to the main purpose of the document, namely that of clarifying the relations between the Gospel and the church's tradition. Consequently the handling of the issue is not as thorough as one might expect. It is restricted to those aspects which have some bearing on the larger issue at hand.

In fact, the commission seems not to have heard special papers on the specific Lutheran or Catholic understanding of justification. It simply acknowledged and confirmed "the consensus which theological and ecumenical research had produced" in previous decades.[6]

It is useful to keep these limitations in mind as one examines the statements on justification.

Consensus on Justification

In keeping with its character the "Malta Report" begins by spelling out those features in the dialog partners' positions which make an agreement appear possible.

"In the issue of justification the Catholic theologians, too, emphasize that God's gift of salvation is not tied to any human conditions on the believer's part" (No. 26).[7]

THE DOCTRINE OF FAITH

It is significant that the report refers to the stand taken by Catholic theologians, rather than by the Roman Catholic Church. Presumably for this reason it does not adduce evidence to substantiate its claim, as it does rather frequently in other sections.

It is significant, too, that the statement is negative. It denies something, namely that God would grant salvation on the condition that the believer fulfill certain requirements.[8] It does not say positively how God imparts, and the believer becomes partaker of, the salvation gift.

The account of the Lutheran position also begins negatively: "Lutheran theologians stress that the act of justification is not restricted to individual forgiveness of sins and do not regard it as a declaration of the sinner's being righteous that remains purely external."[9]

According to this statement Lutheran theologians deny two misrepresentations of justification, which consist in regarding it as being identical with the remission of sins, or as being "purely forensic" in the sense that God's *declaring* the sinner righteous does not really *turn* him righteous.[10]

This negation makes one expect the positive description, which the report immediately adds—presumably as the common understanding of both sides. It reads: "On the contrary, through the justification message the divine righteousness realized in the Christ event is imparted to the sinner as a reality that overtakes him, and thereby the believer's new life is set up" (No. 26).[11]

On the basis of this statement one would presume that justification consists in an act or process whereby God's righteousness transmitted in the "justification message" envelops and overtakes the sinner and sets the basis for the new life shared by all believers. It is clear that in this act or process God's righteousness, "realized in the Christ event," plays a key role as a personal and fairly irresistible power. Justification is clearly regarded as God's act and as prompted by His very own dynamism—"by grace alone," as traditional language would say. It remains unclear *how* justification occurs in a person, or how the sinner overpowerd by righteousness comes to share in the believers' new life.

Other Statements on Justification

These statements on justification are complemented elsewhere. One reads in the section on the ministry: "Lutherans and Catholics are agreed in the [common] conviction that we owe salvation exclusively to God's act of salvation in Jesus Christ effected once for all times as it is testified in the Gospel" (No. 47).

This joint statement establishes a necessary connection between God's act of salvation in Jesus Christ and our salvation. It stresses Christ's exclusive role in providing the conditions for (the sinner's) justification. One could say, then, that for both Catholics and Lutherans justification is due to Christ alone.

A statement that appears in the section on intercommunion states that the Lord's Supper "is the acceptance of men for reconciliation through Jesus Christ's work of redemption" (No. 72). Even though it expresses the Lutheran understanding, it is significant because it employs "acceptance" and "reconciliation" to describe the reality elsewhere called the "justification event."

Inclusiveness

The report reflects the commission's effort to determine whether justification can be understood as expressing the totality of the salvation process. It regards other representations found in the New Testament as being entirely adequate to express the salvation process of which the Gospel testifies.

The commission holds that Paul sharpened the edge of his comprehensive witness to God's righteousness in the battle against Jewish legalism. Therefore, in its estimation, the justification message as affirming Christian liberty in face of legal conditions set up for receiving salvation must ever be articulated anew as explanation of the center of the Gospel (No. 27).

This diplomatically worded formulation evidently reflects a compromise between the Lutherans' high regard for justification as "the main article of the Christian faith" and the critical view which regards justification as one of many representations of the core of the Gospel. The formulation grants that the doctrine of justification is but a response to a specific threat, yet affirms its significance for all time inasmuch as it recognizes that the threat of legalism is ever present in the church. This allegedly indicates "a considerable measure of agreement."[12]

IMPLICATIONS

With regard to the implications of the doctrine of justification for the teaching and life of the church, the report first sets forth the Lutheran position. It requires from ecclesiastic traditions and institutions that they promote true proclamation of the Gospel and do not obscure the unconditional character of the reception of salvation (No. 29). The report concludes the section on justification by affirming that both Lutherans and Catholics share the conviction that the Gospel establishes Christian freedom, so that the church must understand itself and operate as an institution of liberty (No. 30).

DIVERGENCES

The Malta Report does not call attention to divergences. In fact there were some. The report on the Zurich meeting released in 1969 indicates that a wide consensus on the doctrine of justification seemed possible, but that there were questions as to its place and function in theology. It was an issue, too, whether both sides had identical views of its implications for the church's doctrine and life. A published comment on a partial report tells us plainly that, despite mutual concessions, there still was "no unanimity on the question of the place and function of the doctrine of justification." It was regarded as a problem demanding further debate.[13]

The text of the "Malta Report" sounds like a compromise: It quotes the Lutheran position (No. 29), omits any Catholic reservations, and concludes with a common statement on Christian liberty (No. 30).[14]

This review of the "Malta Report" on justification provides the material for an analysis of its relation to the AC.

THE GOSPEL

The two documents differ in their approach to the question of the Gospel. The AC, in keeping with its sources, assumes that the Gospel is summarized in the Creeds' recital of God's deeds "for us and our salvation." It takes for granted that Lutherans and Catholics are agreed on the "story" the Creeds tell. Therefore it argues that the common confession of God's deeds should result in consensus on the reception and use of God's benefits, for these are "part of the story" (AC, XX, 23).

For the AC, therefore, the divergence does not concern the Gospel as recital of God's deeds for our salvation (Gospel in a wide sense), but the Gospel as Christ's specific promise and offer of forgiveness and righteousness. The divergence concerns, more precisely, the *reception and use* of the Gospel in the proper and limited sense of the word.

The "Malta Report" concentrates on the present understanding of the Gospel in the wide sense of the term. It establishes, as expected, that today Lutheran and Catholic theologians have the same understanding of the Gospel and even of its "center," God's "eschatological act of salvation in Jesus' cross and resurrection."

The report does not ask how this common stance relates to the churches' (once) common confession of the Gospel and to their historical divergence as to the nature and use of the Gospel in its strict sense. This "lack of memory" involves an inconsistency, at least on the Lutherans' part. They state that the church's Confessions have authority as adequate interpretations of Scripture (No. 19), yet do not appeal or refer to these authoritative interpretations as they formulate their own today. It is a question whether they took the AC seriously as *interpretation of Scripture.*

Jesus Christ

On account of its approach the "Malta Report" does not relate its statements on God's eschatological action in Jesus to the confession of Christ's work in the Creeds and in the AC. As a result, it does not present a comprehensive statement on Jesus Christ's person and role. Above all, it does not state that He suffered and acted *for us,* as the New Testament formula *hyper* abundantly expresses. Consequently the report is not in a position to affirm that justification occurs *because of Christ,* as the AC does.

In fact, the report reflects reluctance to speak of Jesus as an active person—especially after the resurrection. In keeping with its theological and hermeneutical presuppositions, it prefers to speak of a Christ *event* while regarding *God* as active subject and Jesus as the means *in* whom salvation takes place—this, well understood, *in* the Gospel that is part of the world's historical process.

One wonders whether this rather abstract discourse on Jesus Christ is more apt to communicate than what the AC writes of Jesus, the person, who acts for us as Ruler and Sanctifier (AC, III).

The "How" of Justification

In its consideration of the "core" of the Gospel, God's action in Jesus Christ, the report uses two key terms, "salvation" and "righteousness." It does not define nor relate them to the historical Confessions. It is clear, however, that the commission's understanding of how salvation and righteousness are conveyed in the Gospel, together with its approach and scope, led it away from asking the main question, namely: *How* are people justified? *How* do they get a share in God's salvation and righteousness?

Because the report does not view the Gospel as Christ's specific promise and offer that both demands and calls forth faith, it is unable to state—as does the AC—that it is *through faith* that people become righteous, since it is *by faith* that they accept and receive the gifts of righteousness and salvation offered and imparted by Christ.

Even though the report refers to "the believers' new life" that results from God's righteousness, it does not at all discuss the justifying nature and function of faith in Christ. Thus the report avoided *the* question that brought about the Reformation.[15]

On account of the commission's approach, scope, and presuppositions the report discusses only *God's* action in justifying, without explaining how His action on a *subject* engages the latter's activity. This is why the commission could reach and proclaim an impending consensus.

There has hardly ever been any doubt between Lutherans and good Catholics that justification is God's (unmerited) doing and that it effects new life. The question—which the commission avoided—has always been how God's action involves man's as well.

It is manifest that the commission operated with a rather narrow and critical view of the Lutheran doctrine of justification. It fails to see that justification, as described in the AC, does not exclude other concepts, such as redemption, reconciliation, liberty, new life, and new creation, but rather involves them in many respects as presuppositions, synonyms, or sequels.

The commission understands justification exclusively as the *sinner's* justification (*iustificatio impii*) and does not take into account that the AC and the Apology affirm a justification of the *reconciled* as well.[16]

The commission seems to find justification expressed only in those writings in which justification terminology is used, namely in the apostle Paul's epistles. Apparently it does not regard Jesus' frequent word, "Go in peace, your faith has made you well," as an expression of justification.

In short, here the commission followed rather uncritically the exegetes it heard; it assumed that their views were in keeping with historical evidence.

In view of its limited scope, the report does not deal with the specifically Lutheran question of how the righteous can be treated as such even though he is imperfect in his new life and still has sin. For the same reason the question of how the new life issues from faith is not treated.

Change of Climate

In spite of these limitations and shortcomings the "Malta Report" unearthed common concerns and intentions that the controversy had covered up. It showed that Lutheran and Catholic theologians are closer to each other than one might suppose, inasmuch as they embrace assumptions and methods of contemporary exegesis and leave the churches' creeds or confessions out of consideration.

The report encouraged a climate of mutual understanding and created favorable conditions for new projects like that of a Catholic recognition of the AC, which we shall discuss in the next section.

"All Under One Christ" (1980)

The document to be analyzed in this section, "All Under One Christ: A Statement by the Joint Roman Catholic-Lutheran Commission on the AC," was issued in Augsburg on Feb. 23, 1980, in view of the 450th anniversary of the Confession.[17] It expresses the commission's stand on the possibility of a Catholic recognition of the AC and the implications this might have for relations between the Roman Catholic and Lutheran churches.

The suggestion that the Roman Catholic Church should recognize the AC as catholic had claimed the commission's attention since 1974.[18] Commission members took active part in the public discussion of the issue, especially in Germany.[19] Several collaborated in a joint Lutheran-Catholic commentary designed to explore the catholicity of the Confession for the sake of its recognition.[20] The commission as a whole kept abreast of the debate. It analyzed and confirmed the findings of the "Joint Commentary." Its official statement relates the outcome of the debate with the results of the ongoing dialog between the Catholic and the Lutheran churches.[21]

In view of these facts "All Under One Christ" must be read and understood in light of the "Joint Commentary" and in connection with the commission's previous statements.

Conclusions of the "Joint Commentary"

The Lutheran and Catholic authors who were investigating the AC, mostly in interconfessional teams, approved a concluding statement at their second meeting in September 1979 to summarize their findings on the catholicity of the Augustana.[22] As they expressly state (No. 8), their commentary is a contribution to the question of the recognition of the AC by organs of the Roman Catholic Church as a valid expression of catholic faith.

As a result of the dialog on the common Christian faith, the experts concluded that the AC is indeed catholic in the sense that its assertions must be understood as to a high degree expressing the common catholic faith. As they recurred to the Augustana, they were able to reach a common understanding of the center of the Christian faith (Nos. 1–2).

Catholicity

The argumentation carried on by the authors of the commentary suggests that "catholic" is whatever both sides, as heirs of a common Christian faith, acknowledge and regard as such by virtue of its own evidence. Catholicity would then be the result of a process of persuasion exerted on Christians by assertions claiming to be catholic.

One wonders whether this is what the Lutherans meant when they held that the bishops could not but agree with them on their teachings and reforms as described in the AC. Did they not rather assume and establish a criterion of catholicity that remained valid regardless of the parties' recognition?

The authors' problem seems to be that they did not relate catholicity to its source, the Scriptures. The AC clearly does so, as it asserts that the teaching it presents is clearly established in Holy Scripture and *in addition to that* (*darzu*) is not opposed to the universal Christian church, not even to the Roman church, as far as can be gathered from the fathers' writings.[23]

This problem of the nature of the catholicity to which the AC lays claim and the Roman church is expected to recognize, was not clarified in the recognition debate. It is significant, too, that most authors have consistently avoided commenting on Melanchthon's qualification, "as far as can be gathered from the fathers' writings," when quoting the passage.[24]

Nor was the catholicity problem solved in "All Under One Christ," for it takes over the reasoning of the commentary conclusion and also omits Melanchthon's qualification. The declaration, however, recasts the thought in more precise wording. It says: The joint investigation has shown that the assertions of the AC realize to a high degree this intention of uttering the faith of the one catholic church and to that extent (*insoweit*) must be regarded as expressions of the common faith. The qualification, "to that extent," makes clear *how catholic* the AC is in the Joint Commission's estimation.

QUALIFIED AGREEMENT

The conclusion of the joint commentary reviews the main doctrinal assertions of the Confession in order to tell how catholic they are or can be considered. On account of the authors' peculiar way of determining catholicity, they do not measure the assertions with the "yardstick" of Scripture, or the magisterium, as one might expect. It is their (more or less) common *understanding* of a given assertion that leads them to regard it as (more or less) catholic, as will be seen in the following.

The authors' consensus was patent as they dealt with the common Christian faith in the triune God and the saving action of Jesus

Christ. This allowed them to conclude that through the Reformation the church was not split apart down to its root. Their "deep agreement" extends to areas traditionally regarded as controversial, such as "the doctrine of justification as the unfolding and application of the faith in Christ," and others (No. 3).

In other parts of their statement the authors argue that the differences between Lutherans and Catholics are found mainly in ecclesiology and explain how they could be overcome (Nos. 4–7)—even with the help of their consensus on justification. They characterize the same as a common understanding on the center of the Christian faith, the salvation that God brought about through Jesus Christ in the Holy Spirit for the whole world.

The authors expect their agreement on the doctrinal core eventually to elicit a common answer on the Virgin Mary's place in the Christian doctrine of salvation and on the issue of the papacy (No. 8).[25]

The "deep consensus" reached on the basis of the AC is not "total agreement" but allows the authors to conclude that this Confession unites, far more than it divides, the Roman Catholic and the Lutheran churches (No. 9). They have rediscovered the AC as a "confession of the one faith," even though differences remain and they were as yet unable to recite it together as a "common confession of this one catholic faith" (No. 10).[26]

This review of the statements on justification in their original setting clearly indicates that they speak in rather general—not to say vague—terms. They do not detail the salvation God brought about through Jesus Christ. They do not tell precisely what it is that faith in Christ believes concerning His role in salvation. They do not explain in which regard justification is "the unfolding and application of faith in Christ." It remains unclear just *how* people come to partake in salvation.

Three interconfessional teams had to deal with justification as they interpreted, respectively, the articles on Christ, sin, and righteousness. The authors' consultation, however, did not pull together their separate insights and findings. The "Joint Commentary" offers no consensus formulation that would detail the justification agreement. The Joint Commission's official declaration does include such a statement, but it is rather enigmatic, too, as will be seen.

LUTHERAN-CATHOLIC DOCUMENTS (1972–83)

Outline

The Joint Commission's official declaration, "All Under One Christ," is made up of three parts. The first describes the realignment that has taken place between the Lutheran and Roman Catholic churches since the Second Vatican Council and the ensuing reappraisal of the AC as embodiment of the ecumenical resolve and catholic intention of the Reformation (Nos. 1–9). The second describes the measure of agreement reached by reexamining the Augustana: a (qualified) recognition of its catholicity (Nos. 10–12), a "basic consensus" on the doctrinal articles of the first part (Nos. 13–18), a "broad consensus" on the second part (Nos. 19–22), and an inventory of "open questions and problems" yet to be resolved (No. 23) on the basis of the consensus already achieved (Nos. 24–26). The third part invites the Lutheran and the Roman Catholic churches to articulate anew and confess together the common Christian faith rediscovered by joint investigation of the AC (Nos. 27–28).

Concerns and Presuppositions

As it discusses the role of theological dialog in bringing the churches together, the Joint Commission stresses that its own dialog was officially authorized by the churches themselves, calls for official recognition of its agreements, and enjoins implementation of church fellowship.

The commission explains that it concerned itself with the AC inasmuch as this confessional document is normative or binding for the Lutheran Church (Nos. 8–9). It expected that agreement on the catholicity of this binding confession would enhance the reception of former agreements and help them to acquire "binding force" as well.[27]

In effect, the Study Commission tried to do without the Confessions of the churches as it produced the "Malta Report." The new Joint Commission apparently is trying to overcome this deficiency in order to expedite the reception of the Malta agreements by the churches. This fact suggests that the agreement on justification in "All Under One Christ" is akin to that of the "Malta Report."

It is significant that the Joint Commission expressly refers to studies which have caused a reappraisal of the partial agreement

THE DOCTRINE OF FAITH

reached between Lutherans and Catholics at the Diet of Augsburg (No. 12). This observation suggests that there is a connection between this agreement and the consensus on justification formulated by the Joint Commission. Furthermore, it will be convenient to regard the lectures and discussions at the Congress on the Confutation as a commentary to "All Under One Christ" and a key for interpreting its consensus on justification.[28]

Agreement Levels

The Joint Commission affirms that by reflecting on the AC Lutherans and Catholics have recovered a "common understanding in basic beliefs" that points to "Jesus Christ, the living center of our faith" (No. 17).[29] This "basic consensus" (No. 18) concerns the articles on God and Christ, justification, the Gospel and the sacraments, and the church. It is reported in the second part (Nos. 13–16) and supported by other documents, such as the "Malta Report," as well.

The paragraphs in question distinguish the levels of agreement achieved on the main issues discussed.

They discern "a basic though not full *commonness*" in the understanding of the church, a *common witness* on the Gospel and the sacraments, as well as a *common confession* on God and Christ. With regard to justification "a far-reaching *consensus*" is said to be *emerging*.

This last formulation is taken over from the "Malta Report."[30] The original predicate, *zeichnet sich ab,* suggests that the "far-reaching consensus" is taking on more distinct contours.

God's Saving Act

The Joint Commission states with regard to Arts. I and III of the AC: "We confess together [the common Christian] faith in the triune God and in the saving act of God through Jesus Christ in the Holy Spirit." Lutheran and Catholic Christians have been and are "one in this central and most important truth of the Christian faith" (No. 13).

The document does not explain in what God's saving action consists. It declares with respect to Art. V of the AC: "We testify together that the salvation obtained by Christ in [His] death and resurrection is proffered and effectively imparted to men through the Holy Spirit in the proclamation of the Gospel and in the Holy Sacraments" (No. 15).

This means that "God's saving action through Jesus Christ in the Holy Spirit" is anchored in the salvation that Christ obtained in His death and resurrection, but extends to the present inasmuch as God imparts Christ's salvation through the Holy Spirit.

JESUS CHRIST'S ROLE

The document does not describe Jesus Christ's role in salvation or justification beyond saying that He was the One through whom God worked salvation, or who obtained salvation "in" death and resurrection. As with other documents studied, silence is maintained concerning the Mediator and Propitiator whom the AC depicts as moving God to justify the person who regards and trusts Him as such. There is silence, too, on Christ's being (permanently) the believer's righteousness (AC, XX, 9).

The same situation prevails in the statement on justification (No. 14): It speaks of faith in "Christ's saving act" (*Heilstat Christi*), but does not specify in what this act consists. Consequently it remains unclear what exactly faith believes concerning Christ.

Nor is the problem solved by the reference to the "Malta Report." All one gathers there is that we owe our salvation exclusively to God's act of salvation in Jesus Christ (No. 48) and that His gift of salvation is unconditioned (No. 26).

One is led to think that the Joint Commission's understanding of Christ's role in justification does not demand, as does Melanchthon's and Luther's, specification of the "saving act" in which faith is expected to believe. The AC definitely finds it necessary to specify that justifying faith believes that *on Christ's account* men are accepted and absolved, just as the Gospel encourages us to believe. Besides affirming that He offered Himself in sacrifice for all men's sins, the Confession insists that Christ must by faith be regarded and resorted to as God's only "cause" for accepting the person who believes this.[31]

The commission's words on Christ sound feeble and reticent if compared with the doxological witness uttered by the AC. If the Lutherans and the Catholics are heirs of "an unbroken core of common Christian faith," and if indeed contemporary discourse on Christ is marked by "loss" and "obscuration," the commission missed an excellent opportunity to join with the AC in a clear witness to Christ.[32]

Our concern is that, as long as theologians refuse to admit that Jesus Christ made satisfaction for men's sins and reconciled God with mankind, their present difficulty in appropriating and restating the AC will persist. It is possible that on this score the consensus between Lutherans and Catholics at Augsburg was indeed greater than that between contemporary theologians, no matter whether Lutheran or Catholic, and the AC.[33] It is indeed a sad result of contemporary theological scholarship that it has in fact split open the hitherto "unbroken core" of the churches' "common confession" to Jesus Christ!

Consensus on Justification

The formulation which, according to the commission, delineates an imminent consensus on justification, reads as follows: "It is only by grace and in faith in Christ's saving act, not on the basis of our merit that we are accepted by God and receive the Holy Spirit, who renews our hearts and both enables and summons us to good works" (No. 14).

If one compares this statement with the corresponding passages in the "Malta Report" or the "Leuenberg Agreement," it immediately becomes apparent that it is cast in the kind of language which the AC employs. The only exception is the expression "Christ's saving act," which stems from contemporary theological language.

In view of the reticence found in the other documents, it is remarkable that faith is mentioned as a justification factor. Yet one is struck by the odd formulation "in faith." One can only wonder why it was preferred to "by" or "through" faith, expressions which are used throughout the AC. Above all, however, one must ask about the meaning and intention of that formulation. How does it relate to the doctrine of faith stated in the AC?[34]

The "Joint Commentary," which underlies the Joint Commission's declaration, is likely to provide the answer.

The Expression "in faith"

In their analysis of Art. IV the joint authors Vinzenz Pfnür and Gerhard Müller argue that the doctrine of justification through faith is imprinted with the same intention as the Scholastic teaching of justification "through the grace which God creates in man" (*per gratiam creatam*).³⁵

The authors, therefore, describe justification "through faith" (as distinct from justification "because of faith") as "the Word-bound regeneration which takes place in man in and through faith." They view justification as God's creative act in which sinful man is turned into a "new man reborn through faith and united with Christ and, therefore, with God."³⁶

Pfnür and Müller hold that in the settlement reached on some issues in Augsburg, 1530, faith and "the grace which renders one acceptable" (*gratia gratum faciens*) were considered as one and the same thing. It was stipulated in the agreement that one should hold that remission of sins occurs essentially (*formaliter*) through grace that makes one acceptable and (through) faith, as well as through the Word and the sacraments as (God's) means. Melanchthon is quoted as having said that faith rather than love should be called *gratia gratum faciens*.³⁷

In this argumentation Pfnür and Müller operate within an understanding of faith that emphasizes faith's passivity and thus views it more as an attitude or condition rather than as an act: "Through faith the promise becomes a reality for me and in me. Faith consists in this, that the righteousness offered because of Christ and through Him becomes real [to me] and reaches me." The expression *through faith* denotes the "subjective side of justification through the [objective] promise," that is, "the arriving of grace at [myself] and in me."³⁸

This understanding of faith and of the Augsburg settlement underlies the consensus formulation hammered out by the Joint Commission. It explains why this formulation says that we are accepted "by grace and in (rather than through) faith in Christ's act of salvation." In this sentence *faith* stands for "the grace (in us) that renders us acceptable."

The statement agreed upon by the Commission actually means

that "it is by God's grace that reaches us and makes us acceptable that we are (then) accepted and receive the Holy Spirit."

CONSENSUS IRRESPECTIVE OF THE CONFESSION?

One may readily grant that the commission members actually agreed on this understanding of the issue. The more fundamental question is, however: Does this understanding reflect the stance of the AC?

Observations made in this study suggest that the commission's agreement misses just what is new and unique in the AC's view of faith and justification. Although the agreement grants and affirms, correctly, that God alone justifies by grace, it fails to perceive just *how* God's action engages man, leading him to acknowledge that God accepts and adopts us *because of Christ*. It fails to recognize that the AC insists on justification *through* faith, because otherwise there is no way to maintain *Christ's glory* as Reconciler and Appeaser.

Careful reading of the AC and its sources indicates that their authors tended to explicate justification "through faith" by apparently tautological appositions like "as we *believe* that it is *because of Christ* that ..."[39]

As we have demonstrated, these appositions are not tautological in character, but are intended to specify *in what precise sense* justification is said to occur "through faith." They convey the definite meaning that faith justifies not as a quality or condition, but as an act of beholding and turning to *Christ* as the only One who moves God to justify. In the Reformers' understanding this act is prompted by the promise of the Gospel, for it proffers Christ as the very Ground for God's mercy and for His willingness to accept those who regard Him as the Ground of Justification. Thus the Gospel leads people to believe, that is, to resort to Christ as Mediator.[40]

The "Joint Commentary," however, did not even so much as notice the equation between "through faith" and "as they/we believe that because of Christ ... " in Arts. IV and XX of the AC. It failed to understand the reason for attributing justification to faith.

The Joint Commission seems to have been misled by the commentary, so that it did not perceive the primary and specific function of faith in justification. It discusses only what we have called the secondary or derivative role of faith, which consists in being a quality, condition, or service that God demands, brings about, and approves (Ap, IV, 57–60, 130–35).

Since the "Joint Commentary" did not properly discern the functions of faith, it did not properly relate the processes indicated by the predicate "to be justified." Pfnür and Müller argue correctly that "to be *made* righteous" and "to be *declared* righteous" are distinct from each other, as events which occur (to different people) at different times. *To be made righteous* indicates that the unrighteous is (initially) granted the status of a righteous person, as he acknowledges that it is because of Christ that God accepts and absolves him. *To be reckoned righteous,* however, means that the person who has been reconciled with God is (thereafter) counted and treated as a righteous person because of Christ, as he acknowledges that on account of *Christ* God is merciful and favorable to him.

As Pfnür and Müller, however, try to relate with each other the events which "to be made righteous" and "to be reckoned righteous" denote, they disregard the argumentative sequence of Arts. IV through VI and of the corresponding three sections of Art. XX of the AC.[41] They do not perceive the function which the assertion, "Faith regenerates," has in this connection. It consists in explaining that only *true* faith can be said to justify. Only true faith apprehends the forgiveness of sins proffered because of Christ in the Gospel promise. Consequently true faith does, but fictive faith does not, lift from death to life amid the terrors of conscience. It follows that one may judge on the basis of the *effect* called regeneration whether one's faith is true or not.

This intention of Melanchthon's argumentative sequence is clearly expressed both in the sources of the AC and in Art. XX. Pfnür and Müller, however, misread Melanchthon as if he were saying that faith "makes righteous" because or inasmuch as it "regenerates," namely, brings the Holy Spirit into the heart, restores a relationship of trust and love toward God, and thus establishes in man that "spiritual righteousness" which God demands, imparts, and approves. "To be made righteous" (*iustum effici*) in the sense of *regenerari,* "to be reborn," would then indicate that God Himself makes man effectively righteous by creating faith, and "to be reckoned righteous" would mean that God would proclaim the believer righteous in view of this tangible righteousness which He Himself produced in man. The underlying assumption is that God proclaims as righteous only those who are indeed righteous in the sense described.[42]

This construction, however, will not stand if one carefully examines the argumentative function of that passage of the Apology which allegedly regards faith as identical with "the grace that renders one acceptable" (*gratia gratum faciens*).[43]

In the section immediately preceding this passage Melanchthon states, yet again, the thesis he wishes to demonstrate, namely, that it is faith in God's promise, not love, that justifies. He draws together, once more, the evidence which establishes his thesis: Since faith receives forgiveness of sins and reconciles one with God, it is by faith that we are reckoned righteous *because of Christ,* as well as liberated from death and restored to life or, to use Melanchthon's term, "regenerated."

Melanchthon assumes that his opponents identify *gratia gratum faciens* with God's "love shed in our hearts" and that they consider it indispensable for justification. In order to make unmistakably clear what he means to say, he even tries to say it in the opponents' language. He states that faith is entitled, more than love, to the name *gratia gratum faciens,* since it performs the functions which the latter is said to perform, while love clearly does not.

It should be clear from the argumentative context that for Melanchthon faith accomplishes in a different and better way that which *gratia gratum faciens* is said to do, namely, to justify and effect good works.

One can only regard *gratia gratum faciens* as the equivalent of faith, that is, as conveying *the same meaning in the same way,* if one disregards the specific feature of Melanchthon's teaching of faith, which is apprehension of and recourse to Christ for one's justification. This *act* has no correspondence in *gratia gratum faciens,* which must basically be regarded as a quality. Correspondence could be established only if one regarded *gratia gratum faciens* as love, and if one viewed love as looking away from itself and resting exclusively in Christ as the Beloved. Then, however, it would be more consistent just to attribute justification to love, as the authors of the Refutation of the Schwabach Articles tended to do in Augsburg.

Scholarly Disagreement

The unwarranted interpretation of "justification through faith" which underlies the Joint Commission's agreement has been consistently advocated by Vinzenz Pfnür, Holsten Fagerberg, and others.[44] It received remarkably little criticism in the debate on the AC.

Wolfhart Pannenberg observed, in a footnote, that Pfnür's representation of *iustificari per fidem* inverts the order or sequence of reconciliation and regeneration, but for some unstated reason this observation was not incorporated into the American translation of his essay.[45]

Hans Jorissen, while not disagreeing with Pfnür's understanding of justification, submitted that between Eck and Melanchthon there was a difference in the understanding of faith which still remains true to this day: While Catholics regard faith as but a frame of mind and presupposition for justification (*fides praecedens*), Lutherans look upon it as something that properly and intrinsically justifies.[46]

Robert Jenson suggested that interpretations of the AC like Pfnür's were reaffirming justification by fulfillment of divine requirements, which Melanchthon denounces as "justification on the basis of the Law" in the Apology of the AC.[47]

Martin Seils argued that Pfnür's reading of the AC could not provide the basis for a Lutheran-Catholic agreement, since this author had definitely taken sides in a debate on the correct interpretation of Art. IV of the Apology, even though Protestant scholars are still carrying it on without a final decision.[48] His warning, however, seems not to have reached the Joint Commission.

Justification and Acceptation

The Joint Commission avoids getting entangled in the question of the distinction and relationship between "becoming (being made) righteous" and "being reckoned righteous." It prefers to speak of "being accepted."

This verb is used in the Latin text of Art. IV of the AC. It indicates that which faith believes in keeping with the Gospel promise, namely, that because of Christ we are accepted and absolved. *Being accepted,* then, refers to "the beginning," when the sinner (first) becomes righteous "through faith," that is, by apprehending and resorting to Christ as Mediator.

Since the commission uses the expression "in faith," in the sense of "grace which renders one acceptable," it probably means that man is accepted in view of that faith which God created in him to restore the original relationship of trust and love. This understanding evidently differs from that which the AC envisions, namely, that man is accepted as he acknowledges that *on Christ's account* God is willing to receive and effectively take him into divine favor and fellowship.

Emphasis on Renewal

The Joint Commission's emphasis in the agreement definitely rests on the reception of the Holy Spirit and the doing of good works, which God both requires and makes possible.

Here, as in other documents, one misses the teaching expressed in the first printed edition of the AC, which holds that only on account of Christ apprehended by faith is a person together with his deeds accepted and reckoned righteous.[49] The commission seems to assume that the good works which the Holy Spirit provokes in the accepted person are, as such, acceptable.

Assessment

In short, if one understands "All Under One Christ" in the light of the "Joint Commentary," it becomes plain that the Joint Commission's consensus on justification is based on a rather particular interpretation of the AC. This interpretation, in our opinion, is questionable on two counts: First, it misinterprets Melanchthon's witness on the justifying role of faith and, second, it misrepresents the relationship between regeneration and justification by faith. In this respect the commission agreed *on its members' understanding,* not on the AC.

This means that the consensus between the Catholic and the Lutheran churches on this point is not as profound and deeply rooted as the commission assumes and proclaims.

The value of the commission's agreement rests in its clear understanding that (initial) justification is not the result of merit, since it holds that it is "not on the basis of merit" that we are accepted by God and receive the Holy Spirit. Unfortunately, however, the commission did not explain what *merit* means in this connection.

Perhaps Lutherans and Catholics should still be able to agree on a formulation that would replace the dubious *in faith* by that which faith intends, namely, Christ. It could read as follows: "It is only by grace and *because of Christ,* not on the ground of merit, that we are accepted by God."

If Lutheran and Catholic theologians would understand Melanchthon's and Luther's description of the proper role of faith in justification, they might even agree on an addition such as this, cast in the wording of the AC: "We are accepted by God (and receive the Holy Spirit) as we believe that it is because of Christ that God accepts us (and endows us with His Spirit)."

Once Lutherans and Catholics agree on regarding Christ as the sole Ground for God to justify man, it should be possible to come to terms on how we establish and maintain Christ in this role, namely, by believing in Him as sole Mediator. For faith, as we have explained throughout this work, consists precisely in disregarding oneself—and even faith itself—and beholding Christ exclusively, who is our Propitiator and Righteousness by God's generous and unfathomable decision.

This seems to be the direction in which the United States Lutheran-Catholic dialog is moving. Its main consensus formulation suggests precisely that we look away from ourselves and entrust our salvation entirely to Christ alone:

> Our entire hope of justification and salvation rests on Christ Jesus and on the Gospel whereby the good news of God's merciful action in Christ is made known; we do not place our ultimate trust in anything other than God's promise and saving work in Christ. This excludes ultimate reliance on our faith, virtues or merits.... In brief, hope and trust for salvation are gifts of the Holy Spirit and finally rest solely on God in Christ.[50]

In view of such developments one may hope that "All Under One Christ" will not remain the Joint Commission's only and last word on the AC, but that the commission will return to it, attain a proper understanding of its "doctrine of faith" and exploit fully its potentialities for unity in truth. Meanwhile, it will not hurt if the points of divergence are clearly stated, in order that Lutheran and Catholic Christians may wrestle with them in their studies and prayers!

The Aftermath

The 450th anniversary of the AC passed, and the Roman Catholic Church did not formally recognize it as catholic. The spokesman of the magisterium, Pope John Paul II, however, stated in the general audience of June 25, 1980, that the dialog between Lutherans and Catholics made possible by the Second Vatican Council had shown "how broadly and stoutly the common foundations of our Christian faith are fixed." [51]

The president of the the Secretariat for Christian Unity echoed "All Under One Christ" as he confirmed in the Augsburg celebration of June 29, 1980, that the division did not go down to the common root and that the common ground of our faith reaches far deeper and further than that which divides us.[52]

Again, Pope John Paul II told the Council of the German Evangelical Church on Nov. 17, 1980, in Mainz, Germany, that reflection on the AC as well as other contacts recalled that "we believe and confess together that Jesus Christ is the one Mediator through whom we have peace with God and with one another." He referred to the testimony given by the German bishops in the pastoral letter "Thy Kingdom Come," of Jan. 20, 1980: "Let us rejoice for having found not only a partial consensus on some truths, but rather an agreement on central truths of the faith." He encouraged efforts to overcome remaining differences and made very clear that "only full unity grants the possibility of gathering around the Lord's one table with a single mind and just one faith."[53]

These statements indicate that Roman Catholic officials recognized the catholicity of the AC to some degree, but refused simply to recognize it as catholic. This need not be regarded as a disadvantage, if indeed, as Avery Dulles has suggested, a Catholic "recognition" of it "would seem to endorse a 'Catholic' reading of the AC and would thereby tend to obscure its distinctively Lutheran import."[54] Precisely in the central question of justification by faith the "distinctively Lutheran import" will have to be preserved in any reading of the AC.

The Executive Committee of the LWF received a report on the work of the Joint Commission by its co-chairman, George W. Lindbeck, at a meeting held in Augsburg, July 6–11, 1980. He explained that the Roman Catholic Church could have recognized the AC officially only if there had been unrestricted church fellowship between Lutherans and Catholics. He praised the agreement on justification, saying: "Luther would have been extremely happy with it." He expected this agreement to strengthen the Gospel witness within the Roman Catholic Church.[55]

In a "Declaration on the AC" the Executive Committee thanked the Joint Commission for the statement "All Under One Christ," as well as the pope for his greetings.[56]

At a meeting in Turku, Finland, Aug. 4–13, 1981, the Executive Committee issued a statement on "Four Hundred and Fifty Years of the Augsburg Confession." It drew together the results of the joint study of the Augustana (Part II), evaluated the Roman Catholic reactions (Part III), and then expressly appropriated and confirmed the Joint Commission's main conclusions as expressed in "All Under One Christ" (Part IV) and asked the churches to receive them (Part V).

In doing so, the committee characterized God's act of salvation through Christ in the Holy Spirit as being "final and entirely sufficient," a qualification that does not appear in "All Under One Christ." Further, the committee overlooked the Joint Commission's cautious wording that an agreement on justification is "shaping up" or "emerging"; it simply confirmed "an agreement" on the Joint Commission's consensus formulation, without any qualification at all.[57]

It is significant, too, that the committee avoided any reference to the Augustana's intention of renewing the church with the Gospel, as the Lutheran churches of the German Democratic Republic and the Bishops' Conference of the German United Evangelical Lutheran Church (VELKD) stressed in the declarations of June 21, 1980.[58] It preferred to confirm and praise the Joint Commission's findings with a view toward better relations with Rome.

The seventh General Assembly of the LWF in Budapest (July 22– Aug. 5, 1984) took notice of the Joint Commission's statement through the General Secretary's report on behalf of the Executive Committee without further comment.[59]

THE DOCTRINE OF FAITH

"Martin Luther, Witness to Jesus Christ" (1983)

The Joint Commission issued this "word" on Martin Luther on May 6, 1983, in view of the approaching 500th anniversary of his birth. It tries to convey what Lutherans and Catholics can say together on the Reformer's person and role on the basis of the present historical situation. The document, therefore, is not a summary or evaluation of Luther's teachings, but rather a description and explanation of how the Lutheran and especially the Catholic image of Martin Luther has changed since the 16th century: Today Catholics and Lutherans are able to view Luther together as witness to the Gospel, teacher in the faith, and preacher of spiritual renewal.[60]

While there is much in the document that calls for critical comment, the present analysis must restrict itself to the references to the AC, the Lutheran-Catholic agreements, and the concept of righteousness.

The Joint Commission describes in the first part the historical factors that have issued in a new (common to both churches) view of Martin Luther. The joint celebration of the 450th anniversary of the AC led to the insight that there is "consensus in central truths of faith." Inasmuch as the Confession depends on Luther, that consensus created conditions for a mutual affirmation of the Reformer's "essential insights" (No. 5).

In the second part the Joint Commission describes what Luther discovered and bore witness to as interpreter of Scripture and witness to the Gospel. It maintains that he rediscovered "God's mercy, which He gives us as a present through Christ: His is a bestowing rather than a demanding and condemning righteousness" (No. 8). While polemics prevented an agreement in Luther's time, today several factors have made it largely possible for Catholics to acknowledge his thinking, even the justification doctrine, as "a legitimate form of Christian theology." In order to substantiate this claim, the Joint Commission quotes its own agreement on justification as restated in "All Under One Christ," after the joint "Malta Report" (No. 11).

After showing why and how it came to church division (Part III), the Joint Commission explains why and how Luther's legitimate concerns are being met today even by the Roman Catholic Church. Especially in German-speaking areas Catholics have recognized that his reform efforts were justified. They consider his basic insight concerning God's righteousness as bestowed freely in Christ, without any merit on our part, not to be in contradiction with "genuine Catholic tradition," as found, for example, in St. Augustine and Thomas Aquinas (No. 22).

The document concludes with a list of items one may learn from Martin Luther as our "common teacher" (Part V). Among other things he is said to call us to a faith which consists in unconditional trust in God, who showed Himself a gracious God in the life, death, and resurrection of His Son. He is also said to teach us that grace is a "person-bound relation of God to man which is tied to no condition and which frees us before God and for service to our neighbor."

The Joint Commission, once again, quotes its own findings to make evident the Lutheran-Catholic agreement on justification. Yet it seems as though its intention is to form public opinion by sheer repetition. Since, however, it does not quote other authorities, it finally proves only that the theologians who signed the documents agreed on the consensus formulae.

EVALUATION

As to Luther's rediscovery of Christian righteousness, the commission fails to make mention of his assertion that it is *through faith in Christ* that God gives, and we receive, His righteousness.[61] For some untold reason it is unable to state with Luther (and Melanchthon) that faith in Christ is itself Christian righteousness, as he does explicitly in the "Great Confession" and the Schwabach, Marburg, and Smalcald Articles.[62]

The commission speaks of Luther's "doctrine of the sinner's justification through faith alone" (No. 9). It even describes faith as trusting that God is gracious in Christ (No. 26). When speaking of justification, however, it does not with Luther and Melanchthon affirm the justifying function of faith, which consists in apprehending and regarding Christ as our only righteousness. In short, the problem noted in the "Malta Report" remains unsolved; the document on Martin Luther is, just like its predecessors, deficient in its view of faith. The documents operate within a contemporary theology and fail to relate it properly to the Reformers' understanding of faith and righteousness. This in turn entails a remarkable lack of clarity on Jesus Christ's role in justification. Although they say that God's righteousness is given in or through Him, they do not concur with Luther in saying that He Himself is our Righteousness, namely, if and when we regard Him as such, as the promise of the Gospel enjoins us to do.[63]

The progress made in mutual understanding is nevertheless remarkable. One can only hope that the struggle for a *common* appraisal of Luther will not result in lack of sensibility to the specific features of Luther and the AC, namely, their understanding of Christ's and consequently of faith's *specific* role in justification. Rather than pruning Luther down to the size of Thomas or Augustine, one should grant at least the possibility that he may on this score have found in Scripture a pearl which others, under different conditions, may not have seen.

CHAPTER 12

Retrospect and Perspectives

Two questions have guided our effort to understand the nature and significance of the Reformation: In what does the Lutheran doctrine of the righteousness of faith consist? How has this doctrine been expressed in ecumenical agreements of recent years?

Our study of the prefaces and epilogs of the AC indicated that the Reformation leaders regarded the teaching about faith as the main cause and justification for reforms carried out in the teachings, worship, and piety of the church in their territories. They present and defend this teaching in the first part of the AC. In several articles of the second part they adduce it as an argument against the former religious practices and in favor of changes in such matters as the Mass, monastic life, and the distinction of foods. They seek to demonstrate not only that the Lutheran teaching of faith is catholic and Scriptural, but also that it necessitates certain reforms in the teachings, life, and worship of the church.

Catholicity

As a basic account and apologia of the Lutheran Reformation the AC is not restricted to the single purpose of affirming the catholicity of the Lutheran churches. Although it is not a complete account, it does not cunningly omit or play down the traits which might have veiled the claim to catholicity, as has been maintained by some critics. It does express and uphold the peculiar Reformation stand on Jesus Christ and on the manner in which people become partakers of His benefits, namely, by faith in Him, together with the implications this has for Christian worship and piety.

It is useless to water down this peculiar stand in order to dilute it in the stream of "catholic" tradition. The AC claims that the Lutheran doctrine of faith is catholic in a sense in which the church doctrine of those days was not (and the church of our time may not be): that it is intrinsic to the Gospel of Jesus Christ as proclaimed by the apostles.

This claim must be raised anew today in order to challenge churches and movements to examine the Scriptures and verify whether or not this claim is justified. It is all too easy to declare that the doctrine of the righteousness of faith is catholic in the usual sense and thus to silence the question. This puts to rest the conscience of forces that want a ready solution for the problem of disunity among Christians. It would, however, bring back precisely the problems which only this doctrine can overcome, as it teaches man to resort to Christ alone as the Reconciler and liberating Lord. The foremost of these problems is the bad conscience which results from not knowing certainly whether one may count on God's favor in life and death. Such a bad conscience certainly does not issue in spontaneous and joyous service to God.

Thrust

The doctrine of faith which the AC presents and defends was taken from official documents which can be regarded as its sources, namely, the Marburg and Schwabach Articles together with the Wittenberg-Torgau Articles drawn from the Visitation Articles and the *Instructions for Visitors*. It is expressed by a number of assertions that remain constant throughout the sources and drafts of the Confession. These assertions express what we have called the structure of the doctrine of faith, which rests on three fundamental assumptions, namely, that Christ alone is the Reconciler and Lord of righteousness and life, that Christ together with His gifts is made available only through the promise of the Gospel, and that faith in Christ is the only way of obtaining a share in His gifts of righteousness and life, or of making salutary use of Him as Mediator and Savior.

These interrelated assumptions underlie the assertions consistently made in all the documents, albeit not always in the same order: Men are justified by faith alone; faith in Christ is (itself) the righteousness by which Christians are (reckoned) righteous before God; this (justifying) faith consists in acknowledging and holding for sure that on account of Christ God absolves, receives, and favors the person who believes this, as the Gospel invites him to do; therefore this faith engenders new life and issues in love and worship to God, as well as in service to the neighbor and all of God's creatures.

The critics of the Reformation were unable or unwilling to perceive that the Lutheran teaching of justification "by faith alone" was the compelling result of the double conviction that Christ alone is the Dispenser of righteousness and that the promise of the Gospel is the only means whereby the Holy Spirit makes known, offers, and imparts that righteousness.

In their understanding, the teaching of "faith alone" was meant to discourage pious behavior and drive people away from the church and its saving sacraments. As they saw it, Lutheran teaching endangered the salvation of man because it prevented the acquisition of merits and the reception of sacramental grace whereby he becomes acceptable to God. They feared for the Christian commonwealth if people would rest content with "faith alone" and refuse to be pious and do good. They upheld by all possible means what they had learned: Man must prepare himself with good works in order to get grace; having been enabled by divine grace, he must do good works in order to merit further grace and become worthy of eternal life. Therefore they maintained that man is justified not by faith alone, but by faith formed, that is, empowered or activated by love. This is the same as saying that he is justified not by lifeless, but by living, dynamic, operative faith.

The critics of the Reformation had tradition and common sense on their side, to say nothing of ecclesiastical and political power. The Lutheran minority at the Diet of Augsburg was faced with the double challenge of overcoming preconceptions formed by tons of polemical material and communicating a complex matter in simple, persuasive language. In face of these odds the AC stands out in history as one of the most remarkable achievements of Christian apologetics. Although it could not persuade the majority to embrace the Reformation, it won the respect of the Imperial Assembly and ultimately assured the survival of the Reformation in the empire.

THE DOCTRINE OF FAITH

Focus on Christ

As the analysis of the pertinent articles has indicated, the formulation and defense of the doctrine of justification through faith concentrates on two expressions which necessitate each other, namely, *propter Christum* (because of Christ) and *per fidem* (through faith). Since the Holy Spirit, through the Gospel, makes Christ known and imparts forgiveness of sins and righteousness *because of Christ,* who made satisfaction for our sins, the only way to become (and remain) righteous before God is *through faith* in Christ, for it is by faith that one regards and claims Him as the Ground for God's mercy and favor. Because God set Jesus Christ forth as Mediator and Propitiator and made Him Righteousness for all, as the Gospel proclaims, it becomes necessary to regard and embrace Him in this capacity, that is, to depend on Him as the only Way to righteousness and life.

Therefore the doctrine of faith is nothing but the joyous recognition of Jesus Christ as the One who came, lived, died, rose, and rules "for us men and for our salvation," as the church confesses in the Nicene Creed. As such it entails the conviction and assertion that it is only through faith in Him that one recognizes and honors Him in this function. Only through faith, which looks away from itself and gazes at Christ alone, does one behold and claim Christ for one's salvation.

Since the Gospel presents Jesus Christ as the Sacrifice, Priest, and Lord on our behalf and invites us to regard and engage Him as such; and since true faith consists precisely in recurring to Him as the One on whose account God forgives, accepts, and favors us, the AC asserts—on the basis of the correlation between Christ and faith—that men are justified through faith, as they believe that they are forgiven and accepted because of Christ, and that faith is the righteousness on the basis of which God counts the believer righteous because of that Christ in whom he believes in this way.

This correlation between Christ and faith constitutes the core of the Lutheran doctrine of faith. Besides this core, however, it entails the confession of the necessary results of recognizing and engaging Christ as the Author of our salvation. These results take place in the believer and affect his relation to God.

According to the AC the true faith which is called forth by the Holy Spirit through the Gospel promise and entrusts itself to Christ as the Mediator and Redeemer is what regenerates man: It raises him from death to life by overcoming the fear and desperation produced by the preaching of God's judgment over sin.

This new life manifests itself in a new relationship to God. As he is absolved and accepted by God because of Christ, in whom he puts his trust, the believer learns to know God as a merciful Father and therefore loves, worships, and serves Him, spontaneously and gladly, as God expects and demands in His law.

This means that the believer, who is righteous because of Christ in keeping with the promise of the Gospel, becomes righteous in terms of the Law, too, since he begins to fulfill its requirements by and as a result of his faith in Christ. This fulfillment of the Law, however, remains incipient and imperfect; it does not afford perfect righteousness. For this reason, according to the AC, Christ remains Mediator to the end, and the believer must ever cling to Him, for only on His account will he be reckoned righteous and be invested as heir of eternal life.

In view of the Christological concentration and the anthropological and ethical consequences of the doctrine of justification through faith, it should be clear that this doctrine is guided by two concerns, namely, to (re)affirm the honor of Jesus Christ and establish conclusively that the affirmation of His honor entails a specific stand as to how man becomes (and remains) righteous, namely, by that faith which affirms His honor as the only Mediator and Redeemer.

It follows that the AC in its doctrine of faith is not concerned with the nature of justification in the sense of distinguishing between "becoming" and "being (reckoned) righteous." The text simply assumes this distinction and tries to demonstrate that both things happen because of Christ and therefore by faith.

Both expressions are used to express the Lutheran position: *To become righteous* denotes the sinner's (initial) absolution and reception into God's favor on account of Christ; *to be reckoned righteous* indicates that ("thereafter") the believer is counted righteous on account of the same Christ, whom he keeps regarding as his only Mediator.

It is just as clear, however, that one becomes righteous through faith by being absolved and accepted on Christ's account, not by being regenerated through faith and transformed into a righteous person, although this is a necessary result of one's being absolved and accepted.

It should be clear, too, that one is reckoned righteous because of faith for the simple reason that faith regards and holds Christ as the Ground or Reason for God's being favorable. Although faith is indeed fellowship with God and the highest worship, it is reckoned as righteousness not because it is such an excellent quality or relationship, but because of the Christ it beholds and employs as basis for God's approval.

Misunderstandings

Once the Christological concentration and the ethical components of the doctrine of faith are perceived, it becomes clear that partisan criticism is unwarranted.

It has been said, for instance, that this doctrine is peculiar to the apostle Paul's Letters to the Romans and Galatians; that it does not express the totality of the Biblical witness to God's "saving action." This criticism assumes that the AC presents a "doctrine of justification," and that this doctrine is taught only in portions of Scripture that use justification terminology. It fails to see that the document presents a cluster of teachings on *faith* as the necessary correlate of *Christ* and His *promise* of forgiveness and redemption. This means that whenever the apostolic and prophetic writings present Christ as the Redeemer and whenever they proclaim God's salvation, they are calling for that faith whereby one grasps the Redeemer and apprehends His salutary gifts.

The "Lutheran" doctrine of faith, therefore, is found in all of Scripture, even and especially in the gospels. Here the Messiah's own voice enjoins faith: "The kingdom of God is at hand; repent and *believe* in the Gospel." He tells the afflicted that hoped for Israel's redemption through Him: "Go in peace, your *faith* has made you well."

It has been charged that the Lutheran doctrine of faith is focused on the needs of the individual conscience and results in exaggerated concern for one's own salvation (*Heilsegoismus*). This criticism fully disregards the Christological orientation of the doctrine of faith. It overlooks that texts such as Art. XX of the AC first point to Christ, the Mediator and Propitiator, and only thereafter indicate that this faith which appeals to Christ in His God-appointed role also raises up and consoles the terrified conscience.

It has also been charged that the Lutheran doctrine of faith is ethically deficient. But Melanchthon clearly and repeatedly states that the doctrine of faith intends and brings about true Christian service to God. By attributing justification to Christ alone, it frees the conscience from the compulsive need to justify itself by ingenious practices and liberates it for spontaneous and unselfish service to God in keeping with one's calling in the world.

Crisis

The doctrine of faith which the AC expresses so plainly and vigorously has not found adequate expression in the ecumenical documents examined above.

In fairness to the authors of these documents it must be recalled that they did not intend to give a full report of the doctrine of justification, as they call it. They discuss it only to the extent to which it was necessary to formulate an agreement on central Christian doctrines as prerequisite for church fellowship. Therefore one should not expect more than the documents are able and willing to give.

Nevertheless, the sponsors of these documents have proclaimed consensus on the ever-controversial doctrine of justification. This claim indicates that the discussion of the matter was not as incidental as a superficial reading might suggest. There must be other, deeper reasons why this doctrine was poorly expressed.

Before considering these reasons, it should be recalled once more that the doctrine of faith, as understood by the AC, deals with the heart of the Christian faith: It determines whether and how Christ, the Center of faith, will be used or not in the Christian religion. Consequently, the soundness of a given theology can be ascertained by determining whether and how it engages Christ for salvation. This means that the view of justification presented in the documents says more about the theology of its writers than one would at first expect.

It is plain and clear that all the documents dissociate themselves from the Christology of the AC in some respect. They want to leave behind the representation that Jesus "made satisfaction" for sin and functions even now as Mediator and Propitiator. They try instead to develop and apply a conception of the righteousness of God which manifests itself in history, notably in the life, death, and resurrection of Jesus, but which does not require substitutionary atonement.

In this connection the death of Jesus undergoes a significant reinterpretation. He is said to have died "to demonstrate God's love for sinners" ("Leuenberg Agreement," No. 9). Reference is made to the apostolic *witness* to His resurrection, but little is said about its significance for justification.

In keeping with this view of the "Christ event" as the manifestation of God's righteousness, the documents view the continuity between the death of Jesus and the Acts of the Apostles in a way that differs most significantly from Luther's and Melanchthon's in the AC. While the Reformers testify that Christ, the Lord, Himself charged the apostles with proclaiming the Gospel upon reception of the Holy Spirit—and Melanchthon is wont to quote Luke 24:47 to substantiate this point—the documents envision the apostles as developing and formulating a "message of justification" as their *understanding* of the "Christ event," albeit by the power of the Holy Spirit, in connection with the process of the manifestation of God's righteousness in history.

This means that *Gospel* has divergent connotations for the AC and the ecumenical documents. For the former it is the proclamation of forgiveness and grace or righteousness because of Christ, through faith in Him. For the ecumenical documents, especially the "Malta Report," however, the Gospel is a "message of justification" which—independently of Jesus' resurrection—conveys God's righteousness to the believer by the power of the Holy Spirit, although it is (merely) the expression of the apostles' *understanding* of the "Christ event."

In keeping with this understanding of Christ and the Gospel, the documents conceive of justification as an accomplishment of the "justification message" in the sense that God imparts His righteousness to people without regard for their qualities or merits and actually makes them righteous by engendering the new life of faith which consists in service to God in the world.

In contrast to the presumption that justification could be God's response to human efforts, this view emphasizes that God's grace is "unconditional" and that "we owe our salvation exclusively to God's saving deed in Jesus Christ" ("Malta Report," Nos. 26 and 48).

In contrast to a "one-sided forensic understanding," it is stressed that justification "is not restricted to individual forgiveness of sins," but actually changes the sinner into a new person in Christ.

While these concerns must be regarded as valid, it is nevertheless true that such an understanding of justification can do perfectly well without faith in its proper, justifying role, as defined and highlighted by the AC. At the most (as presumably in "All Under One Christ"), faith is regarded as being the state or condition which God Himself effects in man in order that, in view of such actual righteousness, He may reckon him righteous—without exposing Himself to criticism for having declared righteous someone who does not have actual righteousness of his own.

This means that the ecumenical documents actually do not represent the doctrine of faith as found in the AC. Because they do not share its view of Christ (as the One who suffered and acts *for us*) and its understanding of the Gospel, and because they focus their attention on a "doctrine of justification," the ecumenical documents fail to grasp and express that distinctive view of faith which the AC promotes.

The AC's doctrine of faith evidently assumes, as the Apology (IV, 75) expressly states, that the first thing required in justification is the remission of sins, since all human beings are under sin. It assumes further that the sinner, who has departed from God's presence, must be restored to the fellowship of His children. It does not challenge at all the common conviction that the justified becomes a new person.

The only question this doctrine raises and answers is: Which is the ground and reason for God to forgive and accept the sinner and finally grant him eternal life? The answer is clear and definite: It is *Christ,* whom the Gospel presents as the Mediator and Propitiator; He won, and assures us of, God's (permanent) favor.

We call it the doctrine of faith simply because it holds that *to believe in Christ* on the basis of the Gospel is the only possible way to regard, hold, and employ Him as Mediator and Propitiator.

Challenge

If indeed the ecumenical documents examined here do not reflect the Lutheran doctrine of faith in their understanding of justification, it follows that the agreement on justification was reached not on the basis, but possibly at the cost of, the AC. Peter Manns feared that the struggle for the recognition of the Confession as catholic would result in "ecumenism at Luther's cost."[1] The ecumenical documents confront us with the prospect of "ecumenism at the cost of the AC"—at least as far as the understanding of Christ, the Gospel, and justifying faith is concerned.

It is true that none of the documents examined has the purpose of understanding the AC in its own terms. They were meant to express consensus between the churches *today*. Only "All Under One Christ" expressly intended an agreement based on the Confession. If, however, the AC is truly catholic in the sense of (re)affirming the common Christian faith expressed in the apostolic writings of the New Testament, as well as in the ecumenical creeds, it must be asked whether the Lutheran churches can afford to formulate agreements which are not expressly based on this catholic Confession.

Unless the Lutheran churches want agreements that exclude the specific stand of the AC on faith, they will have to reexamine this confessional document on its own terms, especially with regard to this central teaching. Declarations such as "All Under One Christ" and "Martin Luther, Witness to the Gospel" seek to determine what Lutheran and Catholics can say *together* on the basis of the AC. The Lutheran churches, however, will not know what they themselves have to say, unless they understand their fundamental confession as it testifies to the function which Jesus Christ must have in any Christian church and theology.

The implications of these findings for the question of church fellowship seem to be clear. The Lutheran Church must intensify its theological homework in order to recover the poignant confession of Christ which is found in the AC and its other confessional documents. This confession must resound in all the agreements approved by the Lutheran churches. As it is now, the common understanding of the Gospel affirmed in the "Leuenberg Agreement" is not as close to the AC as the signers of the document assume. Fellowship with the Roman church will not occur as readily as the Joint Committee suggests, if the AC is seriously taken into consideration in its witness to Christ and faith in Him.

The ecumenical documents have tended to declare that remaining issues are "not church-dividing," that they need not prevent church fellowship. Our investigation, however, has shown that the divergence has to do with the focus of the Christian faith, that is, Christ's significance for salvation. This divergence must be resolved, in our estimation, before unity in truth can be achieved.

Since there are unproclaimed divergences between the AC and contemporary theology, as reflected in the ecumenical documents, on such fundamental issues as Christ, the Gospel, and faith, the Lutheran as well as the Reformed and the Roman Catholic churches will have to reexamine the assumptions on which these theologies rest.

It should have become clear through the present study that some of the current interpretations of Christ and the Gospel result in a doctrine of justification that no longer upholds the Lutheran teaching on justifying faith. If theology is meant to serve the proclamation of the Gospel, the churches will have to determine whether or not the Christology whereby the AC undergirds its "because of Christ" in justification is true to the New Testament. The churches further will have to decide whether they want to embrace a theology which refuses to say that justification occurs *because of Christ,* or whether they will hold to the doctrine of faith and justification that rests precisely on Jesus Christ, the Word of God incarnate, as the sole and sufficient Ground of justification.

Hope

There is reason for hope, however. As Johannes Cardinal Willebrands affirmed in Augsburg in 1980, the division has not split the common root, and the common ground of our faith reaches deeper and farther than that which divides us.[2] And as Joseph Cardinal Höffner maintained, scores of Catholics find themselves on Luther's side, over against many who claim his name, in clinging with him to predictable truth, to the Godhead and resurrection of Jesus and to the sacraments of Baptism and the Eucharist.[3]

If Lutherans and Catholics can find a common basis in Christology, in keeping with the Ecumenical Creeds and the AC, they could and should come to a deeper agreement on the doctrine of justification by grace through faith for Christ's sake, since this doctrine, as we have seen, explicits what Christ represents and how He is to be used in the Christian religion.

Such an agreement could take the shape of the formulation we developed in the preceding chapter on the basis of assumptions common to both sides.

Another consideration is that the time may have come for a different ecumenical methodology. Rather than trying to produce joint statements, oftentimes on the basis of "reinterpretation," it might be helpful if the dialog partners would state openly their divergences and tell plainly why each party is unable to accept the other's stand on particular issues. Such openness might help more toward mutual understanding than hiding the differences in general and ambiguous formulations.

These references to the ecumenical dialog, however, should not give the impression that the Lutheran doctrine of justification through faith is a problem between the churches. It is not a problem, but a solution to the deepest human need. It places man where he belongs, namely, before his Creator. It identifies God as the loving Father who receives us as His children on account of His Son. It returns us to the world as fortunate laborers in the Father's vineyard. It projects our hopes on the day of the Lord's coming. Then our life, which now is hidden, will be revealed, as the apostle Paul writes to the Colossians (3:4).

In face of the divisions caused by the Reformation, Emperor Charles V, as defender of the Christian faith and protector of the church, challenged the Estates of the Imperial Assembly to live in unity within the single fellowship of the church, for they stood and were fighting under one and the same Christ. The leaders of the Lutheran Reformation accepted the challenge. Their Augsburg Confession testifies for all time, on the basis of the Scriptures and the Creeds, how Jesus Christ becomes and remains our Lord, namely, through *faith* in the Good News that proclaims and makes Him our Lord by the power of the Holy Spirit. This confession also indicates how all Christians may become one in Him, namely, by the same true faith in Him as Lord.

Our investigation of the Lutheran doctrine of faith has attempted to clarify the Lutheran stand as to how Christ effectively becomes our Lord. It hopes to have contributed some insights as to how Christians may become one in Christ's church. Therefore we join the author of the AC in his request: "We beseech [Christ] to regard his afflicted and scattered churches and to restore them to a godly and abiding harmony."[4]

NOTES

Chapter 1

1. "Catholica et quasi extemporalis responsio," IV, 19, *Die Konfutation des Augsburgischen Bekenntnisses,* ed. Johannes Ficker (Leipzig: J. A. Barth, 1891), p. 19, 2–5. Henceforth referred to as *RC.*
2. "The Gospel and the Church: Report of the Joint Lutheran-Roman Catholic Study Commission," Nos. 26–30, *Evangelium-Welt-Kirche,* ed. Harding Meyer (Frankfurt am Main: O. Lembeck/J. Knecht, 1975), pp. 41–42.
3. "All Under One Christ: Statement of the Roman Catholic-Lutheran Joint Commission," Nos. 13–15, *Lutheran-Roman Catholic Discussion on the Augsburg Confession: Documents 1977–1981,* ed. Harding Meyer, LWF Report 10 (Stuttgart: Kreuz, 1982), pp. 37–38. "Martin Luther, Witness to Jesus Christ: Statement by the Joint Roman Catholic-Lutheran Commission on the Occasion of Martin Luther's 500th Birthday" (Geneva: The Lutheran World Federation, May 1983).
4. "Agreement between Reformation Churches in Europe: The Leuenberg Agreement (*Konkordie*)," Nos. 6–16, *The Ecumenical Review,* XXV (July 1973), 356–57.
5. *Justification Today: Studies and Reports,* Supplement to *Lutheran World,* No. 1, 1965, pp. 2–11.
6. *Confessing One Faith,* ed. George W. Forell and James F. McCue (Minneapolis: Augsburg, 1982), pp. 334–38.
7. "All Under One Christ," Nos. 10–18, *Lutheran-Roman Catholic Discussion,* pp. 36–39.
8. Heinz Schütte, "Gesprächsbericht: Die Theologie Luthers und die reformatorische Bekenntnisbildung," *Ökumenische Erschliessung Martin Luthers,* ed. Peter Manns and Harding Meyer (Paderborn: Bonifatius/Frankfurt am Main: O. Lembeck, 1983), p. 138. Cf. *Luther's Ecumenical Significance* (Philadelphia: Fortress, 1984), p. 107. See also Peter Manns, "Zur Lage der Ökumene nach dem Luther-Jahr?" *Martin Luther 'Reformator und Vater im Glauben': Referate*

NOTES

aus der Vortragsreihe des Instituts für Europäische Geschichte Mainz, ed. Peter Manns (Stuttgart: Steiner, 1985), p. 294.

9. Martin Seils, "Zu einigen Problemen der Interpretation von Artikel IV der Confessio Augustana in der Anerkennungsdebatte," *Die Confessio Augustana im ökumenischen Gespräch,* ed. Fritz Hoffmann and Ulrich Kühn (Berlin: Evangelische Verlagsanstalt, 1980), p. 153: "For the evangelical confession Melanchthon as author of the Augsburg Confession is the 'mouth' of Luther's reformatory theology."

Chapter 2

1. M. Reu, ed., *The Augsburg Confession: A Collection of Sources with an Historical Introduction* (Chicago: Wartburg, 1930), pp. 69*–72*.
2. Johannes Fabri, *Christenliche underrichtung ... uber ettliche Puncten der Visitation, sso im Churfürstenthumb Sachssen gehalten, und durch Luther beschriben, Welche antzunehmen und zuverwerffen seyend* [Dresden: W. Stöckel, 1528]. Johannes Cochlaeus, *Septiceps Lutherus, ubique sibi, suis scriptis contrarius, in Visitationem Saxonicam per ... Ioannem Cocleum, editus* (Leipzig: Valentinus Schumann, 1529).
3. Heinrich Bornkamm in the critical edition of the Lutheran Confessions, *Die Bekenntnisschriften der evangelisch-lutherischen Kirche*, 4. Aufl. (Göttingen: Vandenhoeck & Ruprecht, 1959), p. xvi. Hereafter referred to as *BS*.
4. Melanchthon to Luther, 11 May 1530, *WA Br,* V, 314, 2–3: "Mittitur tibi apologia nostra quamquam verius confessio est. Neque enim vacat Caesari audire prolixas disputationes."
5. Melanchthon to Luther, 11 May 1530, *WA Br,* V, 314, 3–6: "omnes fere articulos fidei complexus sum, quia Eckius edidit *diabolikotatas diabolas* contra nos. Adversus has volui remedium opponere." Johannes Eck, "Sub Domine Jesu et Mariae patrocinio articulos 404 ... offert se disputaturum Augustae Vindelicorum ... ," ed. Wilhelm Gussmann, *Quellen und Forschungen zur Geschichte des Augsburgischen Glaubensbekenntnisses,* II (Kassel: E. Pillardy, 1930). Eck's charges will be considered below, ch. 4.
6. Texts in M. Reu, *The Augsburg Confession,* pp. 166*–190*, left cols.: "The Oldest Form of the Augsburg Confession, May 31, 1530." Trans. of the preface, ibid., pp. 137*–143*.
7. Kress and Volkamer to Nuremberg Council, 3 June 1530, *CR,* II, 83.
8. Cf. the elector's March 15 instruction, trans. J. Bodensieck, "Instruction to Hans von Dolzig for the Counts of Nassau and Neuenahr, March 16, 1530," in M. Reu, *The Augsburg Confession,* pp. 72*–77*. On the Dolzig mission see below, ch. 3, in connection with the Schwabach Articles.
9. "Vortrag, mit welchem der Kaiser Karl V. durch den Pfalzgrafen Friedrich den Reichstag eröffnete," found in Karl Eduard Förstemann, *Urkundenbuch zu der Geschichte des Reichstages zu Augsburg in Jahre 1530* (hereafter referred to as *FU*), I (Osnabrück: Biblio-Verlag, 1966), 295–309, especially pp. 305–07.
10. The instruction, *GQ,* I, i, 326–32. The letters, *CR,* II, 92–103 (by June 11). Cf. Brenz to Isenmann, 24 June 1530, *CR,* II, 125: "Non ... libet, ut in hac causa Caesarem pro iudice eligamus et agnoscamus." Melanchthon in an undated

opinion, *FU,* I, 199–202: The emperor may hear, but is not competent to decide the religious controversy.

11. This information is based on a note inserted supposedly by Justus Jonas at the margin of the *praefatio* in a copy of the first Wittenberg edition of the Augsburg Confession, *FU,* I, 460: "reddita e Germanico Pontani tunc per Justum Jonam."

12. Kress and Volkamer to the Nürnberg Council, 15 June 1530, *CR,* II, 105: Melanchthon has not rendered the Latin preface and epilogue into German because they might be composed in the name of the allied princes and estates; June 19, *CR,* II, 112–13: The epilogue has not been composed because the whole affair might take a different course; postscript, ibid., col. 124: The articles are being revised by the counselors and theologians of the Lutheran princes.

13. Peter Manns, "Luther auf der Koburg: Das Reichtagsgeschehen von Augsburg und die Entstehung der Confessio Augustana," *Luther und die Bekenntnisschriften,* Veröffentlichungen der Luther-Akademie Ratzeburg, Band 2 (Erlangen: Martin Luther-Verlag, 1981), pp. 127–29.

14. According to Kolde, *Die älteste Redaktion,* pp. 45–46, and Wilhelm Gussmann, *Quellen und Forschungen zur Geschichte des Augsburgischen Glaubensbekenntnisses,* I, i, 224–26. On this question as well as on Melanchthon's role as spokesman of the Lutherans see the materials discussed and edited by Wolfgang Steglich in, respectively, "Die Stellung der evangelischen Reichsstände und Reichsstädte zu Karl V. Zwischen der Protestation und Konfession 1529/30: Ein Beitrag zur Vorgeschichte des Augsburgischen Glaubensbekenntnisses," *Archiv für Reformationsgeschichte,* LXII (1971), 161–92 (hereafter referred to as *ARG*) and *Deutsche Reichtagsakten unter Kaiser Karl V,* Jüngere Reihe, 8. Band, 2 Halbbände (Göttingen: Vandenhoeck & Ruprecht, 1970/71).

15. *FU,* I, 308–09. According to Bernd Moeller, "Augustana-Studien," *ARG,* LVII, 80–82, the *propositio* created favorable conditions for the Lutherans, since they were treated as a party among others and were asked to submit a document which they had ready. This may explain why Chancellor Brück abandoned the "supplication" tone and composed the new preface in detached and confident terms.

16. Moeller, "Augustana-Studien," *ARG,* LVII, 81, note 25: The text suggest that the Lutherans are the loyal party, since they have responded to the emperor's request.

17. *BS,* pp. 47–49. Appeal for a free council had been made in the protest against the stipulations of the Diet of Spires, 1529. For sources see Steglich, "Stellung," *ARG,* LXII, 167.

18. Moeller, "Augustana-Studien," *ARG,* LVII, 82: The Confession finally presented itself as an impartial proposition in the context of a conciliation process. The elector's original request for articles, 14 May 1530, *WA Br,* V, 264, 37–31, inquired "whether or in which form and to what an extent we may and can suffer negotiations."

19. In the letters Melanchthon calls it *confessio* (*CR,* II, 126, 140, 142, 144, 146 *et passim*) and *apologia et defensio nostra* (*CR,* II, 141); Brenz, *epitome doctrinae nostrae;* Kress and Volkamer, *Unterricht des Glaubens* or *Verzeichnis* (*CR,* II, 124–25, 127–29, 142–43 *et passim*). Moeller, "Augustana-Studien," *ARG,* LVII, 93, note 87 (after F. H. Schubert): Inasmuch as it presents the opinions and

claims of a group of persons to an imperial assembly, the Augsburg Confession actually is an *oratio*.

20. *BS*, p. 84, 13–21; Tappert, pp. 48–49. The request made in the Latin text seems to apply to Eck especially. According to Steglich, "Stellung," *ARG*, LXII, 170, a similar request appears in the 1529 instruction for a delegation to be sent to the emperor. Cf. Steglich, ed., *Deutsche Reichtagsakten*, Jüngere Reihe, VIII, i, 24–42.

21. Moeller, "Augustana-Studien," *ARG*, LVII, 82, note 31, too, discerns a conclusion to the second part and an epilog to the whole document. The distinction is blurred in Tappert, pp. 94–96. As they replied on July 10 to the emperor's question whether they had further articles to present, the Lutheran estates emphasized again the limited scope of the document: It was not meant to list all the abuses, but to summarize the doctrine preached for the souls' benefit in order to demonstrate to the emperor that no unchristian teaching had been received. See *CR*, II, 184. Walter Brandmüller, "Der Weg zur Confessio Augustana," *Bekenntnis und Geschichte: Die Confessio Augustana im historischen Zusammenhang,* her. v. Wolfgang Reinhard (München: E. Vögel, 1981), pp. 47–50, does not reckon with this determined limitation in scope, as he regards the AC an inauthentic expression of the Lutheran position.

22. Here the term *confessio* (*Bekenntnus*) is used with reference to the princes and cities; the expression *summa doctrinae*, with reference to the preachers and teachers. In the preface the term *confessio* applies to both estates and theologians, but with a difference: The document is a confession of the estates' faith and of the theologians' teaching. According to Joachim Camerarius, Melanchthon wanted to submit the document in the name of the theologians, but the estates decided to submit it in their own name. See Ernst Salomon Cyprian, *Historia der Augspurgischen Confession*(Gotha: A. Reyher, 1730), p. 66.

23. Georg Brück, *Geschichte der Handlungen in dem Sache des heiligen Glaubens auf dem Reichstage zu Augsburg im J. 1530*, ed. Karl Eduard Förstemann, *Archiv für die Geschichte der kirchlichen Reformation in ihrem gesamten Umfange*, I, i (Halle: C. A. Schwetschke, 1831), 53. Cf. "Ain kurtze anzaygung und beschreybung Römischer Kayserlicher Maiestat einreyten ... auf den Reychstag und was sich ... daselbst ... verlauffen unnd zugetragen hat, Anno 1530," reprinted by Cyprian, *Historia*, Beilage VI, p. 76.

24. Johannes Bernard, "Zur Katholizität der Confessio Augustana," *Die Confessio Augustana im ökumenischen Gespräch,* ed. Fritz Hoffmann and Ulrich Kühn (Berlin: Evangelische Verlagsanstalt, 1980), p. 29, remarks that, in spite of his careful formulations, Melanchthon betrays a new understanding of catholicity, although he still regards it as identical with the traditional view.

25. An interesting parallel is provided by Martin Chemnitz's definition as reported by Johannes Bernard, "Zur Katholizität," p. 29, on the basis of W. Beinert, *Um das dritte Kirchenattribut: Die Katholizität der Kirche im Verständnis der evangelisch-lutherischen und römisch-katholischen Theologie der Gegenwart*, I (Essen, 1964), p. 104: "quod semper, quod ubique et ab omnibus fidelibus ex Scriptura constanter receptum fuit." Inasmuch as Chemnitz's *ex Scriptura* refers to the Gospel focused on the doctrine of faith, his position is not identical with that of Vincent of Lérins, however, as Bernard tends to assume.

26. According to Bernard, "Zur Katholizität," p. 30, the catholicity of the AC could

be established unequivocally only after agreement on key issues and on the overarching catholicity that holds the Roman and the Lutheran churches together. According to Ulrich Kühn, "Die Frage einer katholischen Anerkennung der Confessio Augustana als Problem ökumenischer Rezeption," *Die Confessio Augustana im ökumenischen Gespräch,* pp. 22–23, the recognition of the AC by the Roman Catholic Church affects the position of the dialog partners and involves a "catholic interpretation" of the document, and therefore the recognition process actually challenges the Roman church to redefine and explicate its self-understanding. These papers, which were discussed in the German Democratic Republic up to the end of 1978, however, seem not to have influenced the discussion in the West.

Chapter 3

1. Wilhelm Gussmann, ed., *Quellen und Forschungen zur Geschichte des Augsburgischen Glaubensbekenntnisses,* I, i (Leipzig/Berlin: B. G. Teubner, 1911), 278–94: "Ratschlag der Nürnberger Prediger zum Reichstag von Augsburg 1530"; I, ii, 47–96: "Ratschlag der Geistlichkeit von Culmbach." Hereafter referred to as *GQ*. Cf. [Lazarus Spengler?], *Ein kurzer auszug aus dem bebstlichen rechten der decret und decretalen in artickeln, die ungeverlich Gottes wort und evangelio gemess sein oder zum wenigsten nicht widerstreben. 1530;* bibliographical information provided in *GQ,* I, i, 408–10, note 13. According to *GQ,* I, i, 69–70, 80–81, 236–41, these sources provided patristic and canonical material to support the Lutheran position, supplied clarifying formulations for Arts. XXII, XXIV, and XXVI, and caused Melanchthon to reformulate the articles on faith and works and episcopal jurisdiction. Wilhelm F. Schmidt and K. Schornbaum, *Die fränkischen Bekenntnisse: Eine Vorstufe der Augsburgischen Konfession* (München: Chr. Kaiser, 1930), pp. 137–38, counter: The indebtedness of the AC to the *Ratschläge* is conjectural. These are dependent on Luther's works, and it is not clear whether Melanchthon drew from them, or directly from Luther's writings and patristic sources. A recent review is found in Vinzenz Pfnür, *Einig in der Rechtfertigungslehre?* (Wiesbaden: F. Steiner, 1970), pp. 5–28. Hereafter cited as Pfnür, *Einig*.

2. Philipp Melanchthon, *Dispositio orationis, in Epistola Pauli ad Romanos* (Wittembergae: Georg Rhau, MDXXX). This is the second reprint of the second edition by Joseph Clug, Wittenberg, February 1530, according to Paul Drews and Friedrich Cohrs, *Supplementa Melanchthoniana,* V, ii (Leipzig: Egers und Sievers, 1929), xli–xliii. Carl G. Bretschneider, *Corpus Reformatorum,* XV (Brunsvigae: C. A. Schwetschke et Filium, 1848), 443–92, reprinted the text of Peucer's edition of Melanchthon's works. Hereafter referred to as *DOR*. According to Wilhelm Maurer, "Studien über Melanchthons Anteil an der Entstehung der Confessio Augustana, *Archiv für Reformationsgeschichte,* LI (1960), 178–79, the *Dispositio* clarifies key concepts of Art. IV of the AC like *imputare, coram Deo, gratis, per fidem, propter Christum.* Hereafter referred to as *ARG*.

3. Philipp Melanchthon, "Articuli de quibus egerunt per visitatores in regione Saxoniae. Wittembergae 1527"; cf. "Articuli Inspectionis Ecclesiarum Saxoniae emendati. 1528," *CR,* XXVI, 7–28.

4. *Instructions for the Visitors of Parish Pastors in Electoral Saxony,* trans. Conrad

NOTES

Bergendoff, *LW*, XL (Philadelphia: Fortress, 1958), 269–320. The apologetic scope of the publication is spelled out especially in Luther's preface.

5. Johannes Fabri, *Christenliche underrichtung . . . uber ettliche Puncten der Visitation, sso im Churfürstenthumb Sachssen gehalten, und durch Luther beschriben, Welche antzunehmen und zuverwerffen seyend* [Dresden: W. Stöckel, 1528], with an epilog by Cochlaeus. Johannes Cochlaeus, *Septiceps Lutherus, ubique sibi, suis scriptis contrarius, in Visitationem Saxonicam per . . . Ioannem Cocleum, editus* (Leipzig: Valentinus Schumann, 1529).
6. See below, note 10. Wolfgang Steglich, "Die Stellung der evangelischen Reichsstände und Reichsstädte zu Karl V. zwischen der Protestation und Konfession 1529/30: Ein Beitrag zur Vorgeschichte des Augsburgischen Glaubensbekenntnisses," *ARG*, LXII (1971), 190–91; cf. Steglich, ed., *Deutsche Reichstagsakten unter Kaiser Karl V*, Jüngere Reihe, VIII, i (Göttingen: Vandenhoeck & Ruprecht, 1970), 623–47. Hereafter referred to as *RTA*.
7. "Confession concerning Christ's Supper," trans. Robert Fischer, *LW*, 37, 360–72. On the relationship between Luther's Confession and the Schwabach Articles see Paul Wernle, *Der evangelische Glaube nach den Hauptschriften der Reformatoren*, I (Tübingen: P. Siebeck, 1918), 269–70; William E. Nagel, *Luthers Anteil an der Confessio Augustana* (Gütersloh: C. Bertelsmann, 1930), pp. 24–32; Wilhelm Maurer, "Studien," *ARG*, LI, 173–74, and "Zur Entstehung und Textgeschichte der Schwabacher Artikel," *Theologie in Geschichte und Kunst: Walter Elliger zum 65. Geburtstag*, ed. S. Herrmann and O. Söhngen (Witten: Luther-Verlag, 1968), pp. 136–43. Cf. also Georg Hoffmann, "Zur Entstehungsgeschichte der Augustana: Der 'Unterricht der Visitatoren' als Vorlage des Bekenntnisses," *Zeitschrift für systematische Theologie*, XV (1938), 438, note 1. Hereafter referred to as *ZST*.
8. Translation of Schwabach Articles by H. E. Jacobs in M. Reu, *The Augsburg Confession: A Collection of Sources with an Historical Introduction* (Chicago: Wartburg, 1930), pp. 40*–44*. Hans von Schubert, "Beiträge zur Geschichte der evangelischen Bekenntnis- und Bündnisbildung 1529/30," *Zeitschrift für Kirchengeschichte*, XXX (1909), 342, suggests the designation, The Saxon-Franconian Confession (*das sächsisch-fränkische Bekenntnis*). Hereafter referred to as *ZKG*. The Elector of Saxony, Margrave George of Brandenburg, and the city of Nürnberg presented the Seventeen Articles as a confessional basis and condition for both a Lutheran alliance and a special delegation to the emperor on 16 October 1529, in Schwabach.
9. Hans von Schubert, *Bündnis und Bekenntnis 1529/30: Vortrag* (Leipzig: Verein für Reformationsgeschichte, 1908), p. 23. Wolfgang Steglich, "Die Stellung," *ARG*, LXII, 185–86; Georg Hoffmann, "Zur Entstehungsgeschichte," *ZST*, XV, 475–82, 485–86.
10. Text of the March 16 instruction trans. J. Bodensieck in M. Reu, *The Augbsurg Confession*, pp. 72*–77*. The instruction mentions a summary of teachings and a printed report on ceremonies. The latter, according to von Schubert (see previous note), pp. 330–31; Gussmann, *GQ*, I, i, 103–05; and Hoffmann, *ZST*, XV, 480–82, refers to the *Unterricht der Visitatoren* or the *Articuli Visitationis*. Hans-Ulrich Delius, *WA RN*, XXX, iii, 14, reports favorably recent studies which assume that only the Schwabach Articles were to be submitted.
11. Campeggio to Sanga, 9 and 12 May 1530, ed. Gerhard Müller, *Nuntiaturberichte aus Deutschland*, 1. Abteilung, 1. Ergänzungsband (Tübingen: Max Nie-

meyer, 1963), pp. 29–30: "Il duca di Saxonia ... ha mandato una sua assertione de la fede; et secondo mi è stato referito: è nel principio la più santa et catholica del mondo, ma nel mezzo et nel fine piena di veleno." Cf. p. 32: "Con questa mando la copia de li articoli del duca di Saxonia, de liqquali supra ho fatto mentione ... "

12. "Die bekentnus Martini Luthers auff den jczigen angestelten Reichstag zu Augspurgk eynzulegen, In siebentzehen Artickel verfasset. Im XXX. Jar," ed. O. Seitz and O. Brenner, WA, XXX, iii, 178–82. Conrad Wimpina, Johan Mensing, Wolfgang Redorffer, Rupert Elgersma, "Gegen die bekanntnus Martini Luthers auff den yetzigen angestelten Reychsstag zu Augspurg, auffs neuwe eingelegt in Sibenzehen Articell verfasst kurtze und Christenlich underricht. MDXXX," ed. O. Seitz and O. Brenner, WA, XXX, iii, 186–93.

13. "Auff das schreien etlicher Papisten, uber die siebentzehen Artickel. Antwort Martini Luthers. Wittemberg. Im M.D. XXX. Jar," ed. O. Seitz and O. Brenner, WA, XXX, iii, 194–97. Cf. von Schubert, "Beiträge," ZKG (1908), 364–66.

14. GQ, I, i, 114–15; cf. p. 452, note 45. Theodor Kolde, *Historische Einleitung in die symbolischen Bücher der evangelisch-lutherischen Kirche* (Gütersloh: C. Bertelsmann, 1907), pp. vii–viii; Kolde, *Die älteste Redaktion der Augsburger Konfession* (Gütersloh: "Der Rufer," [1906]), p. 50, note 2; Kolde, *Die Augsburgische Konfession,* 2. Auflage (Gotha: F. A. Perthes, 1911), p. 34.

15. Assuming that Melanchthon and Luther modified significantly their position on free will and related matters in the late 1520s, Vinzenz Pfnür, *Einig*, pp. 110–39, made the "additional articles" (*Zusatzartikel*), especially Art. XVIII, the key for the interpretation of Arts. IV–VI. This approach resulted in a defective interpretation of Art. IV, as will be demonstrated below in chs. 5 and 9.

16. Martin Luther, "The Marburg Articles, 1529," trans. Martin E. Lehmann, LW, 38, 85–89. On the relationship between the Schwabach and Marburg Articles see Hans von Schubert, "Beiträge," ZKG, XXIX (1908), 350–52, cf. pp. 379–81; Seitz and Brenner, WA, XXX, iii, 95–97; William E. Nagel, *Luthers Anteil*, pp. 38–39; Wilhelm Maurer, "Studien," ARG, LI, 168.

17. CR, XXVI, 7; cf. 2nd ed., notes 3–4: "quomodo fidem doceant, quid fides, quomodo consequamur eam, et quomodo doceant homines iustificari."

18. CR, XXVI, 9–10, 10–12, 12–18.

19. CR, XXVI, 10–11: "primum quid sit fides"; cf. col. 16: "fidei natura."

20. CR, XXVI, 16, note 37: "dicendum [est], quomodo iustificet [fides], sicuti supra [col. 11] exposuimus ... "

21. CR, XXVI, 12: "Nam ea demum fides iustificat, quum credit remissionem peccatorum."

22. CR, XXVI, 18.

23. CR, XXVI, 18: section *De iustitia;* cf. col. 28: *iustitia fidei.*

24. LW, 40, 293–97. Wilhelm Maurer, "Zur Entstehung ... der Schwabacher Artikel," *Theologie in Geschichte und Kunst,* p. 141, however, regards as untenable Thiele's supposition that these sections go back to Luther. Cf. WA, XXVI, 217, note 1.

25. Wilhelm E. Nagel, *Luthers Anteil,* p. 16; Paul Wernle, *Der evangelische Glaube*, I, 270. Wilhelm Maurer, "Studien," ARG, LI, 170.

NOTES

26. *LW,* 37, 365: Robert H. Fischer disregarded the context as he rendered "faith of Christ." John C. Mattes correctly rendered "faith in Christ," in *The Augsburg Confession,* ed. M. Reu (Chicago: Wartburg, 1930), p. 27*.
27. *WA RN,* XXX, iii, 21, 23–29.
28. *WA RN,* XXX, iii, 20, 6–12. M. Reu, *The Augsburg Confession,* pp. 42*–43*.
29. Below, ch. 5 (analysis of Art. IV) and ch. 9 (analysis of the Joint Lutheran-Catholic Committee on the Augsburg Confession).
30. This formulation echoes Luther's preface to the Letter to the Romans (*LW,* 35, 365–80).
31. The Marburg Articles are found in *LW,* 38, 85–89, trans. Martin E. Lehmann.
32. Günther Wartenberg in Martin Luther, *Studienausgabe,* ed. Hans-Ulrich Delius, III (Berlin: Evangelische Verlagsanstalt, 1983), 472, 10: "hernach so wir gerecht unnd heylig dadurch gerechennt unnd worden synndt." We have assumed that Luther's verbs, *gerechennt* and *worden,* refer respectively to *gerecht* and *heylig,* since he used and explained the expression *heylig werden* in the Confession, *WA,* XXVI, 505, 18–20. Martin E. Lehmann's translation (*LW,* 38, 87) overlooks the parallelism, as well as the argumentative import of Luther's *hernach:* "and by which [faith] we are reckoned and have become righteous and holy...." The rendering misses Luther's point. He obviously wants to discern between different "times" or "moments."

CHAPTER 4

1. Friedrich Loofs, "Die Bedeutung der Rechtfertigungslehre der Apologie für die Symbolik der lutherischen Kirche," *Theologische Studien und Kritiken,* LVII (1884), 673–88. Hereafter referred to as *ThStKr.*
2. Carl Stange, "Über eine Stelle in der Apologie: Ein Beitrag zur Rechtfertigungslehre der Apologie," *Neue Kirchliche Zeitschrift,* X (1889), 183–89.
3. A. Warko, "Die Erbsünden- und Rechtfertigungslehre der Apologie in ihrem geschichtlichen Gegensatz zur mittelalterlichen und gleichzeitigen katholischen Theologie," *ThStKr,* LXXIX (1906), 87–90.
4. Johannes Kunze, *Die Rechtfertigungslehre in der Apologie* (Gütersloh: C. Bertelsmann, 1908), pp. 6–9, cf. pp. 21–24.
5. Hugo Lämmer, *Die vortridentinische katholische Theologie des Reformations-Zeitalters aus den Quellen dargestellt* (Berlin: G. Schlawitz, 1858). Gustav Plitt, *Einleitung in die Augustana,* II (Erlangen: A. Deichert, 1868).
6. For instance Vinzenz Pfnür, *Einig in der Rechtfertigungslehre? Die Rechtfertigungslehre der Confessio Augustana (1530) und die Stellungnahme der katholischen Kontroverstheologie zwischen 1530 und 1535,* Veröffentlichungen des Instituts für Europäische Geschichte Mainz, Band 60 (Wiesbaden: F. Steiner, 1970). Hereafter referred to as Pfnür, *Einig.* See also Erwin Iserloh, ed., *Confessio Augustana und Confutatio: Der Augsburger Reichstag 1530 und die Einheit der Kirche,* Internationales Symposion der Gesellschaft zur Herausgabe des Corpus Catholicorum in Augsburg vom 3.–7. September 1979, Reformationsgeschichtliche Studien und Texte, 118 (Münster: Aschendorff, 1980). Hereafter referred to as *CAC.*
7. Johann Eck, "Sub Domini Jesu et Mariae patrocinio articulos 404, partim ad

disputationes Lipsicam, Badensem et Bernensem attinentes, partim vero ex scriptis pacem ecclesiae perturbantium extractos, coram divo Caesare Carolo V ... ac proceribus imperii ... offert se disputaturum Augustae Vindelicorum die et hora consensu Caesaris posterius publicandis," ed. Wilhelm Gussmann, *Quellen und Forschungen zur Geschichte des Augsburgischen Glaubensbekenntnisses*, II (Kassel: E. Pillardy, 1930), 39–46: listing of the collections of excerpts; cf. pp. 37–39: listing of the writings censured. The Lutheran works censured most frequently are: Luther's *De captivitate Babylonica* of 1520 (54 times) and *Resolutiones disputationum de indulgentiarum virtute* of 1518 (30 times) and Melanchthon's *Loci communes* of 1521 (29 times) and *Annotationes in epistolas Pauli ad Rhomanos et Corinthios* of 1522 (21 times). *GQ* refers to Gussmann's edition. M. Reu, *The Augsburg Confession: A Collection of Sources with an Historical Introduction* (Chicago: Wartburg, 1930), pp. 97*–121*, provides a translation of the dedication to the emperor, the preface of the printed edition, and Arts. 66–404.

8. According to Bernd Moeller, "Augustana-Studien," *Archiv für Reformationsgeschichte*, LVII (1966), 89 (hereafter referred to as *ARG*), Wilhelm Maurer's otherwise excellent "Studien über Melanchthons Anteil an der Entstehung der Confessio Augustana," *ARG*, LI (1960), 158–207, are deficient because they did not pay enough attention to Eck's charges. The problem remains in Maurer's *Historischer Kommentar zur Confessio Augustana*, 2 vols. (Gütersloh: G. Mohn, 1978).

9. "Catholica et quasi extemporalis responsio super nonnullis articulis Catholice Cesaree Maiestati Hispanice proximis diebus in Dieta Imperiali Augustensi per Illustrissimos Electorem Saxonie ac alios quosdam Principes et duas Civitates oblatis, MDXXX," ed. Johannes Ficker, *Die Konfutation des Augsburgischen Bekenntnisses: Ihre erste Gestalt und ihre Geschichte* (Leipzig: J. A. Barth, 1891). Hereafter referred to as *RC*.

10. Ficker, *RC*, pp. xxxii–xliii, regards Eck as the main author of the *Responsio*. Erwin Iserloh, *Johannes Eck (1486–1543): Scholastiker, Humanist, Kontroverstheologe*, Katholisches Leben und Kirchenreform im Zeitalter der Glaubensspaltung, 41 (Münster: Aschendorff, 1981), pp. 67–68, summarizes recent views on the question. Eck's role and the relation between his works and the *Responsio* are discussed by Herbert Immenkötter, ed., *Die Confutatio der Confessio Augustana vom 3. August 1530, Corpus Catholicorum*, 33 (Münster: Aschendorff, 1979), pp. 35–37, especially notes 3–4 and 12–13. Hereafter referred to as *CCA*.

11. Herbert Immenkötter, ed., *CCA*, pp. 74–77 and 204–07; cf. Herbert Immenkötter, *Der Reichstag zu Augsburg und die Confutatio: Historische Einführung und neuhochdeutsche Übertragung*, Katholisches Leben und Kirchenreform im Zeitalter der Glaubensspaltung, 39 (Münster: Aschendorff, 1979), pp. 44–45 and 99–100. For Heinrich E. Bindseil's edition of the Latin and German texts see *CR*, XXVII, 81–184 and 189–228 respectively. American translation by H. E. Jacobs in M. Reu, *The Augsburg Confession*, pp. 348*–83*. References to the Confutation will be to Immenkötter's edition, *CCA*.

12. Johannes Eck, *Enchiridion locorum communium adversus Lutherum et alios hostes ecclesiae (1525–1543)*, ed. Pierre Fraenkel, *Corpus Catholicorum*, 34 (Münster: Aschendorff, 1979), pp. 1–2. Hereafter referred to as *FEE*.

13. Conrad Wimpina, Johan[nes] Mensing, Wolfgang Redorffer, Rupert Elgersma,

NOTES

"Gegen die bekanntnus Martini Luthers auff den yetzigen angestellten Reychsstag zu Augspurg, auffs neuwe eingelegt in Sibenzehen Artickel verfasst kurtze und Christenlich underricht, MDXXX," ed. by O. Seitz and O. Brenner (*WA*, XXX, iii, 186–93). The Refutation of the Schwabach Articles will be referred to as ChU. For bibliography on the authors see Immenkötter, *CCA*, pp. 17–23.

14. Conrad Wimpina, *Sectarum, errorum, hallutinationum, et schismatum, ab origine ferme Christianae ecclesiae, ad haec usque nostra tempora, concisioris Anacephalaeōseōs, Una cum aliquantis Pigardicarum, Wiglefticarum, et Lutheranarum haeresum: confutationibus, Librorum partes Tres. Quarum prima in libros partiales secernitur Octo* (Francophordiae ad Oderam: n.p., MCXXVIII).

15. Johannes Mensing, *Bescheidt Ob der Glaube alleyn: on alle gute wercke dem menschen genug sey zur seligkeyt etc.* Darynn vorleget werden die zwey ungegründte und unchristliche lasterbüchlyn Nicol Amsdorffs, Den frommen Christen zu Goslar und Brunschwygk sonderlich zugeschrieben ... ([Leyptzigk: J. Thanner] MDXXVIII). Mensing, *Erretunge des Christlichen Bescheydts: den Glauben und gute wercke belangende, von der lesterlichen und unchristlichen schmehunge, so Nicol Amszdorff vormeynter prediger, und warhafftiger vorfürer zu Magdeburgk, dargegen geschrieben* ... (s.l., n.p., MDXXVIII).

16. Immenkötter, *CCA*, pp. 36, 17, 34. The draft known as *Responsio Theologorum* (henceforth referred to as *RT*) may have served as basis for the composition of the *Catholica Responsio*, Art. IV. It was published by Johannes Cochlaeus, one of the presumable authors, in *Philippicae Quatuor Iohannis Cochlei in Apologiam Philippi Melanchthonis Ad Carolum V. Imperatorem Romanorum* ... (Lipsiae: [N. Faber,] MDXXXIIII), fol. Hiib–iiib, and reprinted by Heinrich E. Bindseil, *CR*, XXVII, 95–97, cf. 85–87, 89–92. See also Ficker, *RC*, pp. xi–xiv, xxx note 3, xxxiv–xxxv.

17. See above, ch. 2, note 2; ch. 3, note 5.

18. *GQ*, II, 17–18, 103–12. Cf. pp. 103, 35–104, 5 and 112, 3–5.

19. *GQ*, II, 104, 9–11; cf. p. 153, note 3. *RC*, V, pp. 21, 13–22, 5.

20. *RC*, IX, p. 38, 4–7: "cur patiuntur Lutherum et Melanchthonem docere: Baptismus neminem iustificat nec ulli prodest?" Martin Luther, *De captivitate Babylonica, 1520*," *WA*, VI, 532, 36–533, 1. Cf. *LW*, 36, 66: "Thus it is not baptism that justifies or benefits anyone, but it is faith in that word of promise to which baptism is added. This faith justifies, and fulfils that which baptism signifies." Philipp Melanchthon, *Annotationes ... in Epistolas Ad Rhomanos et Corinthios* (Norimbergae: J. Stucks, 1522), fol. D6, on Romans 4:11: Baptism does not convey grace or salvation by itself, but because the baptized believes that God receives him into grace, He is reconciled (*conciliatur*) with him and, in order that he may be sure of that, He shows forth the sign or seal whereby He declares that His promise is serious.

21. *GQ*, II, 125, 10–35. M. Reu, *The Augsburg Confession*, p. 107*.

22. Martin Luther, *Disputation and Defense Against the Accusations of Dr. Johann Eck*, 1519, trans. Harold J. Grimm, *LW*, 31, 317, No. 2: "To deny that man sins even when doing good; that venial sin is pardonable, not according to its nature, but by the mercy of God; or that sin remains in the child after baptism;

THE DOCTRINE OF FAITH

that is equivalent to crushing Paul and Christ under foot."

23. Martin Luther, *Explanations of the Ninety-five Theses*, 1518, trans. Carl W. Folkemer, *LW,* 31, 216: "But even a good work which has been done in the best manner is a venial sin, as cited above from the words of St. Augustine: 'The commandments are fulfilled when what is not fulfilled is forgiven.' And this happens in every good work, for according to the Lord's Prayer we must always seek forgiveness."

24. Ibid., *LW,* 31, 121: "No one is sure that he does not always sin mortally because of the most secret vice of pride."

25. *RC,* VI, pp. 26, 16–27, 2: "scandalosissime predicarunt contra bona opera, ut multi simplices existimarent se peccare mortaliter, si opus bonum facerent."

26. *RC,* II, p. 9, 1–4; cf. IX, 38, 7–8.

27. *RC,* XX, p. 63, 16–19: Eck's Art. 153 proves that the Lutherans do not teach the Decalog. Johannes Cochlaeus, *Septiceps Lutherus, ubique sibi, suis scriptis contrarius, in Visitationem Saxonicam . . . editus* (Lypsiae: V. Schumann, MCXXIX), fol. Ciiib: The "swarmer" (*Suermerus*) Luther argues that "even the Ten Commandments do not apply to us," for they were given exclusively to the people led out of Egypt (Ex. 20:2).

28. Arts. 206, 208, and 209 cited under the heading *charitas* hold that one must be sure of having grace (and love) before he may produce good, that is, God-pleasing works. These were not denounced in the *Responsio*.

29. *RC,* XX, p. 68, 19–23; cf. critical apparatus. Luther's inconsistency in defining faith (Arts. 211 and 166) is alluded to on p. 69, 5–7.

30. *RC,* IV, pp. 16, 11–12; 17, 10–18, 1; 18, 3–4, 7–8; 18, 11–19, 2. Cf. *RC,* V, pp. 23, 6–24, 2, and XX, pp. 65, 24–66, 7, especially p. 66, 12–14: According to Leif Grane, *Die Confessio Augustana: Einführung in die Hauptgedanken der lutherischen Reformation* (Göttingen: Vandenhoeck & Ruprecht, 1970), pp. 60–61, in the Thomist conception even Christ's work is—just as faith—a presupposition of justification: He affords help in order that one's work be accomplished on the basis of His.

31. *RC,* IV, p. 18, 11–13.

32. Philipp Melanchthon, *Loci communes* (1521), ed. Robert Stupperich, *Melanchthons Werke in Auswahl,* II, i (Gütersloh: C. Bertelsmann, 1978), 104, 22–28: If grace is exactly described, it is nothing but God's good will (*benevolentia*) toward us or His will full of mercy for us (*voluntas dei miserta nostri*); the word *gratia*, therefore, does not signify any quality in us, but rather God's very will or good will toward us (*ipsam dei voluntatem seu benevolentiam dei erga nos*). Hereafter referred to as *MSA*. Cf. *CR,* XXI, 158. Leif Grane, *Die Confessio Augustana,* pp. 60–61, also contrasts the traditional and the Lutheran views of grace.

33. *RC,* IV, pp. 19, 2–20, 3; cf. critical apparatus. Melanchthon, *MSA,* II, i, 135, 8–13: Although faith alone (*sola fides*) justifies, still love is required as well, namely, the second part of the Law, Rom. 13:9. Love does not justify, because no one loves as much as he should. It is faith that justifies: It relies on God's mercy, not on its own merit.

34. Eck cunningly omits the context and disregards the scope of the passage. Cf. Martin Luther, *Operationes in Psalmos* (1519–1521), on Ps. 14:1; *WA,* V, 396, 13–28: The enlightened teachers of the faith have failed to understand that

faith is active in every single work, ever believing and trusting that one pleases God or rather that He absolves and is favorable. Therefore it is an error to place faith and its action alongside other virtues and actions. One must raise it above all of them and regard it as a kind of constant, general influence over all works. When it moves and acts, all things in man are moved, act, thrive, please [God]. Cf. *RC,* IV, p. 20, 3–8.

35. *RC,* VI, pp. 26, 16–27, 2, cited above, note 25.
36. Martin Luther, *De votis monasticis . . . iudicium* (1521), *WA,* VIII, 600, 33–36. *LW,* 44, 289: "The doctrine of God teaches faith; these men under vows boast that they teach something more than faith. And that something more is nothing but a work, and can be nothing else but a work. But you cannot teach works unless you hurt faith, since faith and works stand at opposite extremes in the matter of justification." Besides disregarding the context, Eck impudently omits the decisive words, "in the matter of justification."
37. Philipp Melanchthon, *Loci, MSA,* II, i, 43, 22–23 (*CR,* XXI, 106) infers from Rom. 8:7 that the fruits of the flesh cannot be good since it does not and cannot submit to the Law.
38. *RC,* VI, p. 27, 9–28, 1. Luther, *The Babylonian Captivity, LW,* 36, 42: "God does not deal, nor has he ever dealt, with man otherwise than through a word of promise, as I have said. We in turn cannot deal with God otherwise than through faith in the Word of his promise. He does not desire works, nor has he need of them; rather we deal with men and with ourselves on the basis of works. But God has need of this: that we consider him faithful in his promises [Heb. 10:23], and patiently persist in this belief, and thus worship him with faith, hope, and love." By pulling the statement out of context Eck conveys a wrong impression. See also Cochlaeus, *Septiceps Lutherus,* ch. IV, fol. Diva; *GQ,* II, 127, cf. note 193.
39. *RC,* VI, p. 29, 9, cf. line 4. Luther, *The Babylonian Captivity, LW,* 36, 60–61: "Thus you see how rich a Christian is, that is, one who has been baptized! Even if he would, he could not lose his salvation, however much he sinned, unless he refused to believe. For no sin can condemn him save unbelief alone. All other sins, so long as the faith in God's promise made in baptism returns or remains, are immediately blotted out through that same faith, or rather through the truth of God, because he cannot deny himself if you confess him and faithfully cling to him in his promise."
40. Luther, *Lectures on Galatians* (1519), [on Gal. 2:11-13], *LW,* 27, 213: "Therefore Paul is fighting against compulsion and on behalf of freedom. For faith in Christ is all that is necessary for our righteousness. Everything else is entirely without restriction and is no longer either commanded or forbidden." The omission of "in Christ" and "for our righteousness" in Eck's article evidently results in misrepresentation of the intended meaning.
41. *RC,* VI, p. 29, 13–30, 1. Luther, *The Freedom of a Christian, LW,* 31, 361: "The following statements are therefore true: 'Good works do not make a good man, but a good man does good works; evil works do not make a wicked man, but a wicked man does evil works.' Consequently it is always necessary that the substance or person himself be good before there can be any good works, and that good works follow and proceed from the good person, as Christ also says . . . [Matt. 7:18]." Once again the statement is taken out of context to convey a false impression.

THE DOCTRINE OF FAITH

42. *RC,* IV, p. 30, 4–6.
43. *RC,* XX, p. 63, 13–16: "Et primo quidem eos non falso accusari quod prohibeant bona opera apertissime ex eorum impiis verbis docuimus articulo sexto, quae brevitatis studio volumus habere pro repetitis."
44. Erwin Iserloh, *Johannes Eck,* p. 66.
45. *Enchiridion Locorum communium aduersus Lutheranos, Ioanne Eckio authore.* Ab authore iam sexto recognitum: & prioribus locis abunde locupletatis, sex locis auctius prodit.... Excusum Ingolstadii: Apianus, 1529 (hereafter referred to as *EE*), fol. 35a–36a. The 1530 German edition of *EE,* fol. 46b: "Sihe Paulus [Gal. 5:6] will not all gelauben gelten lassenn, allain den gutthettigen unnd liebhabenden glauben." Erwin Iserloh, ed., *Enchiridion: Handbüchlin gemainer stell und Artickel der jetzt schwebenden Neuwen leeren: Faksimile-Druck der Ausgabe Augsburg 1533, Corpus Catholicorum,* 35 (Münster: Aschendorff, 1980) p. 26. *FEE,* p. 98. F. L. Battles, trans., *Enchiridion of Commonplaces of John Eck Against Luther and other Enemies of the Church,* 2nd ed. (Grand Rapids: Calvin Theological Seminary, 1978), pp. 59–60.
46. Robert Jenson, "On Recognizing the Augsburg Confession," *The Role of the Augsburg Confession: Catholic and Lutheran Views,* ed. Joseph A. Burgess (Philadelphia: Fortress, 1980), p. 158 (cf. p. 165, note 20): "The formula *fides caritate formata* adds an additional quality in the believer: love." And *love,* as Jenson adequately holds, in fact means *doing works* that are required. Cf. Leif Grane, *Die Confessio,* pp. 60–61.
47. *EE,* fol. 36b–37a. Iserloh, ed., *Enchiridion,* p. 27. *FEE,* p. 100. Battles, trans., *Enchiridion,* p. 61. Erwin Iserloh, *CAC,* p. 375, cf. *Johannes Eck,* p. 69, still holds that the Lutheran position consisted in attributing justification to "loving, benificent faith," which would mean that loving (with the love provided by the Holy Spirit) is that which is justifying about faith. Righteousness then would still consist in fulfillment of God's requirements, which, according to the Reformers, is but *iustitia legis* and falls short of the *iustitia evangelii.*
48. See above, note 30, cf. *RC,* IV, pp. 17, 12–18, 1.
49. Melanchthon, Art. XX of the AC. Tappert, pp. 41–42.
50. This will become evident in the analysis of Art. IV, ch. 5 below. See also Robert Jenson, "On Recognizing the Augsburg Confession," *The Role of the Augsburg Confession,* pp. 158–62, cf. note 47 above.
51. This view has been defended tenaciously by Erwin Iserloh, *Johannes Eck,* p. 69: "So ist der Unterschied zwischen der CA und der Confutatio ein bloss verbaler und nicht einer in der Sache." *CCA,* p. 374: "Ist die Kontroverse bezüglich Glaube und Liebe im Prozess der Rechtfertigung nicht lediglich eine verbale?"

Chapter 5

1. Cf. Wilhelm Maurer, "Studien über Melanchthons Anteil an der Entstehung der Confessio Augustana," *Archiv für Reformationsgeschichte,* LI (1960), 167–72. Hereafter this periodical will be referred to as *ARG.*
2. The objections raised by Ritschl and Harnack against the reception of the

ancient dogmas on God and Christ by the Reformation and against the interpretation of Christ's work in terms of satisfaction rendered to God have been diluted in principle, but still determine the stand of contemporary theologians. For a report on the discussion of the matter by the Theological Committee of the Lutheran Federation between the Minneapolis and the Helsinki Assemblies see Jörg Rothermundt, "Rechtfertigungsgespräch 1958–1963: Ein Forschungsbericht über die Studienarbeit im Lutherischen Weltbund," *Rechtfertigung heute: Studien und Berichte,* Beiheft zur *Lutherischen Rundschau* (Stuttgart: Kreuz, 1965), pp. 39–40. According to Fritz Hoffmann, "Theologische-systematische Strukturen in der Confessio Augustana: Ihre Bedeutung für das ökumenische Gespräch," *Die Confessio Augustana im ökumenischen Gespräch,* ed. Fritz Hoffmann and Ulrich Kühn (Berlin: Evangelische Verlagsanstalt, 1980), p. 72, note 13, Neo-Protestantism still regards the ancient dogmas as peripheral to Reformation theology allegedly concentrated on the Gospel of justification by grace. In view of the presence of those objections in contemporary theologies, Karl Lehmann and Horst Georg Pöhlmann, "Gott, Jesus Christus—Wiederkunft Christi," *Confessio Augustana Bekenntnis des einen Glaubens: Gemeinsame Untersuchung lutherischer und katholischer Theologen,* ed. Harding Meyer and Heinz Schütte (Paderborn: Bonifacius; Frankfurt am Main: O. Lembeck, 1980), p. 75, cf. pp. 60–61 and 67, inquire whether in the estimation of both the Lutheran and the Catholic churches the Christian faith still stands or falls with the fundamental decisions on Christ and the Trinity. Hereafter referred to as *Gemeinsame Untersuchung.* The translation in *Confessing One Faith: A Joint Commentary on the Augsburg Confession by Lutheran and Catholic Theologians,* ed. George W. Forell and James F. McCue (Minneapolis: Augsburg, 1982), p. 84, toned down the question. Hereafter referred to as *Joint Commentary.*

3. Regin Prenter, *Das Bekenntnis von Augsburg: Eine Auslegung* (Erlangen: Martin-Luther-Verlag, 1980), pp. 62–63. Leif Grane, *Die Confessio Augustana: Einführung in die Hauptgedanken der lutherischen Reformation* (Göttingen: Vandenhoeck & Ruprecht, 1970), p. 23: In the Reformers' estimation denying the divinity of the Son and of the Holy Spirit amounted to giving up the Gospel itself. Wilhelm Breuning, "Christologie und Rechtfertigung in der Lehre der römisch-katholischen Kirche und der gegenwärtigen ökumenischen Diskussion," *Zur bleibenden Aktualität des Augsburger Bekenntnisses,* Fuldaer Hefte, 25 (Hamburg: Lutherisches Verlagshaus, 1981), p. 117: Christ's being *homoousios* with the Father is the basis of our salvation. Cf. p. 116: Theological discourse from the Apostles' Creed to the Council of Trent was concerned with explaining that salvation can come from God only; all the efforts to understand Jesus Christ "from below" and to suppress the question of His identity with God have failed.

4. Regin Prenter, *Das Bekenntnis,* p. 65. Leif Grane, *Die Confessio,* pp. 33–36. Jürgen Lorz, ed., *Das Augsburgische Bekenntnis: Studienausgabe* (Göttingen: Vandenhoeck & Ruprecht, 1980), p. 19, note 14.

5. Regin Prenter, *Das Bekenntnis,* p. 74. Leif Grane, *Die Confessio,* p. 32: "Only Christ, true God and true man, can expiate sin. This consequence is drawn from the Christological dogma [by the Reformers]." Cf. p. 36: Only if one teaches correctly on Christ's person can he teach correctly about His work. Peter Brunner, "Die Notwendigkeit des neuen Gehorsams nach dem Augsburgischen Bekenntnis," *Kerygma und Dogma,* VII (1961), 276, underscores

THE DOCTRINE OF FAITH

the teleological orientation of AC III as he speaks of a *heilsteleologisches ut finale* which characterizes the formulation of the text.

6. Philipp Melanchthon and Martin Luther, *WA*, XXVI, 203, 17–20; *LW*, 40, 276. Cf. Peter Brunner, "Die Notwendigkeit," *Kerygma und Dogma*, VII, 272.

7. Regin Prenter, *Das Bekenntnis*, pp. 74–75. The same point is made by Gottfried Voigt, "Christologie und Rechtfertigung nach dem Augsburgischen Bekenntnis," *Zur bleibenden Aktualität*, p. 40. See also Luther's "Great Confession," as well as the Schwabach and the Marburg Articles: The subject of the reconciling is always the Son of God. See above, ch. 3.

8. Cf. AC, Latin text, XV, 3; XXIV, 22; XXVI, 21; XXVIII, 41 and 50.

9. AC, Latin text, XX, 9; III, 3. The German text, less technical, uses *versöhnen* for both Christ's reconciling and man's appeasing, respectively *reconciliare* and *placare*.

10. *LW*, 37, 362, 364 (*WA*, XXVI, 502, 14–15; 504, 20–22). The expression *gnaden stuel*, propitiation or mercy seat, refers to Rom. 3:25. Cf. the *Instructions for Visitors*, *WA*, XXVI, 224, 29 (*LW*, 40, 300): "Christus Ihesus ist allein der mitler, der uns vertrit" (1 John 2:1, Rom. 8:34). AC, XXI, 2: "unum Christum nobis proponit [scriptura] mediatorem, propitiatorium, pontificem et intercessorem"; "[Christus ist] der einige Heiland, der einig oberst Priester, Gnadenstuhl und Fursprech fur Gott, Rom. 8." The insight into Christ's present activity is preserved by Jo. Benedictus Carpzov, *Isagoge in libros ecclesiarum lutheranarum symbolicos*, ed. Jo. Benedictus Carpzov Filium (Lipsiae: J. Wittgau, 1665), p. 205: "Ideo ... iustificamur, quia Christus *nostri vice* Obedientiam praestitit Deo [causa meritoria] et intercessione sua movet Deum, ut iustitiam hanc apprehensam fide nobis imputet [causa impulsiva]."

11. AC, XXVI, 33: "mereri remissionem peccatorum"; "Gnad verdienen." XXVIII, 35: "mereri iustificari"; "Gnad erlangen." XXVIII, 53: "Gnad erlangen" without correspondence in the Latin text. XXVII, 38: "mereri gratiam et iustificationem." XXVI, 21: "mereri gratiam." XV, 3–4; XX, 21; XXVI, 1 and 6: "promereri gratiam." Heiko A. Oberman suggested that the latter be rendered "merit fully," "Das tridentinische Rechtfertigungsdekret im Lichte Spätmittelalterlicher Theologie," *Zeitschrift für Theologie und Kirche*, LXI (1964), 263, 268, 273, 278.

12. Pars. 21, 25, 26.

13. Par. 2; Tappert, p. 30.

14. Cf. also AC, XX, 9 and 28. Leif Grane, *Die Confessio*, p. 38: "The reconciliation is not only the 'objective' basis of justification, but is identical with it inasmuch as the righteousness which is imparted to man can be no other except Christ's."

15. Document "B," *BS*, p. 78, 36–38. *Instructions for Visitors*, *WA*, XXVI, 203, 24–26; *LW*, 40, 276. Visitation Articles, *CR*, XXVI, 11, cf. note 26. Luther's "Great Confession," *WA*, XXVI, 505, 31–37; *LW*, 37, 366. See also above, ch. 3.

16. See Melanchthon's "Scholia" on Col. 2:10b, *Melanchthons Werke in Auswahl [Studienausgabe]*, ed. Robert Stupperich (hereafter referred to as *MSA*), IV (Gütersloh: G. Mohn, 1963), 246, 26–247, 13: "Now then he presents the definition [of Christian righteousness] and explains what Christ accomplishes in the believer, and thus he discerns two parts in Christian righteousness, *mortificatio* and *vivificatio*. *Vivificatio* consists in that the conscience is raised

up through faith or gets confidence (*fiducia*) and consolation by believing that God has forgiven sins because of Christ. As Christ consoles the heart in this way, He brings along eternal life, as He says: 'Whoever believes in Me shall not die.' He brings along other gifts of the Spirit: charity, humility, chastity." Cf. *MSA*, IV, 249, 12–14, where *vivificatio* is said to comprise two things, namely, the forgiveness of sins or grace and the gift of the Holy Spirit or by the Spirit. In AC, V, 2, and XVIII, 3, the creation of faith is explicitly attributed to the Holy Spirit.

17. Document "B," *BS*, p. 79, 29–30. Melanchthon, *Dispositio orationis, in Epistola Pauli ad Romanos* (Wittembergae: G. Rhau, MDXXX), fol. Bvi; *CR*, XV, 451, on Rom. 3:21: "Paul teaches that Christ did not come to bring a law for us to merit righteousness through our works, but that He came in order to justify the believers freely, without our works. . . . Paul here openly distinguishes the Law from the Gospel and teaches that Christ brings righteousness freely (*gratis*), without our merits, that Christ is not a lawgiver, but the Redeemer. The Law was given through Moses, but the forgiveness of sins and the Holy Spirit are given through Christ." Cf. fol. Giv (*CR*, XV, 482): "Christ came not to bring a law, but to give righteousness and the Holy Spirit freely to the believers, and the Gospel is properly this teaching concerning justification (*haec de iustificatione doctrina*)." Eck's position as expressed in the Articles was that the Gospel is a new law and that its precepts must be kept. See above, ch. 4, note 27. The *Dispositio* will hereafter be referred to as *DOR*.

18. *DOR*, fol. Avi (CR, XV, 445): "nisi hoc loco [de iustitia fidei] cognito, non potest intelligi, cur venerit Christus." Cf. the conclusion, fol. Giv (*CR*, XV, 482): "Meminerit autem lector, hunc [quod iustificemur fide, non operibus nostris] esse praecipuum Evangelii locum, sine quo intelligi non potest, cur venerit Christus." Ernst Kinder, "Christus und der Rechtfertigungsglaube," *Evangelisch-Lutherische Kirchenzeitung*, VI (31. Januar 1952), 17c: The Lutheran Confessions view justification as embedded in Christology; it consists in the existential application of the ancient Christology, which is assumed everywhere. Regin Prenter, *Das Bekenntnis*, p. 78: Without the content of Arts. I–III the discourse of justification in Arts. IV–VI becomes meaningless and faith is left without content, for its only content is the triune God with His work. Karl Lehmann and Horst G. Pöhlmann in *Gemeinsame Untersuchung*, pp. 61–62: The AC stands or falls with Art. IV, but this article stands or falls with Art. III and its relation to Art. I. Cf. *Joint Commentary*, p. 74.

Chapter 6

1. According to Gerhard Müller and Vinzenz Pfnür, "Rechtfertigung—Glaube—Werke," *Confessio Augustana Bekenntnis des einen Glaubens: Gemeinsame Untersuchung lutherischer und katholischer Theologen* (Paderborn: Bonifacius; Frankfurt am Main: O. Lembeck, 1980), p. 113, trans. James L. Schaaf, "Justification—Faith—Works," *Confessing One Faith: A Joint Commentary on the Augsburg Confession by Lutheran and Catholic Theologians* (Minneapolis: Augsburg, 1982), p. 123, henceforth referred to as *Gemeinsame Untersuchung* and *Joint Commentary*, respectively, the negative assertion in Art. IV is aimed at "the semi-pelagianism of late Scholasticism" which Luther "presumes to have found in some nominalist theologians" and held responsible for

THE DOCTRINE OF FAITH

anomalies in the teaching and practice of the church. Holsten Fagerberg, "Die Rechtfertigungslehre in Confessio Augustana und Apologie," *Confessio Augustana und Confutatio: Der Augsburger Reichstag und die Einheit der Kirche*, ed. Erwin Iserloh (Münster Westfalen: Aschendorff, 1980), p. 331, also whitewashes the stand of the controversialists as he remarks that Melanchthon's critique of their understanding of *meritum* was beside the point, for he strikes at the merits derived from man's own doing, while they were upholding, on the basis of tradition, especially of St. Augustine, the merits which derive from God's grace. In our estimation these authors fail to see that, rather than discussing how much or how little is to be attributed to grace and human will, the Reformers were raising a question of principle: Is justification a matter of fulfilling divine requirements with no matter how much divine help, or is it a question of grasping a radically different and new kind of righteousness, the *iustitia evangelii* or *fidei?* The work edited by Iserloh will be referred to as *CAC*.

2. *BS*, p. 57, lines 42–43, cf. lines 11–13.
3. AC, XX, 10; XXVI, 4; XXVIII, 36. Cf. AC, XXIV, 24–25 (Latin text), *BS*, p. 93, 23–28: The opinions concerning the Mass which imply that Christ did not make satisfaction for all sins damage "the glory of Christ's passion."
4. AC, XXIV, 30–31. The *beneficia* are made known through the Gospel, as Melanchthon's *Scholia* on Col. 1:12 indicate: "Est autem evangelium sermo, quo beneficia, quae per Christum donata sunt, recitantur." See "Scholia in Epistolam Pauli ad Colossenses 1527," ed. Robert Stupperich, *Melanchthons Werke in Auswahl [Studienausgabe]*, IV (Gütersloh: G. Mohn, 1963), 220, 11–13. Hereafter referred to as *MSA*.
5. This is recognized also by Martin Seils, "Zu einigen Problemen der Interpretation von Artikel IV der Confessio Augustana in der Anerkennungsdebatte," *Die Confessio Augustana im ökumenischen Gespräch*, ed. Fritz Hoffmann and Ulrich Kühn (Berlin: Evangelische Verlagsanstalt, 1980), p. 157, as well as by Müller and Pfnür in *Gemeinsame Untersuchung*, p. 144, note 34.
6. Melanchthon, *Dispositio orationis, in Epistola Pauli ad Romanos* (Wittembergae: G. Rhau, [MC]XXX), fol. Avi. Hereafter referred to as *DOR*. Reprinted in *CR*, XV, 445. The Latin reads: "qua caro se iustificat aut iustam efficit."
7. *CR*, XXVI, 78–81.
8. Melanchthon's letter to Cordatus, 15 April 1537, *CR*, III, 344.
9. As Martin Seils, "Zu einigen Problemen," *Die Confessio Augustana*, p. 157, correctly remarks, *coram Deo* in AC, IV, 1, corresponds to *coram ipso* in AC, IV, 3: Faith makes righteous and is counted as righteousness before the one and same God who is reconciled by Christ, the Mediator.
10. *DOR*, fol. Gv–vi, Avii–viii (*CR*, XV, 483, 446). See also the "definition of Christian righteousness" which includes in its third dependent clause some of the elements which reappear in AC, IV, fol. Bv (*CR*, XV, 451): "Righteousness is to believe that we are received into the Father's grace because of Christ, that Christ is the Redeemer and Propitiation, that we are justified gratis because of Him, without our merits, if we believe." The qualification, "if we believe," evidently refers back to the preceding object clauses.
11. Cf. the quotation in the preceding note and Melanchthon's preface to the *Scholia* on the Letter to the Colossians, *MSA*, IV, 212, 2–5: Paul teaches that

NOTES

justification takes place not because of any merits of ours, but through faith, if we believe that our sins are forgiven us *gratis* because of Christ, as Isaiah wrote (ch. 53), "Notitia eius iustificabit multos." The highest comfort for consciences is to know "that God gives us the forgiveness of sins *gratis* and justifies us *gratis.*"

12. See above, ch. 3, notes 21 (Visitation Articles) and 30 (Schwabach Articles). Cf. the *editio princeps, BS,* p. 57, 46–50: "umb Christus willen aus Gnaden durch den Glauben, so das Gewissen . . . gläubet, daß . . . umb Christus willen. . . ."

13. As Martin Seils, "Zu einigen Problemen," *Die Confessio Augustana,* pp. 157–58, questions Pfnür's methodological procedure, he suggests that the main sentence of Art. IV should have been analyzed first of all in view of the *Nebensatz,* "cum credunt se in gratiam recipi et peccata remitti." Müller and Pfnür did not take the explicative sentence into consideration in *Gemeinsame Untersuchung,* pp. 116–19, cf. *Joint Commentary,* pp. 125–27. The outcome is a misreading of the text of Art. IV.

14. *BS,* p. 58, 8–10. In "B," *BS,* p. 79, 27–31, the "object" of faith is spelled out: "that He has taken away our sins and that He came for the sole purpose of satisfying for our sins, and to forgive sins and give eternal life and all divine gifts, as He declares, John 3. . . ."

15. AC, XII, 7; XX, 6; XXVI, 5; XXVII, 42 and 44 (*rechtfertig werden*).

16. AC, II, 3; XX, 6; XXVI, 41; XXVII, 48. Cf. AC, XXVII, 61–62, *rechtfertigen und frumb machen.* The only instance in which the expression is used to describe the Lutheran position is AC, XXVII, 43. But see also AC, V, 2–3.

17. Pars. 36, 38, 12, and 16, respectively.

18. AC, XXVI, 4; XXVII, 38, 48; XXVIII, 37, 62, 64.

19. *LW,* 37, 366; *WA,* XXVI, 505, 41–506, 3.

20. AC, XXVIII, 9. Cf. the Latin text, *BS,* p. 122, 2–4: "Haec [res aeternae, iustitia aeterna, spiritus sanctus, vita aeterna] non possunt contingere nisi per ministerium verbi et sacramentorum. . . ." Rom. 1:16; Ps. 119:50.

21. The *argumentum ex natura relativorum ductum* reads in the analysis of Rom. 4:13–14, *DOR,* fol. Ciii (*CR,* XV, 455): "Omnis promissio fide accipitur. Iustitia est promissa. Ergo iustitia est fide accipienda."

22. Martin Seils, "Zu einigen Problemen," *Die Confessio Augustana,* p. 158, also calls attention to the fact that "in the Augsburg Confession *iustificari* is explained by *in gratiam recipi* and by *peccata remitti.*" In his estimation Pfnür's analysis failed to do justice to the importance of this fact.

23. AC, II, 3, *propriis viribus rationis;* XX, 6, *fide et operibus;* XXVII, 42, *votis;* XXVII, 44, *per vota et per observationes suas;* XXVIII, 35–36, *per observationem traditionum.*

24. AC, XXVII, 48, 61–62; cf. AC, XXVII, 43–44.

25. AC, V, 3; XXVII, 43, *wellen rechtfertig werden.*

26. It is remarkable that the AC refrains from saying that "faith justifies." The formulation in XX, 6, German text, "faith and works make us righteous before God," describes the opponents' teaching (Tappert, p. 42).

27. AC, XXIV, 28; XXVIII, 35–36; IV, 1–2; cf. VI, 1; XXVII, 39; and XXVIII, 50, where *Gnade verdienen* corresponds to *iustificationem (pro)mereri.*

THE DOCTRINE OF FAITH

28. AC, IV, 2: "[Iustificantur homines] cum credunt se in gratiam recipi et peccata remitti propter Christum." AC, V, 3: "[Iustificat Deus] hos, qui credunt se propter Christum in gratiam recipi." AC, IX, 2: "pueri ... per baptismum oblati Deo recipiuntur in gratiam Dei." AC, XX, 9: "hanc [remissionem peccatorum et gratiam] tantum fide consequimur, credentes, quod propter Christum recipiamur in gratiam." AC, XXVI, 5: "[Ostendit Paulus] iustitiam christianam ... esse ... fidem, quae credit nos propter Christum recipi in gratiam." AC, XXVII, 37; "Et Paulus ubique docet ... contingere eam [iustitiam] per fidem credentibus, se recipi in gratiam a Deo propter Christum."
29. AC, IX, 2. Cf. the *Instructions for Visitors, WA,* XXVI, 213, 1–3: "das Gott ... sich des kindes annemen [wil] "; XXVI, 213, 7–9: "die Tauffe [bedeutet] nicht allein ... das Gott die kindheit wölle annemen, sondern das gantze leben." Cf. also Marburg article XIV (*BS,* p. 63, 30–31; *LW,* 38, 88).
30. *CR,* XXVI, 21. *WA,* XXX, iii, 88, 8–9 (*BS,* p. 57, 26–27). Parallelism between *recepti in gratiam* and *iustificati* is established in *DOR,* fol. Cv–vi (*CR,* XV, 457), on Rom. 5:8-10: "Si recepti sumus in gratiam, cum adhuc peccatores essemus, quanto magis iustificati, nunc servabimur?" Cf. the Marburg article VII, *WA,* XXX, iii, 164, 1–9 (*BS,* p. 57, 36–39); *LW,* 38, 86.
31. *DOR,* fol. Av (*CR,* XV, 443–44). *CR,* XXVI, 18. Philipp Melanchthon, *Loci communes,* 1521 (*MSA,* II, i, 106, 8–9).
32. *DOR,* fol. Cvii (*CR,* XV, 458–59). Cf. above, ch. 4, note 32, and *Scholia* on Col. 1:2, *MSA,* IV, 213, 32–33: "Gratia significat simpliciter remissionem peccatorum seu favorem Dei."
33. *Loci communes, MSA,* II, i, 104, 32–34; 105, 14–15, 19–20. Melanchthon also stresses that along with grace God gives His *donum per gratiam,* the Holy Spirit, who produces His works—faith, peace, joy, love. According to Martin Seils, "Zu einigen Problemen," *Die Confessio Augustana,* p. 159, Melanchthon had learned from Luther that the only way to affirm the gift character of grace was to understand it, on the basis of Scripture, as favor (*Gunst*). In his estimation this point is neglected in Pfnür's *Einig in der Rechtfertigungslehre?* (Wiesbaden: F. Steiner, 1970), hereafter referred to as *Einig,* with the result that *per fidem* is understood as "in us," while the *extra nos* of the Reformers' understanding of grace and justification is almost totally explained away.
34. *BS,* p. 57, 27: "sollen zue Gnaden genommen und Kinder sein in seinem Reich," etc.; AC, IV, 2; *BS,* p. 56, 11–13.
35. *CR,* XXVI, 20–21.
36. Jo. Benedictus Carpzov, *Isagoge in libros ecclesiarum lutheranarum symbolicos,* ed. Jo. Benedictus Carpzov Filium (Lipsiae: J. Wittgau, 1666), p. 205, quoted above, ch. 5, note 10.
37. The expression *Glaube an Gott* appears in AC, II, 1, and XXVI, 4; *Zuversicht zu Gott,* in XX, 25–26; the verbal form *glauben an Gott,* in XVIII, 2. Similarly, *Glaube an Christum* is found in AC, VI, 1, XV, 3, XX, 5, XXVI, 4, and the verbal form *glauben an Christum,* in XXVI, 4. Cf. *credentes in ipsum* in III, 4, and *fides in Christum* in XXIV, 28.
38. *CR,* XXVI, 18; *WA,* XXVI, 220, 21–24; 221, 2–4; *LW,* 40, 297.
39. Tappert, p. 62. See also the Latin text in AC, XXVI, 4, and XXVII, 37, as well as the passages with *credere* and object clause quoted above, note 28.
40. *DOR,* fol. Civ (*CR,* XV, 456): The apostle praises Abraham's faith "ut in hac

imagine ostendat, quomodo fides versetur circa res positas extra conspectum rationis, et supra naturam." See also Melanchthon's *Annotationes in Evangelium Matthaei iam recens in gratiam studiosorum editae,* 1523 (*MSA,* IV, 207, 20–21): "Fidei vocabulum est correlativum ad promissiones Christi sive de Christo, ut patris ad filium, Domini ad servum." Elsewhere (IV, 206, 9–21) faith is said to be "ascensus, quo humanus animus complectitur divinam promissionem" and "se reicere in Deum." Carpzov, *Isagoge,* p. 205, also stresses that faith is *organum apprehensivum* correlated to its "object" and therefore called *apodochē* in 1 Tim. 1:15 and expressed by such verbs as *lambanein* and *katalambanein* in John 1:5, 11, 12.

41. *CR,* XXVI, 7, note 4: "quomodo doceant homines iustificari." Cf. above, ch. 3, note 17.
42. *DOR,* fol. Avi; *CR,* XV, 445.
43. *CR,* XXVII, 464–65. Emphasis added. The same point is made in Melanchthon's letter to Brenz, 19 February 1531, as he explains why justification must be attributed to faith: "because of Christ, the Propitiator, it is necessary to hold that it is by faith that we are justified." See *CR,* II, 501–02, and also Martin Greschat, *Melanchthon neben Luther,* ed. Robert Stupperich (Witten: Luther-Verlag, 1965), pp. 133–34. It should be observed that the expression *modum iustificationis* as used by Melanchthon denotes justification *fide in Christum,* which is overlooked by scholars who seek the specifically Lutheran *modum* only, if not exclusively, in the predicate *iustificari.*
44. Marburg article V (*LW,* 38, 86), cf. VII, *WA,* XXX, iii, 162, 14–163, 2, and 164; cf. *BS,* p. 57, 32–34, 39–41. Schwabach article V, *WA,* XXX, iii, 88, 3–6; cf. *BS,* p. 57, 20–24. "Great Confession," *WA,* XXVI, 504, 17–22; *LW,* 57, 364. The Reformers, however, do not explain "how justification happens" in the sense of describing a justification *process.* In this respect they definitely supersede medieval tradition. This tradition, however, lives on in some contemporary interpretations.
45. Tappert, p. 30, cf. p. 42, renders both the Latin and the German with "when we/they believe that ... " Heinrich Bornkamm, *Das Augsburger Bekenntnis* (Hamburg: Furche, 1965), p. 18, renders: "wenn sie gewiß sind, daß ... " Cf. p. 27: "nämlich wenn wir darauf vertrauen, daß ... " Leonhard Fendt, *Der Wille der Reformation im Augsburgischen Bekenntnis* (Leipzig: H. G. Wallmann, 1929), p. 35, translates: "(nämlich) wenn sie gewiß sind, daß ... " Cf. p. 85: "(nämlich) wenn wir vertrauen, daß ... " Karl Thieme, *Die Augsburgische Konfession und Luthers Katechismen auf theologische Gegenwartswerte untersucht* (Giessen: A. Töpelmann, 1930), pp. 76–96, disagrees with Karl Holl's proposition that *cum credunt* denotes the chronological and factual coincidence of "being justified" and "believing," which implies that from God's perspective justification is identical with the conferral of faith. He counters that *cum credunt* indicates faith as the condition for the fulfillment and realization of justification. He grants that justification is identical with the creation of faith, which brings to completion God's absolving action, but insists that other sources besides Art. IV must be taken into consideration. In our estimation *both* authors failed to perceive the specific function of the appositive *cum credunt* in the thrust of Art. IV. Carpzov, *Isagoge,* p. 207, reads *cum credunt* as referring to *fides specialis,* which is basically correct, in our understanding, but does not meet Melanchthon's full concern.

46. The German text of AC, XXVI, 4, however, does not detail the "object" as it states: "daß Glauben an Christum hoch und weit uber alle Werk zu setzen sei."
47. This traditional view underlies AC, XX, 23–26, as well as the refutation of the fifth Schwabach article in the "Christenlich Underricht," *WA*, XXX, iii, 189.
48. Such influential authors as Holsten Fagerberg, Erwin Iserloh, and Vinzenz Pfnür seem to have difficulty in recognizing and/or spelling out this basic point, as their discussion at the 1979 symposium of the Society for the Edition of the *Corpus Catholicorum* indicates. This explains why they are able to say that the divergence between Melanchthon and Eck at Augsburg was not substantial but ultimately concerned terminological peculiarities on both sides. See *CAC*, pp. 375–88; on Iserloh's stand see also ch. 4, notes 47 and 51, above.
49. This proposition is made and documented by Hans Engelland in *Melanchthon, Glauben und Handeln, Forschungen zur Geschichte und Lehre des Protestantismus*, vierte Reihe, Band I (München: Chr. Kaiser, 1931), pp. 135–36, 141: To affirm that faith alone justifies is to hold that justification is *propter Christum* alone, for faith justifies not because it is a good work or quality in man, but because it takes hold of the promise of forgiveness in Christ.
50. Jörg Rothermundt, "Rechtfertigungsgespräch 1958–1963: Ein Forschungsbericht über die Studienarbeit im Lutherischen Weltbund," *Rechtfertigung heute: Studien und Berichte*, Beiheft zur *Lutherischen Rundschau* (Stuttgart: Kreuz, 1965), p. 26, reports the views of J. Roloff, "Die Schriftverwendung in Apologie IV," published in *Lutherische Rundschau*, XI (1961), 56–73, which can be regarded as representative: "The Apology conceives justification as comfort for terrified consciences and therefore renders it psychological and subjective in a certain sense...." Discerning consideration of Ap, IV, 118, in its argumentative context is apt to restore the proper perspective, as Hans Engelland, *Melanchthon, Glauben und Handeln*, p. 133, also points out.
51. Melanchthon, "Disputatio, quare fide iustificemur, non dilectione," Thesis 37, ed. Johannes Haussleiter, "Melanchthons *Loci praecipui* und Thesen über die Rechtfertigung aus dem Jahre 1531," *Abhandlungen Alexander von Oettingen zum siebenzigsten Geburtstag gewidmet von Freunden und Schülern* (München: C. H. Beck, 1898), p. 254: After saying in Thesis 36 what is meant with *sola fides iustificat*, Melanchthon stresses in Thesis 37 that in Christ, through faith, consciences have a sure consolation and know how to act and which works please God, and that they receive the Holy Spirit through Christ by faith in order to be able to act properly. Cf. *CR*, XII, 449.
52. In a revealing statement in Art. IV of the German Apology, *BS*, p. 220, 46–47, Melanchthon spells out that the concept of faith is indeed the turning point of the controversy: It is easy to respond to the opponents' Scholastic arguments if one knows what faith is, *wenn man weiß, was Glauben ist*.
53. Franz Pieper, *Christliche Dogmatik*, II (St. Louis: Concordia, 1917), 522, on the basis of the Formula of Concord: Inasmuch as it justifies, faith deals with an object placed outside of man; therefore this faith which connects with the justifying object consists in stepping outside of oneself, it is *ein "aus sich selbst Herausgehen," ein "aus sich selbst Herausfahren."* Martin Seils, "Zu einigen Problemen," *Die Confessio Augustana*, p. 155: For ears attuned to the Reformation the expressions *gratis* and *propter Christum* entail an unrevisable *extra nos*, which in Pfnür's analysis recedes and disappears. One should,

however, take into consideration Bengt Hägglund's concerns regarding the reception of Luther's stand by the Formula of Concord. See his "Die Rezeption Luthers in der Konkordienformel," *Luther und die Bekenntnisschriften,* Veröffentlichungen der Luther-Akademie Ratzeburg, 2 (Erlangen: Martin Luther-Verlag, 1981), especially p. 114: Faith means integration with Christ in the sense that man is placed outside of himself and becomes one with Christ; it is more than a mere instrument.

54. Holsten Fagerberg, "Die Rechtfertigungslehre," *CAC,* pp. 339–40, for instance: "Wherever the promise is, there is life-giving forgiveness of sins, which as renovation constitutes the basis for the forensic reckoning righteous." Gerhard Müller and Vinzenz Pfnür in *Gemeinsame Untersuchung,* p. 124, which refers to Pfnür's *Einig,* pp. 164–65: "To be made righteous, to be reborn anew means to stand in living communion with God." Cf. *Gemeinsame Untersuchung,* p. 125: The expression *iustum effici* denotes "regeneration by Word and Sacrament ... which occurs in man in and through faith." The authors unfortunately did not explicate the sentence on pp. 125–26, that "the sinner is made righteous through faith inasmuch as the happy exchange between him and Christ takes place," which could aptly express the Lutheran position. See also *Joint Commentary,* pp. 130–32.
55. This appropriate observation made by Franz Pieper, *Christliche Dogmatik,* II, 517, seems to apply very well to the studies under consideration.
56. Marburg Articles, *BS,* p. 57, 36–37. Schwabach Articles, ibid., lines 24–31.
57. *DOR,* fol. Avi and Bvi; *CR,* XV, 445 and 451.
58. *DOR,* fol. Fv; *CR,* XV, 476–77.
59. *MSA,* IV, 244, 13–28.
60. *MSA,* II, i, 106, 21–23, 4–6.
61. Martin Luther, "Vorrede auff die Epistel S. Pauli an die Römer," *Die gantze Heilige Schrifft Deudsch. Wittenberg 1545: Letzte zu Luthers Lebzeiten erschienene Ausgabe,* ed. Hans Volz (Herrsching: M. Pawlack, n.d.), p. 2257. Cf. *LW,* 35, 369–70, although the translation is defective.
62. Ibid., pp. 2259 and 371 respectively. The *LW* translation is defective.
63. As they discuss Art. IV, 3, in sections 2.3.5. and 2.4.3. of their joint essay in *Gemeinsame Untersuchung,* Gerhard Müller and Vinzenz Pfnür declare on pp. 120–21 that the *imputatio* relies on (*hat ihren Grund in*) the relationship with God "which is characterized by the pledge of grace and by faith," and that faith lives of the promise in the sense that "the believer knows that he is accepted by God and that fellowship with God (*Gottesgemeinschaft*) was established *gratis propter Christum.*" On p. 126 they affirm that for Luther, too, fellowship with Christ (*Christusgemeinschaft*) is the presupposition of *reputatio,* of being reckoned righteous. These rather cautious formulations do not emphasize that the believer is reckoned righteous because of Christ *and therefore because of faith,* since the only way of regarding Christ as one's Righteousness is *believing in Him* as "the Lord, our Righteousness." Holsten Fagerberg, "Die Rechtfertigungslehre," *CAC,* while declaring on p. 339 that "the forensic *iustos reputari* occurs because of the righteousness which man received in faith," affirms on p. 338 that *regeneratio* as understood by the Apology constitutes the basis for *pronuntiatio.* (See also the passage quoted above, note 54). As Martin Seils, "Zu einigen Problemen," *Die Confessio Au-*

gustana, pp. 159–60, observed, these interpretations tend to play down the *extra nos* and highlight the *in nobis* of Christian righteousness. Compare for the sake of contrast Leif Grane's position in *Die Confessio Augustana* (Göttingen: Vandenhoeck & Ruprecht, 1970), p. 39: "When it is said that faith is counted as righteousness, it is not meant that faith is something in itself, but that the only righteousness in relation to God which one can think of, namely Christ's righteousness, is apprehended by faith." But see also p. 41, where the *extra nos* of the *imputatio* is viewed as renovation of the whole person in the sense that he has his righteousness in Christ alone.

64. See above, the quotation documented by note 42, *DOR*, fol. Avi; CR, XV, 445.
65. Luther, postscript on Melanchthon's letter to Brenz, middle of May 1531, *WA Br*, VI, 100—01.
66. The formulation in the *editio princeps*, BS, p. 57, 50–51, "Whoever truly believes, then, he obtains forgiveness of sins, becomes acceptable to God, and is reckoned righteous before God on account of Christ. Romans 3 and 4," indicates with sufficient clarity how Melanchthon wants AC, IV, 3, to be understood. The believer is reckoned righteous *because of Christ* (and therefore because of faith), just as he was accepted and absolved *because of Christ* (and therefore through faith).
67. Hans Engelland, *Melanchthon, Glauben und Handeln*, p. 565: "Faith alone as correlated to the promise because of Christ is the focal point of the Reformation conception."
68. On why the correlation of faith and Word is fundamental in the Lutheran view of justification see Jörg Rothermund's report on Regin Prenter's "Dogmatische Bemerkungen" in "Rechtfertigungsgespräch 1958–1963," *Rechtfertigung heute* (Stuttgart: Kreuz, 1965), p. 32: Our justification requires both Christ's reconciliation and the divine Word of the Gospel, which on God's authority gives me Christ as my righteousness; without the Gospel, Christ's reconciliation would be useless to me. Here Prenter echoes Luther's "Great Confession." See *LW*, 37, 366; *WA*, XXVI, 506, 3–9.
69. This remains a problem even today, as one can gather from Reinhold Weier, "Die Erlösungslehre der Reformatoren: Philipp Melanchthon," *Handbuch der Dogmengeschichte*, ed. Michael Schmaus, III, fascicle 2c (Freiburg, etc.: Herder, 1972), pp. 13–20, who does not explicitly discuss the correlation Christ/promise—faith.
70. Melanchthon, "Disputatio, quare fide iustificemur, non dilectione," ed. Johannes Haussleiter in *Abhandlungen Alexander von Oettingen . . . gewidmet* (München: C. H. Beck, 1898), p. 254; cf. *CR*, XII, 449.

Chapter 7

1. Philipp Melanchthon, *Dispositio orationis, in Epistola Pauli ad Romanos* (Wittembergae: G. Rhau, [MD]XXX), fol. Bvi—viii; hereafter referred to as *DOR*. Reprinted in *CR*, XV, 477–78.
2. AC, V, 1; *BS*, p. 58, 2: "Ut hanc fidem consequamur . . . "; the German text: "Solchen Glauben zu erlangen . . . " Abraham Calov, *Exegema Augustanae Confessionis*, editio altera (Wittebergae: J. Borckard, MDCLXVII), fol. Iii2: The concatenation of Art. V with Art. IV is defined in the opening words; Art. IV

presented *"actus fidei* salvificae *proprius,* qui est iustificatio"; Art. V declares its divine origin and free donation (*gratuita donatio*). Cf. fol. Iii3: The Confession teaches in Art. V "unde nobis fides constet." Iac[obus] Gulielmus Feuerlinus, *Observationes variae in Augustanae Confessionis singulos articulos* (Gottingae: I. F. Hagerius, [1742]), p. 33: "This article deals with the origin and the causes of justifying faith and thus is intimately connected with the preceding article."

3. Cf. Martin Luther's critique of the *Enthusiasten* in the Smalcald Articles, III, viii (*BS,* pp. 453–56; Tappert, pp. 312–13): God will not deal with us except through His external Word.

4. *LW,* 37, 366; *WA,* XXVI, 506, 11–12.

5. *BS,* p. 59, 7–10; cf. p. 59, 17: "der heilige Geist durch Christum gegeben."

6. Gustav Plitt, *Einleitung in die Augustana,* II (Erlangen: A. Deichert, 1868), 184: The *alii* are Melanchthon's "Pelagian opponents." Cf. II, 161–63. See also the *editio princeps, CR,* XXVI, 555: "to *merit* the Holy Spirit by their own preparations and works." Emphasis added. Ap, IV, 66–67, cf. 73; *BS,* p. 173, 20–29, cf. p. 175, 6–8.

7. Schwabach Articles, VII; *BS,* p. 59, 10–14. Marburg Articles, VI and VIII; *BS,* p. 59, 22–29.

8. *WA,* XXVI, 505, 31–33; *LW,* 37, 36. *BS,* p. 59, 16–17, 27–28. Cf. *wirkt und schafft* in the eighth Marburg article, *BS,* p. 59, 24–25.

9. *DOR,* fol. Cv; *CR,* XV, 457.

10. For bibliography on this issue see *BS,* p. 58, note 3. G. Plitt, *Einleitung in die Augustana,* II, 160–84, demonstrates that *ubi et quando visum est deo* was used by Luther before the controversy with the "enthusiasts." On whether or not the expression refers to predestination see Karl Thieme, *Die Augsburgische Konfession und Luthers Katechismen auf theologische Gegenwartswerte untersucht* (Giessen: A. Töpelmann, 1930), pp. 73–74.

11. *WA,* XXVI, 203, 21–26; cf. also XXVI, 221, 7–222, 7. *LW,* 40, 276 and 297.

12. *CR,* XXVI, 21; cf. XXVI, 11.

13. According to Art. IX, however, faith is created also in the infants brought to Baptism. Cf. Jörg Rothermund, "Rechtfertigungsgespräch 1958–1963: Ein Forschungsbericht über die Studienarbeit im Lutherischen Weltbund," *Rechtfertigung heute: Studien und Berichte,* Beiheft zur *Lutherischen Rundschau* (Stuttgart: Kreuz, 1965), p. 29, as he reports on Regin Prenter's "Dogmatische Bemerkungen": The justification realized on the cross occurs in Baptism.

14. *WA,* XXVI, 219, 19–22; *LW,* 40, 295.

15. *DOR,* fol. Avii; *CR,* XV, 446.

16. CA, XII, 5; *BS,* p. 67, 4–8. In Art. XIII the sacraments are called "signs and witnesses of God's will toward us established to provoke and confirm faith in those who use them." Compare the restatement, presumably from memory, in Ap XIII; *BS,* p. 291, 51–54: "sed [dicimus sacramenta] magis esse signa et testimonia voluntatis Dei erga nos, per quae *movet Deus corda ad credendum."* Emphasis added.

17. Franz Pieper, *Christliche Dogmatik,* II (St. Louis: Concordia, 1917), 477 and 478, states very aptly: "The Gospel, 'the Word of faith' (Rom. 10:8), is a Word which itself creates the faith, the acceptance, which it calls for: 'faith cometh

THE DOCTRINE OF FAITH

by hearing' (Rom. 10:17)" (quoted from the translation by Theodore Engelder, et al. [Concordia, 1951], pp. 400 f.). "By proferring grace or forgiveness of sins through the Gospel, God through the same Gospel also effects in the hearts of men faith in the Gospel" (our translation). See also Martin Seils, "Zu einigen Problemen der Interpretation von Artikel IV der Confessio Augustana in der Anerkennungsdebatte," *Die Confessio Augustana im ökumenischen Gespräch*, ed. Fritz Hoffmann and Ulrich Kühn (Berlin: Evangelische Verlagsanstalt, 1980), p. 158: In the Reformers' thinking faith derives from the promise not only in a cognitive but in a causative sense.

18. *LW*, 37, 366; *WA*, XXVI, 506, 7–12.
19. *DOR*, fol. Aviii; *CR*, XV, 446: "Evangelium patefacit iustitiam fidei, quod coram Deo iusti habeantur, qui credunt, se propter Christum in gratiam recipi."
20. *DOR*, fol. Bvi; *CR*, XV, 451: "Addita est circumstantia ad quos pertineat iustitia revelata in Evangelio. Ait enim in omnes, et super omnes credentes . . . "
21. Leif Grane, *Die Confessio Augustana: Einführung in die Hauptgedanken der lutherischen Reformation*, trans. from the Danish by E. Harbsmeier (Göttingen: Vandenhoeck & Ruprecht, 1970), p. 47: "The declaration of what the Gospel is reestablishes the connection with Art. IV. The Gospel plainly is the doctrine presented in this article." See also *Confessio Augustana Bekenntnis des einen Glaubens: Gemeinsame Untersuchung lutherischer und katholischer Theologen*, ed. Harding Meyer and Heinz Schütte (Paderborn: Bonifacius; Frankfurt am Main: O. Lembeck, 1980), p. 121: "The Gospel is nothing else but the message of justification." Cf. *Confessing One Faith: A Joint Commentary on the Augsburg Confession by Lutheran and Catholic Theologians*, ed. George W. Forell and James F. McCue (Minneapolis: Augsburg, 1982), p. 129. Hereafter referred to as *Gemeinsame Untersuchung* and *Joint Commentary*, respectively.
22. AC, VI, 1; XX, 27, cf. 35.
23. The quoted material in these two paragraphs is from Tappert, pp. 31 and 45.—According to Abraham Calov, *Exegema Augustanae Confessionis*, fol. Nnn3b, the *tractatio* has four members, namely, *to hoti*, that faith must beget good works, *to ti ēn einai*, works (if deriving from true faith) are ordered by God, *to pōs*, how do good works occur? . . . *to dioti*, why are good works to be done? both affirmatively, *kata thesin*, and negatively, *kath' arnēsin*.
24. Schwabach Articles, VI, *BS*, p. 59, 20–21; Marburg Articles, X, *BS*, p. 61, 23–26.
25. *WA*, XXVI, 204, 6–7; 206, 41; *LW*, 40, 277, 280.
26. *LW*, 40, 277; *WA*, XXVI, 204, 1–5, "darynn denn alle gute werck verfasset sind." Cf. Visitation Articles, *CR*, XXVI, 25–26: We are free from that part of the Law which does not demand the righteousness of the heart, namely, from ceremonial and civil requirements; the Decalog, however, demands the righteousness of the heart and for this reason is not abrogated, for Christian righteousness is the righteousness of the heart. These statements were not incorporated into the *Instructions for Visitors*.
27. AC, XX, 3; *BS*, p. 76, 3–4: The works formerly demanded by the opponents were *puerilia et non necessaria* (childish and unnecessary).
28. AC, XXVI, 8–11; XXVII, 49–59.
29. *WA*, XXVI, 505, 21–23; "Great Confession," *LW*, 37, 365.

NOTES

30. *DOR*, fol. Bvii; *CR*, XV, 452.
31. Art. XX, par. 28, is even stronger. The Latin has, "Tantum fide apprehenditur remissio peccatorum et gratia." The German reads, "Der Glaub ergreift allzeit allein Gnade und Vergebung der Sunde." These formulations derive from the *Instructions for Visitors, WA,* XXVI, 220, 21–24, and 221, 2–4; *LW,* 40, 297.
32. *DOR*, fol. Ei; *CR*, XV, 466.
33. *CR*, XXVI, 556; *BS*, p. 60, note to line 8 of the German text.
34. In spite of his desire to document Lutheran-Catholic unity at the Augsburg discussions, Vinzenz Pfnür recognizes that Eck and Melanchthon did not agree on the merit of good works. Only he does not explain *why* they were unable to agree on this issue. In our estimation it was because Eck and his colleagues were persuaded of the soteriological function of these merits, which Melanchthon could by no means accept. See *Confessio Augustana und Confutatio: Der Augsburger Reichstag 1530 und die Einheit der Kirche,* ed. Erwin Iserloh (Münster: Aschendorff, 1980), pp. 370–73. In our time the dialog partners would be well advised to consider the relation between Eck's *gratia acceptans* and Melanchthon's *per misericordiam propter Christum,* where they may find a more solid bridge than Pfnür's identification of *gratia creata* and faith. Cf. *Gemeinsame Untersuchung,* p. 116.
35. *WA,* XXVI, 505, 11—15; *LW,* 37, 365.

CHAPTER 8

1. In this respect Melanchthon follows an argumentation sequence very common in Luther too, namely to present first Scriptural, then patristic evidence, and finally arguments drawn from experience.
2. As Leif Grane, *Die Confessio Augustana: Einführung in die Hauptgedanken der lutherischen Reformation* (Göttingen: Vandenhoeck & Ruprecht, 1970), pp. 151–53, voices concerns over Melanchthon's psychologizing, he overlooks that the scope of the argumentation is to affirm and defend the necessity of proclaiming the doctrine of faith in view of its beneficial effects, not to explain faith or justification in terms of its psychological components.
3. AC, XX, 1–8 and 35–40. *BS*, pp. 75, 13–76, 23, and p. 81, 7–22, respectively.
4. Leonhard Fendt, *Der Wille der Reformation im Augsburgischen Bekenntnis* (Leipzig: H. G. Wallmann, 1929), pp. 26–31, and (after him) Heinrich Bornkamm, *Das Augsburger Bekenntnis* (Hamburg: Furche, 1965), pp. 84–88, discern only two parts. They render *praeterea* in par. 27 as *zweitens,* overlooking par. 23, "Admonentur etiam homines . . . " Tappert, pp. 42 and pp. 44–45, adequately discerns three parts: "We begin by teaching . . . Men are also admonished . . . Our teachers teach in addition . . . "
5. Par. 9. Notice that pars. 15–18, on the struggle of terrified consciences, derive from Melanchthon's contention that the preaching of penitence is indispensable for understanding the role and notion of faith.
6. Leif Grane, *Die Confessio Augustana,* p. 150: One's vocation is the right place for good works. "Justified by faith, the Christian is freed to serve God as cooperator in the created universe."
7. See the reply to AC, XX, 10, in the *Responsio Catholica, Die Konfutation des*

Augsburgischen Bekenntnisses: Ihre erste Gestalt und ihre Geschichte, ed. Johannes Ficker (Leipzig: J. A. Barth, 1891), p. 66, 10–13: "No Catholic ever believed that he would merit grace by his powers or works without God's grace, as we have stated in Article IV. As a result of that we do not belittle Christ's merit, but estimate that our works have no merit whatsoever except by virtue of the merit of Christ's passion." But see also Leif Grane, *Die Confessio Augustana,* p. 149: Even though St. Thomas stresses that all merit derives from God's grace, still one cannot make his views agree with those of the Lutherans. "The contrast again roots in Reformation Christology. Man's only possible righteousness is Christ's foreign righteousness. For this reason every merit, no matter if acquired by one's own effort or effected by the assistance of grace, is excluded."

8. Johannes Eck, *Enchiridion locorum communium adversus Lutheranos,* sexta recognitio (Ingolstadii: [Apianus], 1529), fol. 35: "Hic constat verum esse, quod Augustinus inquit hanc haeresim (non enim nova est, sed antiquissima) exortam ex verbis Pauli male intellectis." Cf. Johannes Eck, *Enchiridion,* ed. Peter Fraenkel, *Corpus Catholicorum,* 34 (Münster: Aschendorff, 1979), p. 97.

9. See above, ch. 6, note 50.

10. Philipp Melanchthon, the Visitation Articles, *CR,* XXVI, 11: "Et arguant eos, quia somniant se credere aut fidem habere, cum non habeant timorem Dei ... " Melanchthon and Luther, *Instructions for Visitors:* "Many people, having heard that they should believe and that thereby they will get forgiveness for all their sins, construe some kind of faith and assume that they are pure; they become impudent and secure, and this carnal security is much worse than all the previous errors" (*WA,* XXVI, 217, 34, to 218, 2; *LW,* 40, 293–94).

11. Par. 23; Tappert, p. 44. Italics added.

12. Lowell C. Green, "Faith, Righteousness, and Justification: New Light on Their Development Under Luther and Melanchthon," *Sixteenth Century Journal,* IV (April 1972), 74–75, fails to stress that *fides specialis* and *fides generalis* are correlated to different "objects," even though later he implies the correlation of the former to the promise, as he states on p. 77: "Righteousness is no longer the dominance of virtues in the believer, but the apprehension of Christ and His righteousness through a new relationship of faith as trust."

13. Philipp Melanchthon, *Dispositio orationis, in Epistola Pauli ad Romanos* (Wittembergae: G. Rhau, [MD]XXX), fol. Ci–ii; *CR,* XV, 453–54. Henceforth referred to as *DOR.*

14. Compare also the use of *statuere, gewißlich schleußen,* as synonym of *credere, glauben,* in AC, XX, 15–16.

15. *CR,* XXVI, 11, cf. 21.

16. *DOR,* fol. Ei; *CR,* XV, 467.

17. *DOR,* fol. Di–iii; *CR,* XV, 467.

18. *CR,* XXVI, 25; *WA,* XXVI, 227, 15–19; *LW,* 40, 303.

19. *BS,* p. 83, 13–14.

Chapter 9

1. "Bericht über die Diskussion zum Thema 'Rechtfertigung': Dokument Nr. 75, Erste Fassung"; "Bericht über die Diskussion zum Thema 'Christus heute':

NOTES

Dokument Nr. 75, Überarbeitete Fassung"; "Anhang III: Rechtfertigung heute: Endgültige Fassung des Dokumentes 75," *Offizieller Bericht der Vierten Vollversammlung des Lutherischen Weltbundes, Helsinki, 30. Juli—11. August 1963*, her. vom Lutherischen Weltbund (Berlin/Hamburg: Lutherisches Verlagshaus, 1965), respectively pp. 271–78, 387–92, 522–29. Cf. "Rechtfertigung heute: Das revidierte Vollversammlungsdokument 75," *Rechtfertigung heute: Studien und Berichte*, Beiheft zur *Lutherischen Rundschau*, 1. Auflage, her. von der Theologischen Kommission und Abteilung des Lutherischen Weltbundes (Stuttgart/Berlin: Kreuz, 1965), pp. 5–17 (text received by the assembly on the left, text issued by the commission in the right columns). English translation of both texts, "Justification Today," *Justification Today: Studies and Reports*, ed. by the Commission and Department of Theology, Supplement to *Lutheran World*, No. 1 (1965), pp. 2–11. References to "Justification Today" will be made parenthetically in the text by Arabic numerals which refer to the articles in which the text is divided in all editions.

2. Vilmos Vajta, *Theologische Abteilung: Bericht 1957–1963*, Dokument Nr. 7, Vierte Vollversammlung des Lutherischen Weltbundes (Genf: Lutherischer Weltbund, 1963), p. 13. Wilhelm Andersen, "Das theologische Gespräch über die Rechtfertigung in Helsinki," *Helsinki 1963: Beiträge zum theologischen Gespräch des Lutherischen Weltbundes*, her. von Erwin Wilkens (Berlin/Hamburg: Lutherisches Verlaghaus, 1964), pp. 30–31.

3. Jörg Rothermundt, "Rechtfertigungsgespräch 1958–1963: Ein Forschungsbericht über die Studienarbeit im Lutherischen Weltbund," *Rechtfertigung heute* (cited above, note 1), pp. 19–74, especially pp. 54–60. Peter Brunner's draft was based on "Erwägungen zu einer Erklärung und Wiederholung von CA IV" and published later as "Rechtfertigung heute: Versuch einer dogmatischen Paraklese," *Lutherische Monatshefte*, I (März 1962), 106–16, and reprinted in *Pro Ecclesia: Gesammelte Aufsätze zur dogmatischen Theologie*, Band II (Berlin/Hamburg: Lutherisches Verlagshaus, 1966), 122–40. Warren A. Quanbeck's essay, "The Significance of Augustana IV for America," served as basis for his draft, which became the matrix of the study document (see below, note 4). Vilmos Vajta's draft, later published as *Gelebte Rechtfertigung: Eine biblisch-theologische Meditation* (Göttingen: Vandenhoeck & Ruprecht, 1963), served as basis for a "preliminary draft" (*Vorentwurf*) that was appended to the member churches' reactions to the study document and influenced the first version of Document No. 75.

4. Warren A. Quanbeck, *A Study Document on Justification*, prepared by the Commission on Theology for the Lutheran World Federation Assembly in Helsinki, July 30—August 11, 1963 (New York: National Lutheran Council, 1966). German translation without indication of the author, *Über die Rechtfertigung*, Dokument Nr. 3, Vierte Vollversammlung des Lutherischen Weltbundes (Genf: Lutherischer Weltbund, n.d.). The Commission on Theology's report is cited above, note 2.

5. Kurt Schmidt-Clausen, "Bericht des Generalsekretärs," *Offizieller Bericht* (cited above, note 1), pp. 72–73.

6. Gerhard Gloege, "Antriebe und Absichten: Eine theologische Bilanz," *Helsinki 1963* (cited above, note 2), p. 79.

7. "Helsinki 1963," *Lutherische Rundschau*, XIV (Januar 1964), 4–5; Peter L. Kjeseth, "Dokument 75," ibid., p. 105.

8. *Offizieller Bericht* (cited above, note 1), p. 280.
9. "Helsinki 1963," *Lutherische Rundschau,* XIV (Januar 1964), 4–5.
10. *Offizieller Bericht* (cited above, note 1), pp. 300–01.
11. Ibid., p. 401.
12. "Justification Today: Preface of the Commission on Theology," *Justification Today: Studies and Reports* (cited above, note 1), pp. 1–2. Compare "Stellungnahme zu dem Dokument Nr. 75, II. Fassung: Erarbeitet im Auftrage der Mitgliedskirchen des Lutherischen Weltbundes in der DDR (28. Januar 1964)," *Helsinki 1963* (cited above, note 2), pp. 70–73. The concerns are basically those raised by Ernst Sommerlath at the 10th plenary session of the Assembly. See *Offizieller Bericht* (cited above, note 1), pp. 395–96.
13. "Helsinki 1963," *Lutherische Rundschau,* XIV (Januar 1964), 4–5.
14. Vilmos Vajta, *Im Wandel der Generationen: Der Lutherische Weltbund 1947–1982,* LWB-Report 16, Dezember 1983 (Stuttgart: Kreuz, 1983), pp. 34–36.
15. Wilhelm Andersen, "Das theologische Gespräch über die Rechtfertigung in Helsinki," *Helsinki 1963* (cited above, note 2), p. 50, after Wolfgang Trillhaas, "Rückblick auf Helsinki," *Lutherische Monatshefte,* II (September 1963), 445.
16. Peter Bläser, "Helsinki in der Sicht eines katholischen Beobachters," *Lutherische Rundschau,* XIV (Januar 1964), 77–80.
17. Wilhelm Andersen, "Das theologische Gespräch über die Rechtfertigung in Helsinki," *Helsinki 1963,* pp. 28–29 (cited above, note 2).
18. Wolfgang Trillhaas, "Rückblick auf Helsinki," *Lutherische Monatschfte,* II (September 1963), 446; cf. Hans-Wolfgang Hessler, "Helsinki im Spiegel der Presse," *Lutherische Rundschau,* XIV (Januar 1974), 69. "Justification by Faith," No. 87, *Origins: NC Documentary Service,* XIII (October 6, 1983), 289.
19. "Statement on the Self-Understanding and Task of the Lutheran World Federation," *Budapest 1984: Official Proceedings of the Seventh Assembly of the Lutheran World Federation,* Budapest, Hungary, July 22—August 5, 1984, ed. Carl H. Mau, Jr., LWF Report No. 19/20, February 1985 (Geneva: Lutheran World Federation, 1985), pp. 176–77.
20. "Preface of the Commission on Theology," *Justification Today,* pp. 1–2 (cited above, note 1).
21. Jörg Rothermundt, "Rechtfertigungsgespräch 1958–1963," *Rechtfertigung heute,* p. 61 (cited above, notes 3 and 1).
22. *A Study Document on Justification,* No. 33, p. 18 (cited above, note 4). W. Andersen, "Das theologische Gespräch," *Helsinki 1963,* p. 41.
23. Gerhard Gloege, "Helsinki 1963—Kritik und Krise des Luthertums,"*Gnade für die Welt: Kritik und Krise des Luthertums* (Göttingen: Vandenhoeck & Ruprecht, 1964), p. 74: "Justification of the godless takes place only in the act of faith and cannot be expressed meaningfully without this relation.... It is exactly man's removal out of atheism that occurs in the act of faith."
24. Wolfgang Schanze, August Kimme, Felix Moderow, Ernst Sommerlath, Gottfried Voigt, "Stellungnahme zu dem Dokument Nr. 75, II. Fassung: Erarbeitet im Auftrage der Mitgliedskirchen des Lutherischen Weltbundes in der DDR (Leipzig, 28. Januar 1964)," No. 10, *Helsinki 1963* (Berlin/Hamburg: Lutherisches Verlagshaus, 1964), p. 73: "Our objections against Document 75 II, as our exposition indicates, do not concern specific formulations, but deep-going

NOTES

unclarities in the matter itself. We are not concerned with the theological vocables and terms employed, but that the issue of justification shall come to its full right."

25. "Vorbemerkung der Theologischen Kommission," *Rechtfertigung heute,* p. 5 (cited above, note 1); cf. "Preface of the Commission on Theology," *Justification Today,* p. 1 (cited above, note 1).

CHAPTER 10

1. "Konkordie reformatorischer Kirchen in Europa (Leuenberger Konkordie)," *Konkordie und Kirchengemeinschaft reformatorischer Kirchen im Europa der Gegenwart: Texte der Konferenz von Driebergen, Niederlande (18. bis 24. Februar 1981),* her. von André Birmelé, Ökumenische Perspektiven, Nr. 10 (Frankfurt am Main: O. Lembeck/J. Knecht, 1982), pp. 13–22; hereafter referred to as *Konkordie.* Elisabeth Schieffer, *Von Schauenburg nach Leuenberg: Entstehung und Bedeutung der Konkordie reformatorischer Kirchen in Europa,* Konfessionskundliche und Kontroverstheologische Studien, Band 48 (Paderborn: Bonifatius, 1983), pp. A132–57, prints side by side the 1971 draft and the 1973 definitive text; Tuomo Mannermaa, *Von Preussen nach Leuenberg: Hintergrund und Entwicklung der theologischen Methode der Leuenberger Konkordie,* Arbeiten zur Geschichte und Theologie des Luthertums, Neue Folge, Band 1 (Hamburg: Lutherisches Verlagshaus, 1981), pp. 191–201, prints them in sequence. English translation, "Agreement Between Reformation Churches in Europe: The Leuenberg Agreement (*Konkordie*)," *The Ecumenical Review,* XXV (July 1973), 355–59. The "Leuenberg Agreement" will be referred to parenthetically in the text, the Arabic numerals denoting the articles which make up the document.

2. "Bericht: Lutherische und Reformierte Kirchen in Europa auf dem Wege zueinander," *Auf dem Weg: Lutherisch-Reformierte Kirchengemeinschaft: Berichte und Texte,* her. vom Sekretariat für Glauben und Kirchenverfassung, Band I (Polis 33; Zürich: EVZ-Verlag, 1967), 9–30. "Thesen über Wort Gottes—Gegenwart Gottes; Thesen über das Gesetz; Thesen über das Bekenntnis," ibid., pp. 31–32, 33–35, 36–43, respectively. "Kirchengemeinschaft und Kirchentrennung: Bericht der lutherisch-reformierten Gespräche in Leuenberg (Schweiz) 1969/70," *Auf dem Weg: Berichte und Dokumente des lutherisch-reformierten Gespräches in Europa,* her. vom Sekretariat für Glauben und Kirchenverfassung, Band II (Polis 41; Zürich: Theologischer Verlag, 1971), 8–24; cf. "Bericht der lutherisch-reformierten Gespräche in Leuenberg/Schweiz über Kirchengemeinschaft und Kirchentrennung," *Una Sancta,* XXV (1970), 215–21.

3. Marc Lienhard, *Lutherisch-reformierte Kirchengemeinschaft heute: Der Leuenberger Konkordienentwurf im Kontext der bisherigen lutherisch-reformierten Dialoge,* Ökumenische Perspektiven, Nr. 2 (Frankfurt am Main: O. Lembeck/J. Knecht, 1972), pp. 30–42; hereafter referred to as *Kirchengemeinschaft.* Harding Meyer, "Die interkonfessionellen Gespräche des Lutherischen Weltbundes," *Una Sancta,* XXV (1970), 305–11.

4. "LWF Statement on the Confessio Augustana (1980)," *Lutheran-Roman Catholic Discussion on the Augsburg Confession: Documents 1977–1981,* ed. Harding Meyer, LWF Report 10, August 1982 (Stuttgart: Kreuz, 1982), p. 69.

The German expression is "Grundverständnis des Evangeliums." See *Das katholisch-lutherische Gespräch über das Augsburger Bekenntnis: Dokumente 1977–1981,* LWB Report 10, August 1982 (Stuttgart: Kreuz, 1982), p. 65.

5. Jos Vercruysse, "Die Konkordie von Leuenberg: Randbemerkungen eines katholischen Ökumenikers," *Zeichen der Zeit,* XXVI (1972), 318–19, as referred by E. Schieffer, *Von Schauenberg nach Leuenberg,* p. 446, note 116 (cited above, note 1).

6. George Lindbeck, "Bericht über den römisch-katholisch/evangelisch-lutherischen Dialog," *LWB Dokumentation,* Nr. 4 (Oktober 1980), p. 22.

7. Heinrich Fries in a letter of Feb. 27, 1973, to the Leuenberg Committee (Lukas Vischer) as quoted by E. Schieffer, *Von Schauenburg nach Leuenberg,* p. 458, cf. note 168 (cited above, note 1).

8. M. Lienhard, *Kirchengemeinschaft,* p. 71 (cited above, note 1).

9. E. Schieffer, *Von Schauenburg nach Leuenberg,* pp. 429–35 (cited above, note 1).

10. *Heilsmittlerschaft* is one of those terms devised by contemporary experts in theological communication to convey complex matters in a comprehensible way. It is a question whether such terms communicate better than traditional—allegedly worn-out—ones.

11. "Bericht der lutherisch-reformierten Gespräche in Leuenberg/Schweiz über Kirchengemeinschaft und Kirchentrennung," Nr. 22, *Una Sancta,* XXV (1970), 220.

12. T. Mannermaa, *Von Preussen nach Leuenberg,* pp. 155–75, cf. pp. 54–78 (cited above, note 1).

13. M. Lienhard, *Kirchengemeinschaft,* pp. 73–74: "Separation from Christology is out of the question."

14. AC, III, 3; IV, 2; XX, 9.

15. Ap, IV, 167 (Tappert, p. 130); *BS,* p. 194, 19–20.

16. AC, V, 3. Cf. the exposition of this passage in ch. 7 above.

17. M. Lienhard, *Kirchengemeinschaft,* p. 77.

18. M. Lienhard, *Kirchengemeinschaft,* pp. 75–76.

CHAPTER 11

1. " 'Das Evangelium und die Kirche': Bericht der evangelisch-lutherisch/römisch-katholischen Studienkommission," *Evangelium-Welt-Kirche: Schlußbericht und Referate der römisch-katholisch/evangelisch-lutherischen Studienkommission "Das Evangelium und die Kirche," 1967–1971,* her. von Harding Meyer (Frankfurt am Main: O. Lembeck/Josef Knecht, 1975), 9–32. English trans. by Gustav Kopka, revised by George A. Lindbeck, " 'The Gospel and the Church': Report of the Joint Lutheran/Roman Catholic Study Commission," ibid., pp. 33–58. Reprinted as "Bericht der Evangelisch-lutherisch/Römisch-katholischen Studienkommission 'Das Evangelium und die Kirche,' 1972 ('Malta-Bericht')," *Dokumente wachsender Übereinstimmung: Sämtliche Berichte und Konsenstexte interkonfessioneller Gespräche auf Weltebene 1931–1982,* her. von Harding Meyer, Hans Jörg Urban, Lukas Vischer (Paderborn: Bonifatius; Frankfurt am Main: O. Lembeck, 1983), pp. 248–71. Ac-

NOTES

cording to August Hasler, "Rom schlägt die Fenster zu: Kirchenamtlicher Dialog in Schwierigkeiten," *Evangelische Kommentare,* V (April 1972), 212, the document was initially released without the churches' permission. Cf. "Das Evangelium und die Kirche," ibid., IV (November 1971), 659–64.

2. The English version in *Evangelium-Welt-Kirche,* p. 39, misses the point, as it fails to convey that the actions "in" Christ *and* "in" the Holy Spirit take place *in the Gospel:* "What God has done for the salvation of the world in Jesus Christ is transmitted in the Gospel and made present in the Holy Spirit."

3. August Hasler, representative of the Secretariat for Christian Unity staff, in an interim report, "Das Evangelium und die Kirche," *Lutherische Rundschau,* XIX (Oktober 1969), 487, voiced the expectation that on the basis of the new approach the old controversies would be examined as to their ecumenical relevance and church-dividing effect.

4. "Primäres Kriterium ist, daß der Heilige Geist das Christusereignis als Heilsgeschehen erweist." The translation in *Evangelium-Welt-Kirche,* p. 39, does not reproduce the force of *erweisen,* as it renders, "making ... into a saving action."

5. The original does not say that consensus has been achieved, but that it is "appearing on the horizon": "Heute *zeichnet sich* in der Interpretation der Rechtfertigung ein weitreichender Konsens *ab*" (emphasis added). The rendition, "is developing," used in *Evangelium-Welt-Kirche,* p. 26, suggests more than the original conveys. The qualification of the consensus as "far-reaching" must be regarded as force of expression. Cf. the Zurich interim report, "Das Evangelium und die Kirche," *Lutherische Rundschau,* XIX (Oktober 1969), 469: "a far-reaching agreement in the understanding of the doctrine of justification as such seemed possible." Harding Meyer, staff representative of the Lutheran World Federation, reports, ibid., p. 478: "It was basically held that the doctrine of justification as a dogmatic doctrine hardly is controversial between Lutherans and Catholics."

6. Harding Meyer, *Luthertum und Katholizismus im Gespräch: Ergebnisse und Stand der katholisch-lutherischen Dialoge in den USA und auf Weltebene,* Ökumenische Perspektiven, Nr. 3 (Frankfurt am Main: O. Lembeck/J. Knecht, 1973), p. 52.

7. The original reads: "daß die Heilsgabe Gottes für den Glaubenden an keine menschliche Bedingung geknüpft ist." The translation in *Evangelium-Welt-Kirche,* p. 41, renders freely: "that God's gift of salvation for the believer is unconditional as far as human accomplishments are concerned."

8. What actually happened was that the Catholic delegation expressed approval of the *intention* of the doctrine of justification. Cf. Harding Meyer's report, "Das Evangelium und die Kirche," *Lutherische Rundschau,* XIX (Oktober 1969), 478: "The intention of the doctrine of justification to express God's unconditional and groundless offer of salvation is affirmed by the Catholic side." The Lutheran churches of the German Democratic Republic correctly stressed in 1964 that the doctrine of justification intends more than merely excluding human merit. Cf. "Stellungnahme zu dem Dokument Nr. 75, II. Fassung," *Helsinki 1963: Beiträge zum theologischen Gespräch des Lutherischen Weltbundes,* her. von Erwin Wilkens (Berlin/Hamburg: Lutherisches Verlagshaus, 1964), pp. 71–72: "*Sola fide* intends not only (negatively) to

exclude the significance of works for salvation, but (positively) to stress the necessity for personal appropriation and decision."

9. The original, "sehen in ihm [dem Rechtfertigungsgeschehen] nicht eine rein äußerlich bleibende Gerechterklärung des Sünders," is rendered freely in *Evangelium-Welt-Kirche,* p. 41: "they do not see in it a purely external declaration of the justification of the sinner."

10. In the original formulation the two aspects are identified. Cf. "Das Evangelium und die Kirche," *Lutherische Rundschau,* XIX (Oktober 1969), 478: "Von lutherischer Seite wird betont, daß die Rechtfertigung nicht nur als Sündenvergebung, als forensische Rechtsprechung verstanden werden müße, sondern zugleich als Grund eines neuen Lebens im persönlichen wie im gesellschaftlichem Bereich."

11. Here the original defies rendition: "Vielmehr wird ... die im Christusgeschehen realisierte Gottesgerechtigkeit dem Sünder als eine umfassende Wirklichkeit übereignet und dadurch das neue Leben der Glaubenden begründet."

12. Harding Meyer, *Luthertum und Katholizismus im Gespräch* (cited above, note 6), p. 53.

13. "Das Evangelium und die Kirche," *Lutherische Rundschau,* XIX (Oktober 1969), 469, cf. pp. 478–79.

14. According to Harding Meyer, *Luthertum und Katholizismus im Gespräch* (cited above, note 6), p. 53, the text of No. 28 does not suggest that the question of the place and function of the doctrine of justification remained open or controversial. His paraphrase of Nos. 28–30, however, does read like a compromise.

15. According to the Zurich report, *Lutherische Rundschau,* XIX (Oktober 1969), 469, both sides feared that the multiplicity of historically conditioned confessional and doctrinal formulations would hinder modern man's access to the center of the Gospel. They manifested the hope that the church would be granted the privilege of restating the Gospel in plain terms.

16. AC, XX, in the *editio princeps;* Ap, IV, 86. *BS,* pp. 83, 39–57; 178, 27–33. Tappert, p. 119.

17. "Alle unter einem Christus: Stellungnahme der Gemeinsamen Römisch-katholischen/Evangelisch-lutherischen Komission zum Augsburgischen Bekenntnis," *Wege zur Gemeinschaft* (Paderborn: Bonifacius; Frankfurt am Main: O. Lembeck, 1980), pp. 53–63. Reprinted in *Dokumente wachsender Übereinstimmung,* pp. 323–28 (cited above, note 1), and in *Das katholisch-lutherische Gespräch über das Augsburger Bekenntnis: Dokumente 1977–1981,* her. von Harding Meyer, LWB-Report 10, August 1982 (Stuttgart: Kreuz, 1982), pp. 32–40; hereafter abbreviated *Gespräch.* English trans. by David Lewis in *Lutheran-Roman Catholic Discussion on the Augsburg Confession: Documents 1977–1981,* ed. Harding Meyer, LWF Report 10, August 1982 (Stuttgart: Kreuz, 1982), pp. 34–43; hereafter referred to as *Discussion.*

18. On the origins and development of the debate see the introduction of *Katholische Anerkennung des Augsburgischen Bekenntnisses? Ein Vorstoß zur Einheit zwischen katholischer und lutherischer Kirche,* her. von Harding Meyer, Heinz Schütte, Hans-Joachim Mund, Ökumenische Perspektiven, Nr. 9 (Frankfurt am Main: O. Lembeck/J. Knecht, 1977), pp. 11–16; trans. *The Role of the*

NOTES

Augsburg Confession: Catholic and Lutheran Views, ed. Joseph A. Burgess (Philadelphia: Fortress, 1980), pp. xi–xvi. See also P. Gauly, *Katholisches Ja zum Augsburgischen Bekenntnis? Ein Bericht über die neuere Anerkennungsdiskussion* (Freiburg: Herder, 1980) and *Discussion* (cited above, note 18), pp. 6–8.

19. The essays in *Katholische Anerkennung des Augsburgischen Bekenntnisses?* trans. *The Role of the Augsburg Confession* (cited in preceding note), except for those added in the American ed., stem from a consultation of the High Church Society of the Augsburg Confession at Schwanberg Castle in September 1976. *Confessio Augustana: Hindernis oder Hilfe?* (Regensburg: F. Pustet, 1979) consists of papers presented by Heinrich Fries and others at a joint meeting of the Catholic Academy in Bavaria and the Tutzing Evangelical Academy on April 14–16, 1978, in Munich. *Augsburgische Konfession im ökumenischen Kontext: Beiträge aus anglikanischer, baptistischer, katholischer, methodistischer, orthodoxer und reformierter Sicht,* her. von Harding Meyer, LWB-Report 6/7, Dezember 1979 (Stuttgart: Kreuz, 1979); parallel ed., *The Augsburg Confession in Ecumenical Perspective,* LWF Report No. 6/7, December 1979, resulted from an ecumenical consultation sponsored by the Institute for Ecumenical Research, Strasbourg, at Liebfrauenberg on Nov. 20–24, 1978. *Confessio Augustana 1530–1980: Besinnung und Selbstprüfung,* her. von Vilmos Vajta, LWB-Report 9, Juni 1980 (Stuttgart: Kreuz, 1980); parallel ed., *Confessio Augustana 1530–1980: Commemoration and Self-Examination,* LWF Report No. 9, June 1980, resulted from a study project by the same Strasbourg institute, leading to a consultation on Liebfrauenberg, Oct. 22–27, 1979.

20. *Confessio Augustana Bekenntnis des einen Glaubens: Gemeinsame Untersuchung lutherischer und katholischer Theologen,* her. von Harding Meyer und Heinz Schütte (Paderborn: Bonifacius; Frankfurt am Main: O. Lembeck, 1980), henceforth referred to as *Gemeinsame Untersuchung;* American trans., *Confessing One Faith: A Joint Commentary on the Augsburg Confession by Lutheran and Catholic Theologians,* ed. George W. Forell and James F. McCue (Minneapolis: Augsburg Publishing House, 1982). Henceforth referred to as *Joint Commentary.*

21. Alloys Klein and Harding Meyer, "Lutheran-Roman Catholic Discussion on the Augsburg Confession: Retrospect, Stocktaking, Prospects," *Discussion,* pp. 11–14; *Gespräch,* pp. 12–15. In Art. 59 of *Wege zur Gemeinschaft* (cited above, note 17) the commentary is said to be a good example of the kind of studies that must contribute toward a better understanding of the 16th century and to the overcoming of preconceived notions.

22. "Ergebnis der Studienarbeit," *Gemeinsame Untersuchung* (cited above, note 20), pp. 333–37, cf. p. xv; reprinted as "Confessio Augustana Bekenntnis des einen Glaubens: Ergebnis einer gemeinsamen Studie katholischer und lutherischer Theologen," *Gespräch,* pp. 26–31; English trans., "Confessio Augustana: Confessing One Faith: Conclusion of the Lutheran-Roman Catholic Commentary," *Discussion,* pp. 28–33 (cited above, note 17).

23. Conclusion of the first part, *BS,* pp. 83d, 1–5; Tappert, p. 47.

24. Wolfhart Pannenberg, Heinz Schütte, and Vinzenz Pfnür quote the passage, but do not discuss the qualification in their essays in *Katholische Anerkennung des Augsburgischen Bekenntnisses?* pp. 18 (note 5), 37 (note 8), 75 (note 45)

respectively; cf. *The Role of the Augsburg Confession,* pp. 28 (note 5), 48 (note 8), 16 (note 46) respectively (cited above, note 18). Avery Dulles, "The Augsburg Confession and Contemporary Catholicism," *The Role of the Augsburg Confession* (cited in note 18 above), pp. 131–38, for instance, forcefully contrasts the understanding of catholicity in the contemporary Roman Catholic Church with that of the Augsburg Confession. According to Bernhard Dittrich, *Das Traditionsverständnis in der Confessio Augustana und in der Confutatio,* Erfurter Theologische Studien, Band 51 (Leipzig: St. Benno, 1983), p. 215, both sides at Augsburg appealed to ancient church criteria of catholicity to demonstrate that they belonged to the *ecclesia catholica*. Their diverse understanding of catholicity, however, becomes evident in that the Lutheran theologians viewed it primarily as agreement with "the Gospel" and the ancient church, while the Catholic theologians regarded catholicity as ascertained, beyond that, by the universal dissemination (*Allverbreitung*) of a doctrine or a certain usage. See also the end of ch. 2 above.

25. The direction in which the Joint Commission is moving on the issue of the papacy can be seen in *Einheit vor uns: Modelle, Formen und Phasen katholisch-lutherischer Kirchengemeinschaft,* ed. by Gemeinsame Römisch Katholische-Evangelisch Lutherische Kommission (Paderborn: Bonifatius; Frankfurt: O. Lembeck, 1985), which forsees a "structured fellowship" characterized by a common episcopal supervision. See also Harding Meyer, "Einheit vor uns: Bemerkungen zu dem katholisch-lutherischen Studiendokument," and Andreas Karrer's very critical review, "Kirchengemeinschaft—um welchen Preis? Zehn Fragen zur katholisch-lutherischen Schrift 'Einheit vor uns,' " both in *Materialdienst des Konfessionskundlichen Instituts Bensheim,* XXXVI (Juli/August 1985), respectively pp. 65–66 and pp. 67–70.

26. The translation in *Discussion,* p. 33, misreads the original, *"als ... sprechen,"* as it renders: "we cannot speak *of* the CA as a common confession of this one catholic faith."

27. A. Klein and H. Meyer, "Lutheran-Roman Catholic Discussion of the Augsburg Confession," *Discussion,* pp. 9–10; cf. the appeal made in Art. 75 of *Wege zur Gemeinschaft,* p. 37, that the churches should begin a process of formal reception and decide what ecclesial and ecumenical importance they attribute to the documents stemming from the dialog.

28. *Confessio Augustana und Confutatio: Der Augsburger Reichstag 1530 und die Einheit der Kirche:* Internationales Symposion der Gesellschaft zur Herausgabe des Corpus Catholicorum in Augsburg vom 3.–7. September 1979, her. v. Erwin Iserloh, Reformationsgeschichtliche Studien und Texte, Heft 118 (Münster Westfalen: Aschendorff, 1980), especially Vinzenz Pfnür, "Die Einigung in der Rechtfertigungslehre bei den Religionsverhandlungen auf dem Reichstag zu Augsburg 1530," pp. 346–74, together with the discussion report on pp. 375–88. This collection of essays will henceforth be referred to as *CAC.*

29. The original text of Art. 17 uses the verb *erschließen,* which conveys the idea of exploring something (like a territory) that has always been there, but only now is taken possession of and put to profitable use. The translation in *Discussion,* pp. 38–39, "have *discovered* that they have a common mind on basic doctrinal truths," does not convey the force of expression of the original.

30. "Malta Report," Art. 26: "Heute zeichnet sich in der Interpretation der Recht-

fertigung ein weitreichender Konsens ab"; trans., "Today, however, a far-reaching consensus is developing in the interpretation of justification." *Evangelium-Welt-Kirche,* p. 15, cf. p. 41 (cited above, note 1).

31. AC, III, 3; IV, 2–3; V, 3, as interpreted above, chs. 5 and 6.
32. Karl Lehmann, Horst Georg Pöhlmann, "Gott, Jesus Christus, Wiederkunft Christi," *Gemeinsame Untersuchung,* pp. 78 and 68; *Joint Commentary,* pp. 86–87, 89. Avery Dulles, "The Augsburg Confession and Contemporary Catholicism," *The Role of the Augsburg Confession* (cited in note 18 above), pp. 137–38, maintains, on the basis of the "hierarchy of truths" recognized by the Second Vatican Council, that "the fundamental affirmations of the Catholic faith, articulated in the classical creeds, remain part of the patrimony of both Lutherans and Catholics. In comparison with this immense common heritage, the discrepancies are relatively minor."
33. Joseph Cardinal Höffner, "Luthers Werk und Persönlichkeit geht auch die Katholiken an: Ansprache ... beim Festakt der Evangelischen Kirche in Deutschland ... am 30. Oktober 1983 in Worms,"*Materialdienst des Konfessionskundlichen Instituts Bensheim,* XXXIV (Nov./Dez. 1983), 117: In holding to the truth (that Jesus is God and resurrected and that Baptism and the Eucharist are sacraments) the Catholic Christian finds himself on Luther's side against many who claim his support.
34. *Discussion,* p. 38, renders *im Glauben* with "by faith," overlooking the problem.
35. According to Vinzenz Pfnür, *Einig in der Rechtfertigungslehre? Die Rechtfertigungslehre der Confessio Augustana (1530) und die Stellungnahme der katholischen Kontroverstheologie zwischen 1530 und 1535,* Veröffentlichungen des Instituts für Europäische Geschichte Mainz, Band 60 (Wiesbaden: F. Steiner, 1970), p. 152, the Reformers' *iustificatio per fidem* and the Scholastics' *iustificatio per gratiam creatam* have the same intention of expressing "that we are justified through God's goodness and mercy which becomes entirely ours." This work will henceforth be referred to as *Einig.*
36. *Gemeinsame Untersuchung,* p. 125, as interpretation of *iustum effici,* and pp. 118–19 on the basis of Paul Althaus, *Die Theologie Martin Luthers* (Gütersloh, 1961), pp. 111–12: Justification *per fidem* is God's creative act: the natural man of sin becomes "a new man, who is reborn through faith and is one with Christ and therefore with God." *Joint Commentary,* pp. 132, 127.
37. *Gemeinsame Untersuchung,* pp. 116–18; *Joint Commentary,* pp. 125–27. Cf. Ap, IV, 116; *BS,* p. 183, 50–55; Tappert, p. 123. Thesis and reference stem from V. Pfnür, *Einig,* pp. 152–53, cf. note 86 (cited above, note 35). Pfnür, however, disregards the argumentative context of the passage.
38. *Gemeinsame Untersuchung,* pp. 118 and 116; cf. *Einig,* p. 154. *Joint Commentary,* pp. 125–27.
39. AC, IV, 1–2; XX, 9 (German text).
40. See the interpretation of AC, V, 3, above, ch. 7.
41. See above, ch. 2. Cf. AC, XX, 9 (*Erstlich*), 23 (*auch*), 27 (*Ferner*); *BS,* pp. 76, 79, 80; Tappert, pp. 42, 44, 45.
42. V. Pfnür, *Einig,* pp. 178–81.
43. Ap, IV, 116. *BS,* p. 183, 50-55; Tappert, p. 123.

44. Vinzenz Pfnür, *Einig,* pp. 140–221; "Anerkennung der Confessio Augustana durch die katholische Kirche?" *Katholische Anerkennung,* pp. 60–81, trans."Recognition of the Augsburg Confession by the Catholic Church?" *The Role of the Augsburg Confession* (cited in note 18 above), pp. 27–45; "Die Einigung in der Rechtfertigungslehre bei den Religionsverhandlungen auf dem Reichstag zu Augsburg," *CAC,* pp. 346–74; Holsten Fagerberg, *Die Theologie der lutherischen Bekenntnisschriften von 1529 bis 1537,* übers. v. Gerhard Klose (Göttingen: Vandenhoeck & Ruprecht, 1965), pp. 150–68 (hereafter referred to as *Theologie*); "Die Rechtfertigungslehre in Confessio Augustana, Confutatio und Apologie," *CAC,* pp. 325–45. See also Fagerberg's positive review of Pfnür's *Einig* in *Theologische Revue,* LXVIII (1972), 34–37.

45. Wolfhart Pannenberg, "Die Augsburgische Konfession als katholisches Bekenntnis und Grundlage für die Einheit der Kirche," *Katholische Anerkennung des Augsburgischen Bekenntnisses?* (Frankfurt am Main: O. Lembeck/J. Knecht, 1977), p. 27, note 30; trans. "The *Confessio Augustana* as a Catholic Confession and a Basis for the Unity of the Church," *The Role of the Augsburg Confession,* ed. Joseph A. Burgess (Philadelphia: Fortress, 1980), p. 35, cf. p. 44, note 31.

46. Hans Jorissen in the discussion of Fagerberg's and Pfnür's papers, *CAC,* pp. 381–82; cf. Jorissen's final remark, p. 595: "One may question whether at that time the divergences concerning the concept of faith were totally resolved, since later these divergences erupted again in full measure."

47. Robert Jenson, "On Recognizing the Augsburg Confession," *The Role of the Augsburg Confession* (cited in note 18 above), pp. 157–62. See also Gottfried Hoffmann's critical review of the joint commentary in *Lutherische Theologie und Kirche,* June 1983, pp. 79–81.

48. Martin Seils, "Zu einigen Problemen der Interpretation von Artikel IV der Confessio Augustana in der Anerkennungsdebatte," *Die Confessio Augustana im ökumenischen Gespräch,* her. v. Fritz Hoffmann und Ulrich Kühn (Berlin: Evangelische Verlagsanstalt, 1980), p. 160; cf. p. 150: "It is rather uncommon that the solution of an interconfessional question of wide significance should rest on a piece of research and that ecclesial consequences should be drawn before this work could prove itself sound in the research dialog." The "Joint Commentary" therefore was supposed to provide a broader basis for convergence and consensus.

49. AC, XX, *editio princeps; BS,* p. 83, 15–57.

50. "Justification by Faith (Common Statement)," No. 4, cf. No. 157; *Justification by Faith, Lutherans and Catholics in Dialogue,* VII, ed. H. G. Anderson, T. A. Murphy, and J. A. Burgess (Minneapolis: Augsburg, 1985), pp. 16 and 72. There are in the document some features which would require critical comment, as for instance the use of the expression *in faith* in No. 161 and the repeated description of faith as "response to the Gospel." Faith would be more adequately described as effect of the Gospel, which at the same time apprehends and claims the Christ proffered in the Gospel as the only and sufficient Ground of justification.

51. Papst Johannes Paul II, "Ansprache am 450. Jahrestag der Confessio Augustana," *Gespräch,* p. 57; trans. *Discussion,* p. 60 (cited above, note 17): "how great and solid are the common foundations of our Christian faith."

52. Johannes Kardinal Willebrands, "Confessio Augustana, ein Forum der Begeg-

nung: Grußwort zur Jubiläumsfeier der Confessio Augustana," *Gespräch,* p. 54; *Discussion,* p. 57.

53. Papst Johannes Paul II, "Ansprache in Mainz am 17. November 1980," *Gespräch,* p. 58, cf. p. 52; *Discussion,* pp. 63–64, cf. p. 55. Harding Meyer, "Augsburg, Rom und die Zeitungen," *Ökumenische Rundschau,* XXX (1981), 79, regards the pope's remarks as evidence for the success of the debate over the recognition of the AC.

54. Avery Dulles, "The Augsburg Confession and Contemporary Catholicism," *The Role of the Augsburg Confession,* p. 136.

55. George A. Lindbeck, "Bericht über den Römisch-Katholischen—Evangelisch-Lutherischen Dialog, *LWB-Dokumentation Nr. 4,* Oktober 1980, pp. 19, 21.

56. "Erklärung des LWB zur Confessio Augustana" (Augsburg, 6.–11. July 1980), *Gespräch,* p. 65.

57. "450 Jahre Confessio Augustana: Stellungnahme des LWB-Exekutivkomittees" (Turku, 4.–13. August 1981), *Gespräch,* pp. 68–75.

58. "Evangelische Kirchen in der DDR: Erklärung zum Jubiläum des Augsburger Bekenntnisses," No. 5; "VELKD-Bischofskonferenz: Erklärung zum Jubiläum des Augsburger Bekenntnisses," Nos. 6, 7, *Gespräch,* pp. 48–49, 43–44.

59. Carl H. Mau Jr., "Report of the General Secretary on Behalf of the Executive Committee," *From Dar es Salaam to Budapest: Reports of the Work of the Lutheran World Federation 1977–1984,* LWF Report No. 17/18, April 1984 (Stuttgart: Kreuz, 1984), pp. 23-25. The report actually read to the Assembly not so much as mentioned the Joint Commission's statements on the AC and Martin Luther. See Carl H. Mau Jr., "Report of the General Secretary," *Budapest 1984: Official Proceedings of the Seventh Assembly of the Lutheran World Federation,* Budapest, Hungary, July 22–Aug. 5, 1984, LWF Report No. 19/20, February 1985 (Geneva: Lutheran World Federation, 1985), pp. 166–68.

60. "Martin Luther—Zeuge Jesu Christi: Wort der Gemeinsamen römisch-katholischen—evangelisch-lutherischen Kommission anläßlich des 500. Geburtstages Martin Luthers," *Materialdienst des Konfessionskundlichen Instituts Bensheim,* XXXIV (Mai/Juni 1983), 55–57; trans. "Martin Luther—Witness to Jesus Christ: Statement by the Joint Roman Catholic-Lutheran Commission on the Occasion of Martin Luther's 500th Birthday," May 6, 1983, mimeo, The Lutheran World Federation, Geneva.

61. Uuras Saarnivaara, *Luther Discovers the Gospel* (St. Louis: Concordia, 1951), pp. 36–37: "I began to understand that the righteousness of God is that gift of God by which a righteous man lives, namely, faith, and that this sentence: The righteousness of God is revealed in the Gospel, is passive, indicating that the merciful God justifies us by faith, as it is written: 'The righteous shall live by faith.' " Cf. Martin Luther, "Vorrede zum ersten Bande der Gesamtausgaben seiner lateinischen Schriften, Wittenberg 1545," *WA,* LIV, 186, 5–8: "ibi iustitiam Dei coepi intelligere eam, qua iustus dono Dei vivit, nempe ex fide, et esse hanc sententiam, revelari per evangelium iustitiam Dei, scilicet passivam, qua nos Deus misericors iustificat per fidem, sicut scriptum est: Iustus ex fide vivit."

62. *WA,* XXVI, 504, 17–21; cf. 505, 16–17. *BS,* p. 57, 21–31, 32–41; cf. p. 415, 14–20 (Tappert, p. 292): "Inasmuch as this must be believed and cannot be

obtained or apprehended by any work, law, or merit, it is clear and certain that such faith alone justifies us. "
63. *WA,* XXVI, 504, 19–22; *LW,* 37, 364: "it is impossible that there should be more saviors, ways, or means to be saved than through the one righteousness which our Savior Jesus Christ is and has bestowed upon us, and has offered to God for us as our one mercy seat, Romans 3 [:25]."

CHAPTER 12

1. Peter Manns, "Zum Vorhaben einer 'katholischen Anerkennung der Confessio Augustana': Ökumene auf Kosten Martin Luthers?" *Ökumenische Rundschau,* XXVI (1977), 426–50.
2. See above, ch. 11, note 52.
3. Joseph Kardinal Höffner, "Luthers Werk and Person geht auch Katholiken an: Ansprache... aus Anlaß des Gedenkens an den 500. Geburtstag Martin Luthers am 30. Oktober 1983 in Worms," *Materialdienst des Konfessionskundlichen Instituts Bensheim,* XXXIV (November, Dezember 1983), 117.
4. Ap, Preface, 18; Tappert, p. 99.

www.ingramcontent.com/pod-product-compliance
Lightning Source LLC
Chambersburg PA
CBHW020756160426

43192CB00006B/343